Customer Analytics

FOR

DUMMIES®

A Wiley Brand

by Jeff Sauro

FOR

DUMMIES®

A Wiley Brand

Customer Analytics For Dummies®

Published by: **John Wiley & Sons, Inc.,** 111 River Street, Hoboken, NJ 07030-5774, www.wiley.com

For general information on our other products and services, please contact our Customer Care Department within the U.S. at 877-762-2974, outside the U.S. at 317-572-3993, or fax 317-572-4002. For technical support, please visit www.wiley.com/techsupport.

Wiley publishes in a variety of print and electronic formats and by print-on-demand. Some material included with standard print versions of this book may not be included in e-books or in print-on-demand. If this book refers to media such as a CD or DVD that is not included in the version you purchased, you may download this material at http://booksupport.wiley.com. For more information about Wiley products, visit www.wiley.com.

Library of Congress Control Number: 2014946670

ISBN 978-1-118-93759-4 (pbk); ISBN 978-1-118-93762-4 (epub); ISBN 978-1-118-93763-1 (epdf)

Manufactured in the United States of America

10 9 8 7 6 5 4 3 2 1

Contents at a Glance

Table of Contents

Introduction

W elcome to *Customer Analytics For Dummies.* This is a book about using data to make better decisions about — and for — your customers. With this book, you find out valuable ways of quantifying your customers' journey, before, during, and after a product or service experience. You discover methods and metrics to improve a customer's experience with a product, service, and brand.

About This Book

You might already be familiar with some form of customer analytics through product development, marketing, sales, and customer services. But the heart of customer analytics is staying focused on the customer, which might be a new concept for you.

In *Customer Analytics For Dummies,* I discuss the finer points of customer analytics. Customer analytics involves gathering data about your customers at various stages of the buying experience, detecting patterns from that data, predicting actions your customers will take, and then making decisions about how to improve your business to attract more customers and keep the customers you already have.

I also include real-world examples from some of the dozens of organizations I've worked with, both big and small, to collect, analyze, and help improve the customer experience. These examples, which include actual data and the methods used, show you what you can accomplish through customer analytics.

You don't need to read this book cover to cover. You can if that appeals to you, but it's set up as a useful reference guide to dip into as you need. Stumped by a certain situation? Look in the table of contents or index, find the topic you need, and then flip to the page to resolve your problem.

Whether you're new to customer analytics or an experienced market analyst, you'll find something that will help you.

Foolish Assumptions

To get the most from this book, you need to be interested in using data to improve the customer experience. And I assume you are, since you are holding this book (for which your humble author thanks you, by the way!). I also assume you are comfortable with computers and working with numbers and data. And although it isn't necessary and I don't assume you have it, it would helpful if you had access to a spreadsheet program, such as Microsoft Excel (and are familiar with how it functions). You should also have access to customer data, be able to collect customer data, or at least want to collect and analyze customer data. Of course, I provide tips throughout this book to help you get started. (I'd be foolish not to, right?)

Icons Used in This Book

Throughout the book, you'll see these little graphic icons to identify useful paragraphs.

The Tip icon marks tips and shortcuts that you can take to make a specific task easier.

The Remember icon marks the information that's especially important to know. To siphon off the most important information in each chapter, just skim through these icons.

The Technical Stuff icon marks information of a highly technical nature that you can safely skip over without harm.

The Warning icon tells you to watch out! It marks important information that may save you headaches. Warning: Don't skip over these warnings!

Beyond the Book

Customer Analytics For Dummies includes the following goodies online for easy download:

- ✔ **Cheat Sheet:** Here you'll find the necessary methods, metrics, and sample-size tables to help you collect and analyze customer analytics.

  The cheat sheet for this book is at

  `www.dummies.com/cheatsheet/customeranalytics`

- ✔ **Extras:** I provide a few extra articles, step lists, and case studies at

  `www.dummies.com/extras/customeranalytics`

Where to Go from Here

Knowing your customers is a vital step in building your business. With this book, you have all the information you need to get started on that journey. If you're completely new to customer analytics, I recommend starting with Chapter 1. Otherwise, take a look at the table of contents and start with a topic that interests you.

Part I

Getting Started with Customer Analytics

getting started
with
Customer
Analytics

Visit www.dummies.com for great Dummies content online.

In this part . . .

✔ Discover exactly what customer analytics is.

✔ Accurately measure with quantitative and qualitative data.

✔ Collect descriptive, behavioral, interaction, and attitudinal data from customers.

✔ Choose the right metrics, methods, and tools.

✔ Visit www.dummies.com for great Dummies content online.

Chapter 1

Introducing Customer Analytics

*T*he purpose of business is to create and keep a customer. This statement was made by Peter Drucker, the acclaimed 20th-century management consultant. A simple statement that reveals in just a few words that the long-term viability of a company is not just about maximizing revenue and minimizing costs. Long-term viability is about understanding what it takes to attract customers by continuing to meet and exceed their physical and psychological needs.

Good customer management comes from good customer measurement. Metrics are numbers assigned to everything from website visitors, same-store sales, and profit margin to call-center wait times. Analytics are metrics plus the methods that drive meaningful decisions. You can think of metrics as "informational," while analytics are "strategic." So while not all metrics are analytics, all analytics come from metrics. You need metrics to get analytics.

Increasingly, decisions are made on numbers. If you know the numbers better, and can articulate what those numbers mean and how you can differentiate a product, organization, or brand, you can distinguish yourself from your competitors.

Defining Customer Analytics

Although it might not be called customer analytics, chances are, you're already familiar with some form of customer analytics. The efforts and activities of product development, marketing, sales, and services are driven to anticipate and fulfill customer needs. That is, you can't sell a product unless someone has a need for it.

Customer analytics is a new term and is broadly used, but it generally includes the following actions and activities:

- **Gathering data:** Pull together customer purchase records, transactional data, surveys, and observational data at all phases of a customer's journey.

- **Using mathematical models to detect patterns:** There are many number crunching, statistical analysis, and advanced modeling techniques that help turn raw data into more meaningful chunks.

- **Finding the insight:** From the patterns of the data come insights into causes of customer behavior.

- **Supporting decisions:** Understanding past behavior helps predict future customer behavior from data instead of relying on intuition.

- **Optimizing the customer experience:** Detect problems with features, purchases, and the product or service experience.

- **Mapping the customer journey:** From considering, purchasing, and engaging with products and services, mapping the touchpoints and pain points helps identify opportunities for improvement.

Customer analytics is different from many of the other metrics within an organization. The four critical ingredients of customer analytics are:

- **Customer focused:** The first word in customer analytics is customer. This means that the metrics collected need to come from customer actions or attitudes, or are derived in some way that's connected to customers.

- **At the individual customer level:** You need access to the lowest level of customer transaction data, not data rolled up at the product or company level.

- **Longitudinal:** Customer analytics involves looking at customer behavior over time.

- **Behavioral and attitudinal:** You need a mix of what customers do and what customers think. Although customer actions (purchasing, recommending) are ultimately what you care about, attitudes affect actions — so measuring and understanding customer attitudes helps to predict future behavior.

The benefits of customer analytics

The benefit of customer analytics is that better decisions are made with data, which leads to a number of tangible benefits:

- **Streamlined campaigns:** You can target your marketing efforts, thus reduce costs.

✔ **Competitive pricing:** You can price your products according to demand and by what customers expect.

✔ **Customization:** Customers can select from a combination of features or service that meets their needs.

✔ **Reduced waste:** Manage your inventory better by anticipating customer demands.

✔ **Faster delivery:** Knowing what products will sell when and where allows manufacturing efforts to anticipate demand and prevent a loss of sales.

✔ **Higher profitability:** More competitive prices, reduced costs, and higher sales are results of targeted marketing efforts.

✔ **Loyal customers:** Delivering the right features at the right price increases customer satisfaction and leads to loyal customers, which are essential for long-term growth

In the following sections, I go more in-depth about the data you collect with customer analytics.

Multidisciplinary

The realm of customer analytics crosses departments, skills, and traditional roles. It's multidisciplinary and typically involves input from and output to:

✔ **Marketing:** This encompasses the messaging, advertising, and the customer demographics and segments.

✔ **Information Technology (IT):** The IT department usually has access to the databases of customer transactions and data.

✔ **Sales:** Front-line contact with customers, knowledge of pricing, revenue, transactions, and reasons for lost customers are included here.

✔ **Product development:** This includes product features, functions, and usability.

Multimetric

No single metric can define customer analytics. It requires a combination of both behavioral and attitudinal data. Some common ones include:

✔ **Revenue:** Simple enough, this is your top line and you're probably tracking this for your accountant already.

✔ **Transactions:** How many transactions are you completing in a given time frame? Digging deeper into the data, transactions become important for finding patterns.

✔ Customer Lifetime Revenue: The total top line revenue a customer generates over some "lifetime," which can be days, months or years (see Chapter 6).

✔ **Future intent:** Will your existing customers buy from you again (see Chapter 11 and Chapter 12)?

✔ **Likelihood to recommend:** How likely will customers recommend your company and products (see Chapter 12)?

✔ **Product usage:** Which features are your customers actually using (see Chapters 10 and 13)?

✔ **Website visits:** Are potential customers finding your website and doing what you expect — finding information or buying a product (see Chapter 10)?

✔ **Return rates:** How many products are being returned due to dissatisfaction (see Chapter 11)?

✔ **Abandonment rates:** Did a customer start a transaction and then quit before completing (see Chapter 10)?

✔ **Conversion rates:** How many potential customers do you convert into actual customers (Chapter 10)?

✔ **Satisfaction:** Are customers satisfied with your product, company, and service (Chapter 9)?

✔ **Usability:** Do customers have problems using your products (see Chapter 15)?

✔ **Findability:** Can customers find the features they're looking for in your products, or find what they're looking for in your website? I discuss findability in Chapter 15.

Multimethod

No single method defines customer analytics. Some common methods, most of which are discussed throughout this book, include:

✔ **Surveys analysis:** This involves collecting, analyzing, and posing decision questions directly to your customers. Chapter 9 has more details on what to ask.

✔ **Customer segmentation:** Not all customers have the same backgrounds, goals, or buying patterns; grouping your customers into similar patterns helps identify opportunities for better marketing and product development. Chapter 4 has more details.

✔ **Customer journey mapping:** Understanding the process customers go through as they engage with a service uncovers pain points and opportunities for improvement (see Chapter 7).

✔ **Transactional analysis:** This examines the purchase frequency, amount, and the type of products purchased together for patterns and predictions.

✔ **Factor analysis:** This statistical technique helps identify clusters of similar customers (see Chapter 4) and similar response patterns from survey results (see Chapter 9).

✔ **Cluster analysis:** Similar to factor analysis, this statistical technique groups customers together into clusters (see Chapter 4) and identifies the best labels for customers to find items in website navigation (see Chapter 15).

✔ **Regression analysis:** This statistical technique identifies the key variables that have the biggest impact on customer satisfaction (see Chapter 9) and customer loyalty (see Chapter 12).

✔ **Neural networks/machine learning:** Advanced software programs can adapt to patterns learned from data mining and better predict customer needs. This is covered in *Predictive Analytics For Dummies* by Anasse Bari, Mohamed Chaouchi, and Tommy Jung (Wiley).

Using customer analytics

Customer analytics are used across industries in both small and large organizations. Examples of customer analytics at work include:

✔ **Retail:** Targeted promotions based on past purchase for individual customers mean retailers anticipate needs and send coupons for things like home improvement or diapers.

✔ **Finance:** Credit card companies can understand when customers are more likely to cancel their account based on non-usage, as well as detect fraud based on unusual purchases.

✔ **Online:** An understanding of which designs, layouts, navigation structures, and even how the color of buttons affect customer purchases (called conversion rates) is used extensively across most Internet retailers.

✔ **Software:** Customers who need sales force automation software often also need accounting software and human resources software.

Professionals who *specialize* in customer analytics typically have a background that includes a mix of mathematical and software skills. These individuals typically go by titles such as:

✔ Data scientist

✔ Statistician

✔ Database analyst

Just as most organizations are already measuring customer analytics, most businesspersons also can use customer analytics. You don't need a PhD in statistics or even a specialization in math. All you need is some desire to better understand a customer and a willingness to answer business questions with data. Customer analytics is therefore also done by

- ✔ Business analysts
- ✔ Project managers
- ✔ Product developers
- ✔ Designers

Compiling Big and Small Data

Customer analytics is often associated with big data. *Big data* refers to extremely large datasets, often containing millions or billions of customer transactions or records. These large datasets are analyzed with sophisticated software to reveal patterns, trends, and associations. Big data allows you to detect very subtle trends and patterns that may have a large impact on revenue.

But customer analytics is also about small data. While not as trendy as big data, *small data* refers to finding insights with datasets that often contain less than 30 customers. With small data, you're limited to seeing larger patterns in attitudes.

While the field of customer analytics is still being defined and varies across organizations and industries, it usually involves some combination of the following:

- ✔ **Past behavior:** Customer analytics is about using data from the past to predict future behavior. This is both a definition and a warning. What customers did in the past is no guarantee of what they will do in the future. If a certain type of customer purchased one type of product in the past, he is probably more likely to do so again in the future; however, there's no guarantee.

- ✔ **Predictive modeling:** Software programs are able to detect patterns in behavior, even subtle ones that are difficult for humans to detect with intuition or just inspecting data. For example, software can determine quickly that a certain segment of customers, such as higher-income mothers, are more likely to purchase certain products and aren't sensitive to changes in price.

A model is a description of a customer interaction, process, or behavior that can be used to predict future outcomes. For example, the sales price of a house can be estimated by its total square footage. In general, bigger houses sell for more than smaller homes in the same neighborhood.

This book focuses on the methods and metrics that help answer business questions and set the groundwork for predicting. There is a special branch of customer analytics that deals exclusively with making predictions with software. See the appendix for a primer on getting started with prediction.

✔ **What-if scenarios:** Customer analytics allows you to test "what-if" scenarios by looking at past customer data and estimating how future data may change based on manipulating things like product features, prices, messaging, or some combination of those elements.

✔ **Customer experience:** While customer analytics often involves the hard numbers of transactional data, sales, and profitability, it also involves understanding the customer's experience with a product or service.

Measuring the customer experience involves collecting metrics for the entire journey a customer has with a brand or organization — including awareness, purchasing, and long-term usage. This involves collecting a mix of metrics about behaviors and attitudes.

Customer analytics includes the metrics for the customer experience. It's as much about how the customer uses a product as it is about what goes into the product.

Chapter 2

Embracing the Science and Art of Metrics

Customer analytics largely involves turning customer actions and attitudes into data. Not all data is the same, and knowing what type of data you're dealing with guides you through what you can do with it. When you can interpret the data that's available to you, you can start making better decisions about product features and service experiences.

In this chapter, I help you understand the different types of data, and show you how to work with quantitative and qualitative data. I also cover best practices for identifying the best metrics to manage.

You'll have to put on your analytical thinking cap (the science of metrics) and your creative thinking cap (the art of metrics). If you aren't a numbers person and decide to hire someone who is, that's okay. But this is still a useful chapter because you need to know how to talk to your analytics person. And you still need to know how to interpret the numbers so you can make sound decisions about how to improve your business.

Adding up Quantitative Data

Quantitative data is information that's broken down by concrete numbers — for example, how many products a customer places in the shopping cart (3) or how much revenue you earn from a specific customer ($2,000).

Quantitative data falls into two categories:

- ✔ Discrete (countable items)
- ✔ Continuous (measurements)

You encounter a lot of numbers when quantifying customer experience with products and services. Knowing whether the data is discrete or continuous dictates the method you use in your analysis and reporting.

Discrete and continuous data

Discrete data has finite values, or buckets. You can count them. For example, the number of questions correct would be discrete: There are a finite and countable number of questions.

Other examples of discrete data are

- ✔ Number of products in your catalog
- ✔ Number of employees you have
- ✔ Number of customer reviews for a specific product

Continuous data technically has an infinite number of steps, which form a continuum. The time to find a product on a website is continuous because it could take 31.627543 seconds. Time forms an interval from 0 to infinity.

Other examples of continuous data are

- ✔ Dimensions of a specific product
- ✔ Miles to your retail store from a customer's location
- ✔ Time for a customer to find the information he or she is looking for on your website
- ✔ Days until a product ships to a customer

You can usually tell the difference between discrete and continuous data because discrete data can't be broken into smaller meaningful units. You can't have half a customer, but you can have half a minute.

Levels of data

Another way customer analytics data gets divided is by the four levels of measurement. They're levels because they start with data that's more limiting in the type of analysis you can perform to the least limiting:

✓ **Nominal:** This includes discrete data such as the name of your company, type of car you drive, or name of a product. *Nominal* means essentially "in name only"; if you have a name, it belongs in this category. Nominal data is qualitative data.

✓ **Ordinal:** This includes data that has a natural ordering. The ranking of customers by oldest to newest, the order of callers in a queue for a call center, the order of runners finishing a race, or more often, the choice on a rating scale, such as from 1 to 5.

With ordinal data, you cannot know with certainty whether the intervals between each value are equal. In measuring customers' attitudes toward their experience with products and services, you have to rely heavily on questionnaire data that uses rating scales. For example, on an 11-point rating scale, the difference between a 9 and a 10 is not necessarily the same as the difference between a 6 and a 7.

✓ **Interval:** This is data that has equally split intervals between each value. The most common example is temperature in degrees Fahrenheit. The difference between 29 degrees and 30 degrees is the same magnitude as the difference between 78 degrees and 79 degrees (I much prefer the latter of these two examples).

✓ **Ratio:** This is interval data with a natural zero point. For example, time to find a product on a website is ratio, because 0 time is meaningful. Degrees Kelvin has a 0 point (absolute zero). The steps in both these scales have the same degree of magnitude.

Whenever you can establish that data is ratio, you can make reasonable deductions, such as "customers are twice as satisfied using a new product version compared to an old version."

Just because customers' average rating on one product is a 4 and the rating on another product is a 2 doesn't mean customers are twice as satisfied. The first rating is definitely twice as high, but unless the scale is both ratio, and calibrated so the numbers correspond to customer behavior, making such claims is risky. It's best to simply say the rating was twice as high.

Many organizations, statisticians, and even software programs use this hierarchy so it's important to understand the terms when you encounter them. Some analysts even restrict their analysis based on it (see the sidebar "The history of levels of measurement" for more information).

Figure 2-1 shows how the levels of measurement fit into the broader categorization of qualitative and quantitative data.

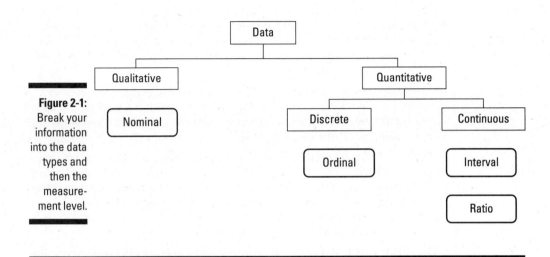

Figure 2-1:
Break your information into the data types and then the measurement level.

The history of levels of measurement

Where did the levels of measurement come from and why should you care? Well, you should at least care about identifying nominal or categorical data. If it isn't nominal, then it's quantitative. So why all the fuss?

In the 1940s, when behavioral science was in its infancy, there was much concern about trying to make the practice as legitimate as possible. Psychology and other social and behavioral sciences are considered soft sciences as opposed to the hard sciences of chemistry and physics. It was thought that applying some of the same thinking from the hard sciences would improve the legitimacy of these soft sciences — as well as the veracity of the claims made.

One approach was to map types of scaling to more natural laws (something akin to the physical laws of gravity and motion). This classification system was proposed in 1946 by S.S. Stevens. In the article, Stevens went so far as to say that you should only take averages on at least interval and ratio data. Nominal and ordinal data should only be counted and described in frequency tables — no means and standard deviations.

One of the more famous articles showing the fallacy of such rigid thinking was by an eminent statistician named Lord, who in his article "On the Statistical Treatment of Football Numbers" showed how the means of nominal data can be meaningful too!

In practice, rating scales are ubiquitous in companies and rarely have they been shown to have interval, much less ratio scales (what is the 0 point of customer satisfaction ?)

In summary, it's generally OK to take means and apply statistical tests to ordinal data, just be careful about making ratio claims such as "twice as satisfied."

Variables

A *variable* is a characteristic of a product or service that varies, which can often be manipulated. For example, price, delivery time, and color are product variables. Customer variables can include gender, income, geography, new customer versus existing customer, and type of industry, to name a few. When you look at product and customer variables, you can understand how different product attributes attract more or less sales and how different customers respond to different products and feature combinations.

There are two types of variables:

- Dependent variables are usually the things you care about but can't affect directly, such as profitability, customer satisfaction, and customer loyalty. You can influence dependent variables by changing the independent variables. An example of this relationship is shown in Figure 2-2.
- Independent variables can be directly controlled or manipulated.

  For example, independent variables include price, features, advertising, and usability.

Often, independent variables correlate with dependent variables, but the correlation doesn't equal causation. Other variables that you're not measuring can "mediate" or be responsible for the relationship. For example, higher sales (dependent variable) might be attributed to a new marketing campaign (independent variable) but the increase is actually just due to a growing economy that's helped all businesses (mediator variable). See the appendix for more discussion on measuring correlation and causation between variables.

You can think of independent variables as the ingredients you use to cook a stew. The soup is the dependent variable (what you care about), but adjusting the ingredients and their combinations is what you can control.

Variables often come in the form of words instead of numbers — for example, new customer or existing customer, male or female, high income or low income. To make analysis of these qualitative values easier, you can code them into dummy variables by assigning them a number (for example, new customers get coded a 1 and existing customers get coded a 0; men get coded as 1 and women coded as 0 [or vice versa]).

With your variables coded as 1s and 0s, you can compute the percentage of customers with each variable.

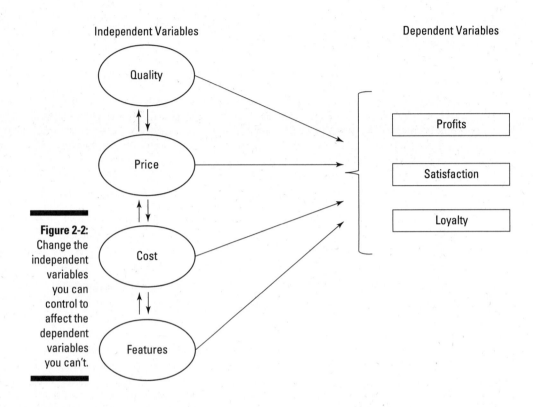

Independent Variables

Dependent Variables

Quality

Price

Cost

Features

Profits

Satisfaction

Loyalty

Figure 2-2:
Change the
independent
variables
you can
control to
affect the
dependent
variables
you can't.

Quantifying Qualitative Data

Qualitative data is often helpful by itself to explain the "why" behind low sat-isfaction rates, higher sales, or high customer turnover rates. For example, if you see customers complaining that they don't know what the total price of their order is in local currency or how to change the currency in a website shopping cart, you know what you can fix.

Comments provide immediate insight and potentially action (improve the currency display on checkout).

Always take the time to sort and count customer comments. Just because customer information is qualitative doesn't mean you can't use quantitative methods to interpret qualitative data to make better decisions. If you find that a significant portion of comments revolve around a specific issue (say 20% of the comments center around currency issues), you've just turned your quali-tative data into quantitative data.

Quantifying iTunes experiences

My company asked 56 customers to rate their experience with iTunes. Customers answered several questions about the ease of use and quality of iTunes and whether they would recommend it to their friends. (See Chapter 12 for more on customer loyalty.) Customers who provided low scores were asked to briefly describe what motivated the rating.

For example, one customer said

I used to use iTunes much more often before they raised their prices from 99 cents to $1.29 per song. I still use the iTunes player to transfer songs to my iPod but I usually buy songs on Amazon. com now because it's a much better deal.

And another said

I dislike iTunes. It's unnecessary and can be annoying and difficult to use.

In total, 16 customers were rather dissatisfied with the iTunes experience. To understand the main drivers behind the dissatisfaction and the prevalence of some of these issues in the larger population, similar comments were first grouped, followed by the total number of comments in each of the groups. This table shows the results.

Category	# of Comments	Total Comments	%	95% CI Low	95% CI High
Difficult to use	4	16	25	9	50
Proprietary	4	16	25	9	50
Necessary to use	3	16	19	6	44
Conversion process	2	16	13	2	37
Installation	1	16	6	1	30
Price of songs	1	16	6	1	30
Slow	1	16	6	1	30

Conclusions from this data indicate that one of the primary reasons users are unlikely to recommend (called detractors) iTunes is because it is difficult to use, with four users making comments about ease.

Usability is often a key driver of product loyalty, and iTunes is no exception. (See Chapter 14 for more on usability.) I was 95% confident that between 9% and 50% of all iTunes detractors feel ease of use is one of the main reasons for not recommending the product to a friend.

I generated a 95% confidence interval around each group of comments using the online calculator (www.measuringu.com/wald.htm) to get an idea about how prevalent these reasons would be in the whole iTunes user population.

Quantifying the frequency of customer comments helps you understand how prevalent a certain attitude may be in your entire customer population. Some examples of open-ended responses (often called *verbatim responses*) are common for things such as:

- Reasons why customers are not recommending your product
- Observations from customers using a product at their workplace
- Product complaints in customer service calls

Here are three steps you can follow to turn qualitative data into quantitative data to estimate the prevalence of responses:

1. **Group similar comments and behaviors.**

   Customers will use their own words to describe how they feel. Group similar phrases, behaviors, or concepts together. Some comments will be virtually identical and grouped easily. Others will differ and require additional layers of grouping.

   There can be a high amount of variability between people grouping items. If possible, consider having multiple people independently categorize comments.

2. **Count the frequency.**

   Count the number that appear in a category and the total number. If 5 out of 50 comments are related to price, for example, then an estimate of how often price is a concern is 10% (5/50).

3. **Estimate the frequency.**

   You can estimate how common an issue is with the entire customer base by using a confidence interval (discussed later in this chapter).

Collecting data from a sample of customers costs a lot less and takes a lot less time than measuring every customer. The level of precision you get from even a small sample is usually sufficient to make decisions from the data.

Determining the Sample Size You Need

It would be good to know what customers think or what product features they like so you can build better products. How do you get this information? By asking your customers to take a poll.

But the problem is you rarely can ask all your customers to take your poll. That would be too time intensive and expensive, and you'd be swimming in data. Instead you collect data from a sample of customers. Your sample size can be small — 5 to 10 customers, or very large — 10,000+ customers. The data you collect from your sample represents all your customers.

Polling sample sizes

In August 2014, Gallup reported the presidential job approval rate was 41% with a margin of error of +/- 3%, using a 95% level of confidence.

Gallup derived this approval rate by asking 1,500 representative voters. Fifteen hundred responses represent some 240 million citizens, or just .001%!

This small proportion has a small margin of error. If Gallup were somehow to ask every voter whether he or she approved of the president, the best estimate of the job approval rating is between 38% and 44% (41% - 3% and 41% + 3%, respectively). This range is created by adding and subtracting the margin of error to the sample percentage.

Surveying a sample of customers is a tried and true method. Polling agencies that measure electoral votes take the same approach: They ask only a subset of the voting population to predict how the entire electorate will vote.

You can achieve a rather low margin of error after just sampling a small fraction of the entire population. There is a diminishing return from increasing sample sizes beyond a certain point. While you want your estimate to be accurate, you have to determine the sample size you can afford based on your budget and company resources.

Table 2-1 shows a table of confidence intervals around different sample sizes. You can see how the margin of error and width of the confidence interval decrease as the sample increases. As a general approximation, you need to quadruple your sample size in order to cut your margin of error in half.

Table 2-1	Confidence Intervals (CI)		
Sample Size	*Margin of Error (+/-)*	*95% CI Low*	*95% CI High*
13	24%	26%	74%
21	20%	30%	70%
39	15%	35%	65%
46	14%	36%	64%
53	13%	37%	63%
63	12%	38%	62%
76	11%	39%	61%
93	10%	40%	60%
115	9%	41%	59%
147	8%	42%	58%

(continued)

Table 2-1 *(continued)*

Sample Size	Margin of Error (+/-)	95% CI Low	95% CI High
193	7%	43%	57%
263	6%	44%	56%
381	5%	45%	55%
597	4%	46%	54%
1,064	3%	47%	53%
2,398	2%	48%	52%

For example, at a sample size of 381, your sample estimate will have a margin of error of approximately plus or minus 5%. That means if a survey to customers indicates that 50% say they would repurchase their subscription in the following year, you can be 95% confident that between 45% and 55% of all customers actually will. The sample size needed when making comparisons (say, between different product designs) will differ, and is covered in Chapters 10, 14 and 15.

Estimating with a confidence interval

Rarely will you be able to survey every customer. Instead you need to take a sample of customers and use this sample to make inferences about all customers. You have to accept that the sample estimate has a risk of being inaccurate.

Even if your sample size is small, you can still use it to make sound decisions, especially when you use techniques like confidence intervals.

You can measure the amount of error with a confidence interval. Confidence intervals tell you how much you can expect sample estimates to fluctuate based on sample size. They provide you with the most likely range for the unknown customer population numbers you're trying to predict. The larger the sample size, the better the estimate is. By building a 95% confidence interval around a sample, you can expect that 95% of the time your interval will contain the actual customer population average.

Confidence intervals and all data you collect will only accurately predict the customer population if your sample is representative of the actual customer population. If you sell products mostly in Europe but most of your survey data comes from the U.S., it's unlikely your estimates will be accurate (unless U.S. customers respond similarly to European customers).

Computing a 95% confidence interval

To compute a 95% confidence interval, you need three pieces of data:

- ✔ The mean (for continuous data) or proportion (for binary data)
- ✔ The standard deviation, which describes how dispersed the data is around the average
- ✔ The sample size

In the following sections, I show you how to calculate a confidence interval when you have continuous data or discrete data.

Continuous data example

Imagine you asked 50 customers how satisfied they were with their recent experience with your product on an 7-point scale, with 1 = Not at all satisfied and 7 = Extremely satisfied. These are the steps you would follow to compute a confidence interval around your sample average:

1. **Find the mean by adding up the scores for each of the 50 customers and divide by the total number of responses (which is 50).**

   If you have Microsoft Excel, you can use the function =AVERAGE() for this step. For the purpose of this example, I have an average response of 6.

2. **Compute the standard deviation.**

   You can use the Excel formula = STDEV() for all 50 values. I have a sample standard deviation of 1.2.

3. **Compute the standard error by dividing the standard deviation by the square root of the sample size.**

   ```
   1.2 / √(50) = .17
   ```

4. **Compute the margin of error by multiplying the standard error by 2.**

   ```
   .17 x 2 = .34
   ```

5. **Compute the confidence interval by adding the margin of error to the mean from Step 1 and then subtracting the margin of error from the mean, like this:**

   ```
   6 +.34 = 6.34
   6 -.34 = 5.66
   ```

   You now know you have a 95% confidence interval of 5.66 to 6.34. The best estimate of what the entire customer population's average satisfaction is ranges between 5.66 and 6.34.

If you have a smaller sample, you need to use a multiple greater than 2. You can find what multiple you need with the online calculator available at www.measuringu.com/ci-calc.php.

Discrete data example

Imagine you asked 50 customers if they are going to repurchase your service in the future. Using a dummy variable, you can code Yes = 1 and No = 0. If 40 out of 50 report their intent to repurchase, you can use what is called the Adjusted Wald technique to find your confidence interval:

1. **Find the average by adding all the 1s and dividing by the number of responses.**

   ```
   40 / 50 = .8
   ```

2. **Adjust the proportion to make it more accurate.**

   a. Add 2 to the numerator (the number of 1s).

   ```
   40 + 2 = 42
   ```

   b. Find the adjusted sample size by adding 4 to the denominator (total responses).

   ```
   50 + 4 = 54
   ```

   c. Divide the result to find the adjusted proportion.

   ```
   42 / 54 = .78
   ```

3. **Compute the standard error for proportion data.**

   a. Multiply the adjusted proportion by 1 minus the adjusted proportion.

   ```
   .78 × (1 - .78) = .17
   ```

   b. Divide the result (.17) by the adjusted sample size from Step 2.

   ```
   .17 / 54 = .0031
   ```

   c. Determine the square root of the value from the preceding step.

   ```
   √.0031 = .057
   ```

4. **Compute the margin of error by multiplying the standard error (result from Step 3) by 2.**

   ```
   .057 × 2 = .11
   ```

5. **Compute the confidence interval by adding the margin of error from the proportion from Step 1 and subtracting the margin of error from the proportion.**

   ```
   .78 + .11 = .89
   .78 - .11 = .67
   ```

The 95% confidence interval is .67 to .89. The best estimate of the entire customer population's intent to repurchase is between 67% and 89%.

Values are rounded in the preceding steps to keep them simple. If you want a more precise confidence interval, use the online calculator available at www. measuringu.com/wald.htm.

Determining What Data to Collect

The art and science of customer analytics means turning metrics into insights. But you need metrics to begin with. Metrics can be found all across an organization and a customer's journey (see Chapter 7). I discuss in detail the right metric to collect depending on your goals and methods throughout this book. But first it's a good idea to get a better understanding of problems and opportunities for your customers.

You need to collect data from each of the following four customer analytics data types.

- **Descriptive:** The descriptive data becomes the template for whom you measure. It includes demographic data like gender, age, geography, and income. It also includes self-described attitudes and preferences toward products, categories, and technology. From this data, you can create meaningful segments (for example, early adopters or value-seekers) and personas (see Chapter 5).

  You can collect this data from purchases, registrations, surveys, interviews, and contextual inquiries.

- **Behavioral:** The behavioral data becomes the framework for testing experiences. It is the general pattern customers exhibit when using your products and services. It includes making purchases, registering, browsing, and using different devices.

  For example, customers of certain product categories, like consumer electronics or home furniture, tend to browse products on their tablet at night and make purchases on their desktop during the day.

- **Interaction:** The interaction data becomes the task scenarios that you simulate and measure during a usability test (see Chapter 14). It includes the clicks, navigation paths, and browsing activities found on websites and software.

  The classic usability test typically focuses on this level of granularity by simulating real interactions. You can use real-time data from A/B testing, Google Analytics, and lab-based or unmoderated testing to collect data for this grouping (see Chapter 10).

- **Attitudinal:** Preference data, opinions, desirability, branding, and sentiments are usually captured in surveys, focus groups, and usability tests. This is where questionnaires like the SUPR-Q (www.suprq.com), System Usability Scale (SUS; www.measuringu.com/sus.php), or the Net

Promoter Score (www.netpromoter.com) quantifies how interactions and behaviors affect attitudes. These attitudes will then affect some self-described descriptive attributes quantified in the descriptive grouping (see Chapter 9).

Improvements you make that affect attitudinal data, like increased trust and loyalty, drive further buying behavior.

Managing the Right Measure

If you can't measure the customer experience, you can't manage it. Improving the customer experience starts with measuring. But you must be sure you're getting the right measure (or usually measures) to manage. The right measure(s) will:

- ✔ Identify problem areas
- ✔ Track improvements over time
- ✔ Be meaningful to the customer

The wrong measure(s) can:

- ✔ Identify wrong areas of focus
- ✔ Miss problems all together
- ✔ Lead to unintended consequences
- ✔ Alienate customers

Here are some different ways of thinking about measuring experiences:

- ✔ **Conversion rate versus number of conversions:** Conversion rates are the central metric for testing better designs, ads, and campaign effectiveness (covered in Chapter 10). The ratio of total users who purchase, register, or click (convert) to all users who viewed the page is an effective ratio because you can compare low traffic and high traffic pages.

  While this is a convenient metric, the total number of conversions likely has a bigger impact on your bottom line than the rate. Wouldn't you rather have 100 conversions from 100,000 page views than 10 conversions from 100 page views?

- ✔ **Number of clicks versus time to destination:** When you're trying to make a more efficient experience, reducing the number of clicks to accomplish a goal seems like a good way to measure. Putting all functionality and content on one page would certainly reduce the number of clicks, but that probably is not what your customers have in mind.

Too much functionality or content on one page makes for an overwhelming experience; just make sure the paths customers need to complete a task are clear (see Chapter 15).

✔ **Call time or call satisfactorily resolved:** Wonder why those often scorned customer service agents you call to complain to speak so quickly? If you want to reduce call time in a customer support center, you can instruct agents to get off the phone faster, but have you really increased service or quality if customers have to call back?

Often a simple follow-up question sent via email can solve this problem.

✔ **Customer satisfaction as a bonus motivator:** Many companies pay bonuses based on achieving and exceeding certain customer satisfaction goals. Unfortunately and not surprisingly, this can lead employees to improve their chances for getting the bonuses in ways that make measures less meaningful.

✔ **Likelihood to recommend or likelihood to repurchase:** With the popularity of the Net Promoter Score (see Chapter 12), it may seem like word of mouth is the only measure you should care about. But if everyone already knows about and owns your product or visits your website, likelihood to purchase again might be a better measure of growth.

For measuring customer loyalty, I recommend using both repurchase rates and likelihood to recommend. This provides a mix of both behavior and attitude.

✔ **On-time arrival versus on-time departure:** Have you ever been on a plane that pulled away from the Jetway only for it to sit on the tarmac waiting for mechanical issues or other delays? You then arrive at your destination late? It's likely that the flight segment still counted as an on-time departure. You can't argue with the measure: The plane did pull away from the Jetway on time and that does mean something. However, that action just doesn't mean that much to the customer sitting in the idled plane.

Measuring is good. Knowing what to measure is better. Finding the right measure means taking multiple measures and seeing which one best tracks customer sentiments and revenue.

Chapter 3

Planning a Customer Analytics Initiative

*L*aunching a customer analytics initiative can be confusing on where to start and which method to use when. In this chapter, I review the best practices for defining, collecting, and analyzing your customer analytics to help make better decisions from your customer data.

There are a number of ways of thinking about goals, methods, and outcomes. Your organization may already have a project scoping process that you can adapt for your customer analytics initiative. In this chapter, I use an approach based loosely on the Six Sigma methodology, tailored to customer analytics. It's a framework that's flexible and familiar and works across disparate products and companies.

The basic framework is to define what you want to do, find the right ways to measure it, do something about the measures, and put processes in place to continue using customer analytics to make better business decisions.

A Customer Analytics Initiative Overview

Before you start on your initiative, keep these four things in mind:

✔ **Access to the right data:** It's hard to increase the frequency of customer purchases, conversions, or attitudes if you don't know what customers are purchasing, when they are purchasing it, or what they are thinking. Be sure you know that the data you need exists, or that you'll be able to collect and analyze it.

✔ **Customer level data:** To do the most with customer analytics, you'll want to gather data for each customer, not aggregated data at product or company levels.

Because customer analytics is about understanding the customer from past data to predict future data, you need to identify transactions, revenue, and survey data for each customer. You can then roll this lower level customer data up to product or company level summaries as needed.

✔ **Analytics that focus on the customer:** The "right" analytics depend on the method. But one thing that all good customer analytics have in common is that they are meaningful to the customer. Just like airlines should care more about on-time arrivals than on-time departures, your analytics should be felt by customers at all phases of their journey.

If you want to improve the customer support experience, customer satisfaction with the call outcome is a better metric than the number of calls answered in an hour. The latter is an example of company centric and the former is customer centric.

✔ **Getting buy-in:** Planning, collecting, and analyzing data is only good if something is going to be done about the insights.

All too often, I see organizations spend a lot on research and customer measurement projects but the results stop at the executive presentation meeting. Unfortunately, insights aren't acted upon because the people who can change the product, price, or experience aren't involved with the data collection and planning. They are naturally resistant to outsiders telling them what to do. This can happen with both internally and externally collected data. Get buy-in from the people you need to implement your insights and minimize the "not invented here" attitude.

Customer analytics should be shared with not only executives, but also with product development, sales, and support staffers. As part of the planning and getting buy-in, be sure the analytics will cross customer touchpoints and be accessible across the organization.

Not all customer analytics initiatives lend themselves well to the more systematic methodology I include here. So don't try to force extra steps or complexity just to meet this framework.

A lot of creative thinking goes into making a plan. Don't feel like you need to fit every project into this process. That's especially the case if your goals and methods are narrow in scope. The rest of this chapter covers the details of putting together your customer analytics initiative.

Defining the Scope and Outcome

The first stage is goal setting: where you define the scope and outcome of your project.

Don't overlook or rush through this stage. Collecting customer analytics takes time and money. You can easily exceed your budget if you compiled the wrong data.

1. **State the goals of the initiative.**

   Think in terms of the intended outcome (for example, an increase of 10% in revenue of a product line over the next year). The more specific you can be, the more attainable the endeavor.

2. **Write down the questions you want to answer.**

   Data is meaningless unless it's collected for a reason. Articulate what business questions you're hoping to answer. Avoid being vague and large in scope. Start small and specific and itemize your questions.

   You want to be SMART: Specific, Measurable, Attainable, Realistic, and Timely.

   Some examples of questions customer analytics can answer include:

   - Which product feature should I add to this product?

   - What is preventing customers on the website from completing a purchase?

   - What labels should I change in the website navigation?

   - Why are customers not recommending a product and how can I improve positive word of mouth?

   - What percent of high-income mothers are aware of the brand and website?

   - Who are the most profitable customers?

   - How long until a customer makes a repeat purchase?

There's a good chance you aren't the first person to collect and use customer analytics in your organization. Look for past initiatives, past projects, and what worked and what didn't work. The documents, results, and people involved in past initiatives will save you a lot of effort and prevent you from reinventing the wheel.

Identifying the Metrics, Methods, and Tools

During this step, identify the metrics and methods you'll use to answer your questions and achieve your goals:

- ✔ **Look for metrics that are meaningful to customers.** Think on-time arrivals instead of on-time departures. See Chapter 2 for ideas on the right data to collect.

- ✔ **Identify what tools you'll need for data collection.**

  Consider collecting customer data by surveying existing customers. Even something as simple as surveying customers requires several inputs.

Table 3-1 shows how you can go from question (from the preceding section) to metric to method, and finally to the right tools for the two examples of customer loyalty (see Chapter 12) and findability (see Chapter 15).

Table 3-1		Metrics and Tools	
Question	*Metric*	*Method*	*Tools*
Why aren't customers recommending a product?	Net Promoter Score	Survey existing customers to understand their current likelihood to recommend and identify the root cause of why they are or not recommending	Survey software Access to customers *A method to invite customers **A method to analyze the data
What labels need to be changed to improve website navigation?	Findability rate	Findability study using tree testing and card sorting	Tree testing software Access to prospective customers *A method to invite customers **A method to analyze the data

* This can be through email, after a transaction, via phone, or embedded into a product.
** You need software and people with the right skills to conduct advanced statistical analysis such as cluster or factor analysis.

You also need to understand your baseline scores. It's hard to know if you've improved anything if you don't have a baseline measure.

After surveys, customer transactions and purchase data are popular sources for finding baseline data. You need

✔ **Access to customer data:** This is often guarded in organizations because it contains both sensitive company and customer data.

✔ **Transaction data at the right level of detail:** Total revenue by product is often at too high a level to understand what's driving purchases. In many cases, you want to obtain customer transaction data at the product level. This way, you can understand who these customers are (demographics and so forth), when they made the purchase, for how much, and how often (for repeat purchases).

Some of the most important insights companies gain from their customer analytics comes from merging survey data with transactional data. One of the biggest challenges is being able to properly match customer survey results with past and future transactions. You may need the help of a database administrator or IT person to be sure you can merge survey data with transactional data.

Setting a Budget

Every project requires a budget — whether it's large or small. Consider the following as you prepare your project:

✔ **Software:** If you have millions of customers and as many monthly transactions, you'll benefit from sophisticated software that integrates into sales and accounting systems. Products offered from SAS, IBM, and Oracle can cost upwards of six figures to implement and service.

Some of the best insights still come from simple calculations in Excel or a calculator. Don't think you need to wait to get approval to purchase expensive software to begin making decisions from customer analytics.

✔ **Time:** You can spend a lot on the hard costs of software and services as well as the softer costs of employee time. Software packages that can fit the budget for single-person companies to the largest enterprises are available. Throughout this book, most methods and analysis can be conducted with Excel, free web software, or options that don't require very expensive software.

Sampling over census

With faster computers and better software and the buzz around big data, there's a tendency to want to measure every customer scenario and every transaction over years (like a census). While this will provide all the relevant data, many business questions can be answered from sampling a subset of transactions or customers for a fraction of the cost and effort.

For example, the Internal Revenue Service has piles of taxpayer information contained in bloated documents for millions of people. It's estimated that in 2012, $6.7 billion in taxes went uncollected from almost half a million taxpayers simply because the IRS couldn't find the people who owed the taxes!

To find the root cause of this problem, the IRS reviewed a sample of that year's reports and investigated what happened. The major reason in almost 60% of the reports was that IRS employees didn't follow all the steps to locate people.

Using a confidence interval on this sample, the IRS can be 95% confident at least 54% of all the half-million returns would also have this as the main problem. (See Chapter 2 for how to compute confidence intervals.) A sample of just .01% of the data of interest can lead to the same insights. More importantly, something can be done about the findings a lot quicker.

While it's easy to calculate the cost of purchasing software and services or hiring additional employees to handle an initiative, be sure to consider the cost of business as usual:

✔ How many customers are defecting to a competitor?

✔ What percent of customers are not returning?

✔ How many customers are discouraging others from using your product or service?

Determining the Correct Sample Size

If you aren't measuring every transaction or surveying every customer, you'll have to deal with the uncertainties that come with sampling a portion of your customer population. Even if you sample everyone, you'll likely want to make estimates about future customers or future transactions, and to do so, you'll still have to deal with the uncertainty.

In general, it costs more money and takes more time to either sample or analyze data from a large database, so you must put some thought into how large of a sample size you need.

I include ways of coming up with the right sample size for each method in each chapter. In general, you should consider two important concepts when planning your sample sizes:

✔ **You need larger sample sizes to detect smaller differences.**

A new design, promotion, or feature may improve customers' attitudes or sales, but if the increase is small (something like a 5% increase), unless your sample size is large enough, that difference won't be distinguishable from random fluctuations in the data.

✔ **For very large sample sizes, almost all differences will be statistically significant.**

Statistically significant essentially means that the differences are not likely due to sampling error. However, statistically significant does not mean the findings are noteworthy or important. Will customers notice a one-second reduction in the time it takes to rent a car online? Probably not. Although it's a good idea to drive increases in positive attitudes and sales, watch out for spending a lot of effort for little return. See the appendix for more of a discussion of statistical significance.

Analyzing and Improving

In the analyze phase, you want to be able to describe the current state of the customer, often by segment (see Chapter 4), and identify the root causes of problems or insights to make improvements.

For example, if you're measuring customer loyalty, you'll have customers' likelihood to recommend scores, satisfaction ratings on other parts of an experience, and open-ended comments. From this you can

✔ Compute the baseline Net Promoter Score

Examine the open-ended comments for the reasons for ratings

✔ Conduct a key driver analysis to understand which features or attributes of the experience are having the biggest impact on customers' likelihood to recommend

See Chapter 12 for more on this approach.

Improving is often the most challenging part of any project, and that's making changes to a product or process. The goal of the improving phase is to implement solutions that address the root causes of customers' pain points.

During the improving stage, you use the data collected in the measure phase to show quantifiable improvements (or reductions) in your metric. This can include

- Conversion rates (converting more browsers to buyers online)
- Improvements in customer attitudes
- Increases in revenue
- An increase in the number of repeat purchases

One of the worst things that happens is collecting analytics that clearly show a problem with the customer experience but then doing nothing about it. It can frustrate customers and lead to analytics initiatives that were just an exercise in measuring.

- For some methods, the improvement process is built into the measure step.

  For example, when conducting an A/B test on a website (see Chapter 10), the improvement has to be built so implementation is easy.

- In other cases, making changes is much harder. If you find that one of the primary reasons customers aren't repurchasing or recommending your product or service is because of price, making changes to the price usually involves corporate politics, entrenched ideas, and shareholders.

Controlling the Results

A lot of effort can go into planning and collecting data. You can prevent waste and rework by putting in place systems to reduce the time between data collection and action. Some things to consider are

- **Automatic reporting:** Look for ways to output key dependent variables to executive and team dashboards or scorecards that provide real-time insights into customers' experiences.

- **Access to data:** It can take a long time to jump through corporate hoops to get access to purchase history or customer details. Have a documented process that others can follow and a way for your employees and data scientists to get creative with the data.

- **Putting the right people and procedures in place:** You don't want to have an initiative that's entirely dependent on the knowledge of one person. Be sure to document

  - Procedures for how to get access to the data
  - Methods that go into analyzing it
  - People who are responsible for the analysis and decision-making
  - Who is impacted by the results

A few words of caution

If you can't measure it you can't manage it. But sometimes more measurement brings more management. Some analytic initiatives receive enormous funding and also scrutiny from companies. Once processes are in place for measuring customer satisfaction, loyalty, repeat purchases, referrals, or any number of metrics, it seems inevitable that companies use these new metrics to decide on their employees' promotions, bonuses, pay — and even terminations.

While it's good to have accountability toward customer-facing metrics, be careful about tying employee performance to those metrics.

Employees will start to "game the system" by finding ways of inflating scores or working around the metrics so the numbers improve while the customer experience doesn't.

To minimize the negative effects of having a measurement system drive undesirable behavior, consider having steps in place, such as

- ✔ Multiple sources of data
- ✔ Third-party audits
- ✔ Periodic review to see if the reward system is causing more harm than good for the employees and customers

Part II
Identifying Your Customers

Visit http://www.dummies.com/extras/customeranalytics for great
Dummies content online.

In this part . . .

✔ Segment your customers for better targeting.

✔ Know your customer segments better with personas.

✔ Find what value different customers bring to your company.

✔ Visit `http://www.dummies.com/extras/customeranalytics` for great Dummies content online.

Chapter 4

Segmenting Customers

. . . .

In This Chapter

▶ Applying the advantages of segmenting customers

▶ Following the segmentation process

▶ Transforming customer data into segments

. . . .

*U*nless you have only one customer, you'll want to understand how your customers differ and how you can adapt to the differences. Customer segmentation is a powerful technique to focus efforts and serve customers better.

A customer segment is a grouping of customers that share certain characteristics. Understanding your customers — their similarities and differences — is one of the most fundamental and essential steps in quantifying the customers' relationship with your product and company. Not only does segmenting customers tell you how to better serve current customer demographics, but it also allows you to discover any unmet needs and deliver better products and services in the future.

In this chapter, you discover how customer segmentation can improve the way you do business and increase your profits. First, I discuss the advantages of customer segmentation. Then, I introduce you to the type of information you need about your customers in order to build a sound segmentation strategy. Finally, you discover how to objectively segment your customers and determine which segments are the most profitable.

Why Segment Customers

Customer segments enable you to understand the patterns that differentiate your customers. However, collecting and analyzing data just to understand patterns and differences is not useful unless you're going to do something with the information. Analyzing customer segments enables you to customize your products, services, prices, and marketing strategies to better increase profitability and customer satisfaction for your segment. Some of the valuable results of segmentation enable you to effectively:

- ✔ **Identify the most and least profitable customers.** All customers are not created equal. An examination of revenue by customer segment usually reveals that a minority of customer segments is responsible for the majority of profits. This is called the *Pareto Principle*.

  Identifying more profitable segments allows you to focus your efforts on keeping these customers happy while increasing their purchases. What's more, segmenting can reveal underserved customers for whom specially designed and marketed products or services can be created.

- ✔ **Improve marketing focus.** Segments often have different interests, values, tastes, and reasons to purchase what you offer. Vastly disparate segments may not respond to the same marketing messages or campaigns.

- ✔ **Predict future purchase patterns.** Knowing that certain customers are more likely to purchase other products based on past purchases helps with planning and marketing. If you've ever watched a show on Netflix or purchased a book on Amazon, then you've seen the value of segmenting to predict and encourage future purchases.

  This practice is called *predictive analytics.*

- ✔ **Build loyal relationships.** Fully meeting the customers' expectations through customized service and uniquely designed products at a price they can afford helps build customer loyalty. Loyal customers are more likely to do business with you again and recommend you to their friends and colleagues.

  In addition, segmentation may reveal what kinds of incentives cause each segment to choose your business over the competition over and over again.

- ✔ **Price products differently.** Why lose money by reducing prices if some customers aren't motivated by price? By acquiring an in-depth knowledge of customer motivations and gauging how much they are willing to spend (price sensitivity), you can develop more effective pricing strategies.

- ✔ **Develop better products and customize products or service features.** Segmentation provides the knowledge you need to tailor your products and services to maximize your profits within each segment:

  - *Do you lose sales because your product lacks prestige for the target segment?*

  - *Is the product's large number of features making its price prohibitive?*

> • *Are customers more interested in the competition's products because it has better features?*
>
> • *Do you need to develop a whole new line of products?*
>
> Properly customizing products for each segment becomes easier as more understanding of the target segments is acquired.
>
> ✔ **Create personas.** A persona is a fictional person who represents the characteristics and goals of a customer segment. Personas are used to help make better product development and marketing decisions. See Chapter 5 for more information on creating personas.

This list is not exhaustive. The advantages of segmentation depend on the type of product or service you offer. Once you become more acquainted with the process of segmenting and researching your customers, you will find which ones apply to your business and possibly discover other unexpected advantages. For now, identifying a few objectives and positive outcomes is a good place to start.

One of the first steps to take in customer segmentation is to think about what makes sense for your organization. Is the gender of a customer something that determines what products he or she buys or is it the time of purchase? Or is gender just a proxy for another important variable? For example, an online sports website typically has men purchasing shirts and jerseys most of the year. During the Christmas shopping season, however, the gender balance shifts to women. Is that because women start appreciating sports around the holidays or are customers purchasing gifts for the men in their lives? Gender in this case is just a proxy for the time of purchase.

As another example, airlines want to segment their customers by how frequently they fly. A customer who flies once a year for pleasure is different from a customer who flies over a hundred thousand miles a year for business. The occasional traveler spends a lot less money with the airline, less time on the website and with customer service, but also has different needs and expectations. Email marketing and promotions should be tailored differently to both types of travelers. While airlines, like most companies, want to retain as many customers as possible, some segments are more valuable in terms of annual and lifetime revenue, something I cover in Chapter 6.

It is helpful to decide what you want to know about your customers before starting. While the type of product or service determines the customer attributes that are worth segmenting, there are some fundamental attributes most organizations should be familiar with. These are key areas on which data should be collected.

Tips for successful customer segmentation

Customer segmentation is more than a simple process. It requires a combination of facts and intuition to put yourself in your customers' shoes. Follow these guidelines to success:

✔ **Start with the end goal in mind.**

Define what you will do with the segmentation data before you begin. If your segmentation goal is to increase the sales of one of your product's optional features, data should be gathered about who buys the feature, which income bracket they belong to, and what their motivations are (low-cost solution or a premium high-quality option).

✔ **Be open-minded.**

Patterns emerge from data analysis. It's fine to have preconceived ideas about what to expect, but don't let that dictate how you look for patterns. Let the data do the talking.

One of the goals of segmentation is to learn new and possibly unexpected things about how your customers are similar. For example, when my company wanted to understand the most important features to customers on a healthcare web application, the stakeholders felt they already knew what those features were. However, the survey results from a representative set of customers showed the top three features were different from what the stakeholders were sure they knew.

✔ **Use existing data.**

The data you need may already exist. There's no need to commission an expensive survey if the data is already collected, say, for example, during the process of a sale or while on a call to customer service. What's more, you don't want to overburden your customers with questions about their details if you already have them. When my company wanted to know which versions of a software product customers were using, instead of asking them, we were able to find the information by reviewing the software purchase data.

✔ **Use multiple sources of data.**

Try not to rely on a single source of data. Look at existing customer lists, surveys, and third-party reports.

For example, on a customer segmentation survey my company conducted for a software company, we looked at the response rates by product lines and compared them to actual sales by product line. We ensured that the composition of customers responding to questions about their product usage would match the actual breakdown by product. Running smaller surveys with open-ended questions and conducting a few interviews can provide a lot of insight into what questions to ask. Customer surveys are usually easy to implement. Some companies offer perks such as drawings or a discount on a future purchase as a reward for participating in a survey.

When possible, use more than one source and plan on cross-referencing data.

Segmenting by the Five W's

Segmenting customers can seem daunting: Where do you start and how do you segment? While the answer depends on your goals and products, it can be helpful to think in terms of the five W's (*who, where, what, when, why,* and *how*) when segmenting.

Okay, it's actually five W's and an H.

Who

At the most basic level, you should know the demographics of your customers. Characterizing customers based on demographics is the simplest and easiest way to start segmenting. Demographic questions are not subjective: They give you real, verifiable information about your customers.

The core "who" demographic subjects include:

- ✔ Gender
- ✔ Age
- ✔ Income
- ✔ Education level
- ✔ Occupation
- ✔ Marital status
- ✔ Number and ages of children

Knowing these basic demographics is interesting in itself. For example, an airline company interested in determining who the most frequent users of its company-brand credit card are may find that they are high-paid men who travel for business. This type of information helps with identifying effective sources of advertising or products that this group is more likely to purchase.

Figure 4-1 displays two core demographics, gender and age, for a photography company. The data came from 4,000 responses to a customer survey. The results show an even split in gender. One consequence of this split is that gender-based marketing messages or targeted selling would likely exclude half the customer base. If the gender split was more like 80% to 20%, targeting one gender would likely make more sense.

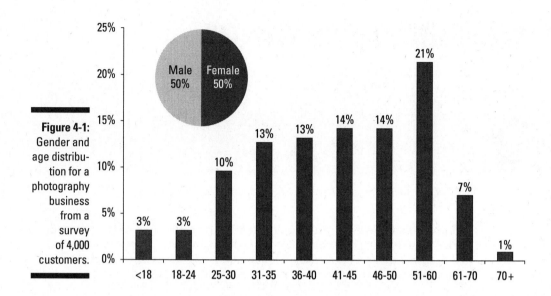

Figure 4-1:
Gender and
age distribu-
tion for a
photography
business
from a
survey
of 4,000
customers.

However, it's clear from the data that around 92% of the customer base is between 25 and 70 with the largest age segment being baby boomers between the ages of 51 and 60.

When analyzing demographic customer data, one strategy is to understand where your customer segments are disproportionate relative to the total population. In comparing this age distribution to the latest U.S. Census data, the age groups from 25 to 60 represent a higher percentage than the general U.S. population. While this age range is a bit wide, it can still narrow the focus of marketing activities and product strategies to this age range. It may also suggest to the company that there is an underserved market for younger and older photography enthusiasts.

Where

Knowing where customers live isn't just an exercise in placing pins on a map. Instead, it's about understanding the geographic diversity or concentration of your customers. It helps with locating better business locations, decreasing delivery time/distance, and so forth. If most of your customers live far away from your physical location, you may decide to open a new location that is closer to them.

Geographic attributes can include:

✔ Rural versus urban

✔ Domestic versus international

✔ City names and market size (for example, San Francisco versus St. Louis)

✔ Regions and states

✔ Zip codes

My company conducted a study for a U.S.-based mobile phone carrier to understand problems customers had when purchasing phones and paying bills online. As part of the study, the company wanted to understand the geographic breakdown of its online customers so it collected the zip codes of the participants. Figure 4-2 shows the locations of customers who participated in the study, which enabled the company to see the urban concentration and geographic diversity of the participants.

Figure 4-2: Locations of U.S.-based mobile phone customers who responded to a survey about their online account activity.

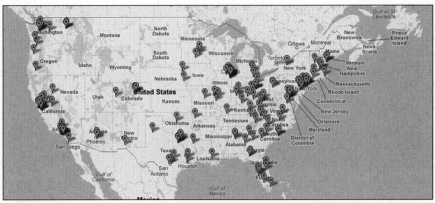

What

In thinking about the "what," you should think about past, present, and future. What have customers done, what are they doing, what are they thinking, and what are they likely to do?

What they have done

The easiest place to start is the past. What have customers done that distinguishes them? If helpful, think in terms of recency, frequency, and monetary value (revenue and profits) for segments:

✔ Most recent purchase

✔ Total number of transactions

✔ Product experience

✔ Total revenue

✔ Total profit

✔ Time spent with support

✔ Actual number of referred customers

From the answers to these questions, you learn how your customers interacted with your business in the past, and who your best customers were. Comparing this data with the data from other W's, you will be able to identify the characteristics of your least and most profitable customers.

For example, Figure 4-3 shows the amount of experience customers have with a software product used for drawing and design. The responses from almost 2,000 customers reveal that most customers have more than ten years of experience using the product.

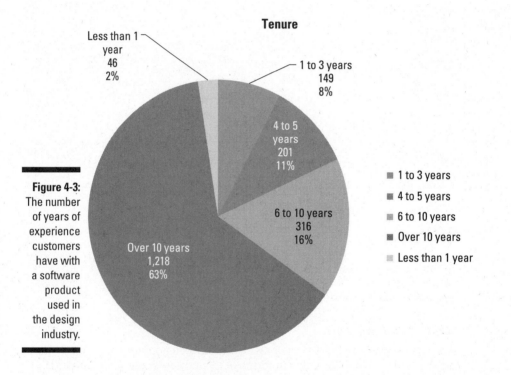

Figure 4-3: The number of years of experience customers have with a software product used in the design industry.

As another example, the retailer L.L.Bean sends different catalogs to customers based on how recently customers have purchased, how frequently they purchase, and the type of products they purchase. That means your neighbor probably has a different L.L.Bean catalog than you do.

What they are doing

Understanding the context, goals, and motivations of customers will help you to identify gaps in product features and opportunities for improvement. Use segmenting to define key areas such as:

> ✔ Motivations: Business or pleasure
>
> ✔ Experience level: Power versus novice user
>
> ✔ Goals: Perhaps looking for a lawyer versus getting answers to a legal question

A customer who uses only a few features of a software product has different needs than a "power user" who uses all the functionality. Power users may be more interested in new features and upgrades than the more occasional or novice user.

What they think

Look to identify attitudes and psychographics that differentiate the following:

> ✔ **Lifestyles:** Traveler versus homebody
>
> ✔ **Values:** Frugal versus spendthrift
>
> ✔ **Technology:** Early adopter versus tech laggard
>
> ✔ **Personalities:** Risk seeking versus risk averse
>
> ✔ **Overall product satisfaction:** Low versus high
>
> ✔ **Investing habits:** Active versus occasional investor

These questions are more subjective than objective, but are nonetheless fundamental. For example, if a majority of your customers typically wait until all their friends have a technology before making a purchase (tech laggard) then marketing that emphasizes cutting-edge technologies won't be appealing.

What they are likely to do

You also want to think in terms of long-term relationships and the lifetime value of a customer. Using a combination of surveys and past behavior can help you estimate:

> ✔ Likelihood to recommend to friends
>
> ✔ Likelihood to repurchase

This helps you identify the customer segments with whom you can reasonably expect to benefit from long-term relationships. Identifying loyal customers is instrumental in keeping them. Offering perks such as discounts when using your company-brand credit card, participation in sweepstakes, or free products and services for their loyalty is an effective way to get customers to choose your company over the competition. Customer loyalty is covered in detail in Chapter 12.

When

There are often significant differences in the types of customers you have, based on when you measure.

- ✔ Seasons: Christmas shopping versus ordinary time
- ✔ Weekends versus weekdays
- ✔ Life events: After a baby, marriage, or move
- ✔ Daytime versus evening
- ✔ Periodic activities: Get haircuts and buy toothpaste every five weeks

Why

The "why" is pretty obvious, isn't it? The customer wants or needs what you have to offer!

As touched on in the beginning of this chapter, customer segmentation can help answer many business questions. Among those include:

- ✔ What are my customer segments and how are they defined?
- ✔ How many distinct groups do we serve — and how are they different?
- ✔ What customer segments deliver the most revenue and profit?
- ✔ What products and services appeal to which customer segments?
- ✔ How can I tailor communication to better address customers' needs?
- ✔ Which consumers tend to shop/interact exclusively online and why?
- ✔ How and where should I leverage my customer loyalty program further?

How

How do customers interact with the product or service?

- ✔ Online versus in store
- ✔ Phone versus in person
- ✔ Through a reseller versus direct

Knowing how customers already interact with your business gives insight into what can be improved and what is already working to its full potential. For example, say you are trying to improve the sales of your software and you realize that most users buy it from a reseller. Perhaps that means that your website is difficult to use and so less tech-savvy people therefore turn to a third party. This is very valuable information and could indicate that your website needs improvement in order to meet the needs of your less tech-savvy customer segment.

It isn't essential to collect every one of these attributes about your customers: Some may not apply and some may not make a huge difference. It all depends on the kinds of products or services you offer and the goals you have in mind. Are you looking for an optimal store location to reach wealthy clientele? Focus on geographical and demographic questions to identify where the well-to-do segment of your customer base resides or shops. Use your judgment and knowledge of your own business to pinpoint the attributes that are the most meaningful to your study.

Analyzing the Data to Segment Your Customers

After you've collected the data, you can do a number of things to make your segmentation as realistic and objective as possible. Customer segmentation, especially when dealing with large volumes of data, needs to be well thought out and organized. Predictive analytics technology can discover automatically which groupings exist in customer data and find relevant patterns that are likely to be much more subtle, extracting much greater predictive insight than traditional segmentation. However, you don't need sophisticated software to uncover the major customer segments. You can manage it by following these four steps.

Step 1: Tabulate your data

The first step is to organize the data in a way that is simple to analyze. It can be helpful to tabulate your data in a spreadsheet.

For example, the data shown in Table 4-1 is a small sample from a larger survey of United Airlines website customers that my company performed in May 2014. In this table, each row is from a different customer and each column contains the answers to specific questions about how each customer typically interacts with the United Airlines website.

Where possible, survey responses should be coded with simple numeric responses. For example, customers who have a United Airlines credit card are coded 1 and those who don't have one are coded 0. For categories that have a natural ordering, maintain the sequence by coding categories from low to high or from high to low. For example, the most frequent visitors in the survey represented in Table 4-1 are coded with a high frequency of 1, for visiting on average once a day, and 5 for once in the last year (low frequency).

Table 4-1	Characteristics of Flyers	
Possess an airline credit card **1: yes; 0: no**	**Frequency of website visits** **1: once a day** **2: a few times a week** **3: a few times a month** **4: a few times a year** **5: once**	**High frequency of website visits** **(1: yes; 0: no)**
1	3	0
1	4	0
0	2	1

You can then create new variables to simplify the segments. The column "High frequency of website visits" is created by reducing the multiple levels in the "Frequency of website visits" column to just high and low frequency (a binary variable). Customers who visit at least a few times a week (scores of 1, 2, or 3) are coded a 1 and those visiting less frequently (scores of 4 and 5) are coded a 0.

Step 2: Cross-Tabbing

Now that your data is tabulated, the next step is to refine your analysis by "crossing" more than one variable. Cross-tabbing helps you visualize interrelations between two variables by explicitly revealing that some customer attributes usually appear (or do not usually appear) in conjunction with other attributes. Table 4-2 illustrates this concept by showing the interrelation between the customers' ownership of an airline credit card and the frequency of their visits to the airline website.

Table 4-2	Cross-Tabbing Customers with Credit Cards and Website Visit Frequency		
	Low frequency of website visits	**High frequency of website visits**	**Total**
Customer owns an airline credit card	56	29	85
Customer does not own an airline credit card	13	13	26
Total	69	42	111

Each cell in Table 4-2 contains the number of customers who fit in the category on the top and side of the table. For example, 29 customers own an airline credit card *and* visit the airline website frequently. Next, to facilitate analysis, the numbers in Table 4-3 can be converted to percentages, using the following simple equation:

% of customers in cell = # of customers in cell* 100%

= total # of customers surveyed

Here, the total number of customers surveyed is 111. Therefore, a new table with percentages can be created and is easier to interpret:

Table 4-3	Cross-Tabbing with Percentages		
	Low frequency of website visits	*High frequency of website visits*	*Total*
Customer owns an airline credit card	50%	26%	76%
Customer does not own an airline credit card	12%	12%	24%
Total	62%	38%	100%

A lot of useful information can be drawn from Table 4-3. For example, there appears to be no association between owning an airline credit card and the frequency of website use (12% low frequency, 12% high frequency). For customers who do own a credit card, a counterintuitive result emerges: A majority of them visit the website infrequently (50% low frequency, 26% high frequency). This initial analysis suggests that airline credit card ownership is not associated with more frequent visits to the airline website.

This data comes from just a sample of customers. Any sample has random variation. To know if the difference between card ownership and website frequency is statistically significant (beyond what you would expect from random variation), you would conduct a Chi-Square Test of Independence. See the appendix on on how to conduct and interpret this statistical test.

When cross-tabbing, look to mix many of the different dimensions to find patterns or valuable segments. You may uncover surprising trends and learn something new about your customers!

Step 3: Cluster Analysis

A more advanced technique used to identify segments is based on clustering algorithms such as cluster analysis, factor analysis, and multiple regression analysis. These techniques identify statistical patterns that are hard to detect intuitively. You'll want to call in the professionals to help with this because it involves both sophisticated software and statistical know-how. You may encounter some output of cluster analysis, however. There is more discussion on finding similarities with customer analytics in the appendix and in the book *Predictive Analytics for Dummies* (Wiley).

A common output of a cluster analysis is a visual map (called a *dendrogram*) that shows how customers cluster based on responses to the same questions. For example, Figure 4-4 shows an example of a dendrogram for how customers shop for consumer electronic devices on their smartphones. Each line represents a particular feature that consumers find important, such as reading consumer reviews, or the capability to customize products or watch product videos. The closer the lines are, the more similar customers each feature. So customers find similar importance with features A, B and with features C, and D. However, features C and D aren't closely related with either feature A or B as they are far apart in the dendrogram.

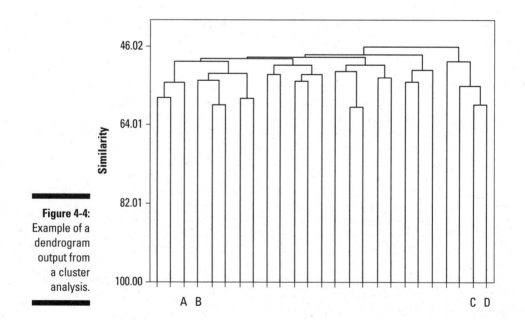

Figure 4-4:
Example of a
dendrogram
output from
a cluster
analysis.

Step 4: Estimate the size of each segment

When your data is organized, you can estimate how many customers are in a particular segment. The purpose of estimating the size of the segment is to understand the total percent of current customers who make up each and to estimate the total size of the segment for non-customers too. If the potential market size is large, then it presents more opportunity for growth.

To estimate the size of each segment, you need to know the total size of your market and some data about the appropriate segment. For example, if marketers at United Airlines want to calculate the size of the segment of its customers who frequently visit its website, United Airlines can use the following equation:

Estimated # of customers

x % of customers who frequently visit the website

= # of customers who frequently visit the website

Unless you survey every single customer, there is a sampling error with your percentages. The best way to understand the sampling error is to use confidence intervals (as covered in Chapter 2). Confidence intervals put boundaries around the upper and lower percentages to understand how much percentages could fluctuate based on your sample. For example, if 5 out of 100 survey respondents are over age 65, a good estimate about this segment is 5%. Using confidence intervals, you can be 95% confident that the actual percentage of all customers over age 65 is between 2% and 11%. In other words, it's highly unlikely more than 11% or fewer than 2% of customers are over age 65.

To compute confidence intervals with binary data, use the free calculator online at http://www.measuringu.com/wald.htm. Figure 4-5 shows a screen shot of what you enter and the results. Enter **5** in the "Passed" box and **100** in the "Total Tested" box. The row labeled "Adj. Wald" provides the confidence interval.

Step 5. Estimate the value of each segment

To determine which customer segments are economically the most important to you, estimate the percentage of customers in a specific segment who are going to purchase your product within a specific time period and the amount of revenue you expect from each sale. Ideally, you already have good estimates from the experience of operating your business and from the information gathered in the preceding steps. The following equation can be used to calculate the revenues expected from a specific segment:

# of customers in the segment

x % of customers who will purchase your product

x revenue per sale of your product (in $)

= potential revenues (in $) from this segment

For example, if there are an estimated 100,000 potential customers in a segment and 5% will likely purchase a $100 product, the potential revenue is 100,000 × .05 × 100 = $500,000.

Input Table		Results Table					
Passed	**Total Tested**	**Confidence Intervals**				**Point Estimates**	
5	100		Low	High	Margin of Error*		
		Adj. Wald	0.0187	0.1146	0.0480	Best Estimate	0.0588
Calculate		Exact	0.0164	0.1128	0.0482	MLE	0.0500
		Score	0.0215	0.1118	0.0451	LaPlace	0.0588
Confidence Level: 95% ▾		Wald	0.0073	0.0927	0.0427	Jeffrey's	0.0545
					Using Alpha: .05	Wilson	0.0666
Likely Population Completion Rate							
Unknown ▾							

Figure 4-5: Compute confidence internals.

Use both the lower and upper boundaries of the confidence intervals to create "conservative" and "best-case" scenarios for estimating the value of a segment.

Using attitudinal variables like the *Net Promoter Score (NPS)* is useful to differentiate between "good" and "bad" profits. The NPS is an indication of how likely customers are to recommend your product or service to a friend or coworker. The scale ranges from 0 (not at all likely to recommend) to 10 (very likely to recommend). If a customer's NPS is:

- ✔ **9 or 10:** The customer is called a *promoter* and is likely to talk positively about your product.

- ✔ **7 or 8:** The customer is called *passive* and probably will not talk positively or negatively about your product.

- ✔ **Below 7:** The customer is called a *detractor* and will likely talk negatively about your product.

The data in Table 4-4 are a small subset from a survey of customers at a large software company.

Table 4-4	Net Promoter Score
Likelihood to Recommend	*Category*
5	Detractor
10	Promoter
8	Passive
7	Passive
. . .	. . .

The proportions of promoters, passives, and detractors among your customers reveal how customers and their friends and colleagues view your product. Customers who generate a high proportion of revenue but who have a bad experience are more likely to say negative things and lead to decreasing revenue streams (bad profits). This topic is discussed in Chapter 12.

You can cross-tab responses to the Net Promoter question with other important questions about future revenue and include confidence intervals. For example, say you want to understand how software renewal rates would differ based on how likely customers are to recommend a product to a friend. Figure 4-6 shows the percentages of customers who said they would renew their software licenses based on whether they were promoters, passives, or detractors. Only 18% of customers who are detractors are likely to renew their licenses. In contrast, 53% of promoters are likely to renew. The small lines that are placed on top of each bar in the graph are visualizations of the confidence interval. They tell you that between 50% and 55% of all customers who are promoters would renew their licenses.

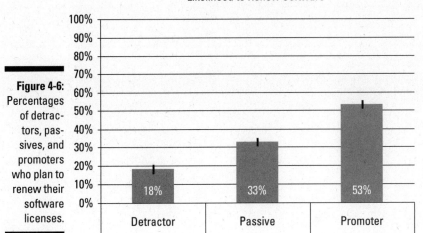

Figure 4-6: Percentages of detractors, passives, and promoters who plan to renew their software licenses.

Don't try to do everything at once. Collect enough data to get a good handle on your customers, but don't hesitate to go in stages. Finally, try to focus your efforts by having some research questions and hypotheses to answer before collecting data, but don't be afraid of following the patterns that emerge from the analysis.

Happy segmenting!

Chapter 5

Creating Customer Personas

*P*ersonas are fictional customers based on real data obtained from customer segmentation analyses, ethnographic research, surveys, and interviews.

The purpose of a persona is to better focus product development and marketing efforts on real customer needs and goals rather than just abstract demographics. To make personas more realistic, they get names like "Marcus" or "Shannon" and have pictures or can even be life-sized cardboard cutouts.

While the people and pictures can be fictional, the details should be factual: Their goals and characteristics should represent the real needs of a larger group of customers.

In this chapter, I discuss the ways personas can help product development and marketing efforts for an organization. I walk you step by step through the persona creation process with examples and show you how they can answer important questions.

Recognizing the Importance of Personas

When you're busy developing a product, it's easy to start wondering what a hypothetical customer could want to do and build in new features to support these possible scenarios.

I've worked with many development teams building consumer and business software products. Product managers and developers spend lots of time discussing all sorts of scenarios. That's part of product development:

understanding what customers need and meeting that need (see Chapter 9). However, there's a difference between making sure a product meets core customer goals and getting bogged down in making sure a product can do everything.

Unusual scenarios are called *edge-cases* and include all the things a customer *might* do with software but probably wouldn't do most of the time. A customer might want to customize the toolbar in a software program. A customer might want to access the command line. A customer might want to code plug-ins.

The problem with the "coulds" and "mights" is that there is an almost endless list of things one customer could do or might want to do with any product. Trying to build for every possible scenario means building a product that doesn't work well for the most common scenarios customers want.

If you try to build for all users, you build for no users. A persona is intended to focus design thinking. If a persona named Marcus represents 70% of your customers' goals, behaviors, and profiles, most design questions can be answered by asking: Would Marcus do this? Personas are powerful if they are specific.

When you understand your customers' motivations, expectations, and abilities, you have a more accurate picture that helps to design better products for them and how to make them choose your product over your competitors' offerings.

Counterintuitively, precisely defining the goals, motivations, and needs of a narrow slice of customers and designing for them will not necessarily narrow your market. On the contrary, it enables you to fully focus your efforts on entirely satisfying these customers, gaining their loyalty, and letting them take care of marketing your product in the most effective way: by recommending it to those around them.

Now boarding

An example of a dramatically successful product that was specifically designed for a comparatively small customer segment is the roller-board suitcase as featured in the book *The Inmates Are Running the Asylum* (Sams - Pearson Education). If you've been on an airplane in the last ten years, then you've seen these getting put in the overhead bins.

The roller-board suitcase, complete with retractable handle and wheels, was not originally designed for you and me, but for airline flight crews. It perfectly met their needs: It was compact, simple, easy to haul around busy airports, and just the right size to fit a few changes of clothes. As a result, flight attendants were extremely satisfied with it and popularized it so much that roller-board suitcases have since become the norm for air travel. Personas can help you design such perfectly adapted products.

It's important to create a persona that represents the primary segment of customers for a product. The advantages of thoroughly researched and well-developed personas are:

✔ **As stand-ins for real users, they guide decisions about design and functionality.**

What is Marcus going to use this product for? If Marcus's needs and skill level are already defined, it is simple to figure out how to serve him better. Personas help prevent programmers or designers from creating products that would be perfect for themselves or from making guesses about what customers want. A persona helps keep the end user involved in the product development.

✔ **They allow you to concentrate on designing for a manageable target who represents a larger group.**

Focusing on one customer segment and fully satisfying it is much more efficient to increase sales and profits. Trying to satisfy all your customers at once does not work.

✔ **They give a common and consistent goal to the design and marketing teams.**

Marcus, with his particular motivations and level of proficiency with the product, needs to be on everyone's mind. If everybody works to satisfy him, not only the design of the product but also the message sent to customers will be consistent and more convincing.

✔ **Prioritizing design elements and resolving design disagreements can be done in an economical way.**

Personas are great communication tools. In explaining decisions to colleagues or people higher in the company hierarchy, use of personas helps refocus the conversation on the target customer.

✔ **Identifying opportunities and product gaps to drive strategy becomes easier.**

Having a precise idea of the target customer, actually trying to see things from his point of view, is an excellent starting point for brainstorming. Novel feature or product ideas can emerge from this single customer-oriented thinking.

✔ **Designs can be continually evaluated and validated based on personas to reduce the frequency of usability testing.**

If the whole programming team strives to make a product designed for Marcus, there should be fewer surprises when conducting real-life testing.

Working with personas

When you embark on the process of creating customer personas, multiple personas typically emerge as you identify various customer segments and use cases. The number and type of personas reflect the diversity of your customer base.

For example, automotive websites like Cars.com, Kelley Blue Book, and Edmunds.com have different types of customers that research information on cars. Some customers are auto enthusiasts, others are parents with kids, and still other significant segments of the customer base are young professionals intimidated by the car-buying process.

One such car company created seven personas from the data it collected from interviews and surveys on how customers researched automotive information online. The company broke the seven personas into four *primary* and three *secondary* personas. Breaking the personas into primary and secondary groups helps website developers decide on the prominence of automotive information. The primary customer segments are embodied in primary personas that want many details about car specifications. The designers then cater to this primary class of users by providing multiple views on engine, body, performance, and feature details. However, they can't ignore the secondary personas who represent another significant portion of website visitors — those who are intimidated or less interested in the minutiae of car specs.

In building the personas, the key characteristics identified in surveys and interviews that defined the persona were the type of car (new versus used) and the emphasis on price versus style.

One primary persona, Bill, is 34, single, and possesses strong opinions about car brands and style. He's less interested in other people's ratings and loves to research cars whenever he has time. His defining quote is: "I have to have a new car every year." An abbreviated version of the Bill persona is shown in Figure 5-1.

In contrast, a secondary persona is represented by Sam (see Figure 5-2). Sam doesn't like researching cars, and this is the first one she's buying on her own. She's just out of college and is looking for a good deal on a used car. She wants something reliable but fun. Her defining quote is: "Buying cars is intimidating but I have friends I can ask."

Having the relevant information about primary personas like Bill means the designers should be sure car enthusiasts can get to all the technical specs they want on the website. The designers balance the Bills with the Sams, who will visit the website to look for basic information like features and reviews.

Sam isn't interested in technical jargon, so the designers have summary information and graphics to denote high and low gas mileage vehicles and price, and display the rates prominently on the car detail page.

Bill: 34 Single, lives in Los Angeles

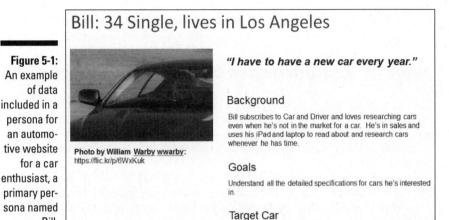

Photo by William Warby wwarby:
https://flic.kr/p/6WxKuk

"I have to have a new car every year."

Background

Bill subscribes to Car and Driver and loves researching cars even when he's not in the market for a car. He's in sales and uses his iPad and laptop to read about and research cars whenever he has time.

Goals

Understand all the detailed specifications for cars he's interested in.

Target Car

New Car | Brand over Value

Figure 5-1:
An example of data included in a persona for an automotive website for a car enthusiast, a primary persona named Bill.

Sam: 23 Single, lives in Denver

Photo by Goonk Vilaivanh goonkvilaivanh
https://flic.kr/p/hUssEW

"Buying cars is intimidating but I have friends I can ask"

Background

Sam is 1 year out of college in her first job. Her parents purchased her only other car and she's looking to make her first purchase. She is comfortable with technology but does not use her iPhone to research cars.

Goals

Looking for a fun car, hates to "haggle" and looks to others for advice.

Target Car

Used Car | Price and Value are the most important. She's interested in ratings and reviews.

Figure 5-2:
An example of data included in a persona for an automotive website for a first-time car buyer named Sam.

It's common to use stock photography for personas (as in this chapter). While it's fine to use actual customer pictures, it can be difficult based on customer privacy concerns. Give the persona a face, but don't be too concerned if it's a model rather than a real customer.

Getting More Personal with Customer Data

A few simple steps are required when you need to build an effective persona.

Step 1: Collecting the appropriate data

The most important rule in building a persona is that the information you use for it should not be made up or based on opinion. Base your persona on actual data. Collecting, aggregating and analyzing customer data from customer databases and social media helps provide input into a data-driven persona process.

That said, although you want customers to like your product, the best data to start with is not obtained by asking your customers what they like or don't like.

Personas concentrate on what a user does, what frustrates him, and what makes life a bit easier. A good persona is a narrative that describes a person's typical day and experiences, as well as skills, attitude, background, environment, and goals. Personas identify the motivations, expectations, aspirations, and behaviors common to a large segment of customers.

Start with demographic data from a customer segmentation analysis: gender, age, industry, how frequently they use the product, and so forth. This tells you a lot about who your customers are; however, it rarely includes information about motivations and goals, which are essential in building a persona.

To understand what your customers are trying to do, use the following methods.

Conducting a new survey

Surveys are one of the most cost-effective ways of gathering data from lots of customers. You can survey existing customers from customer lists or prospective customers by using panel agencies that recruit qualified customers or prospective customers. In addition to basic demographics, ask questions about motivations, goals, and challenges.

See Chapter 13 for ideas on conducting a top-tasks analysis that gets to the primary things customers really want to do with your product.

Interviewing customers

Interview customers to get a better understanding of motivations, goals, and challenges. You can conduct the interviews in person or over the phone.

Don't cold call customers. When collecting customer information, be sure a customer opts-in to being contacted. Allow customers to opt-out of being contacted again if they wish.

Avoid focus groups if possible. Unless your product or service is used by groups of people at the same time, conduct one-on-one interviews. Group sessions can easily be influenced by personalities and are often best for generating new ideas to test later. In the interviews, have customers talk about their problems, frustrations, and goals.

Observing

Watch users as they use your product, a competitor's product, or just try and solve problems on their own. This is often referred to as ethnographic research or field studies. In observing, you can see things that are hard for customers to articulate.

For example, while I worked at Intuit, we watched customers as they entered their information into point-of-sale cash registers, then exported their sales at the end of the day into QuickBooks. The process of exporting and importing was both time consuming and error-prone. This frustrating process inspired the Intuit design teams to come up with ideas about how to make balancing the books easier.

Usability testing

Have users attempt common tasks with your product or service. Don't ask users what they like or dislike; instead, watch them interact with it and look for pain points and opportunities to improve your offering. (See Chapter 14.)

Secondary research

If interviews cannot be conducted or surveys commissioned, partial secondhand information can be obtained from within your company: in sales, marketing, product, customer support, and tech support. While it's not ideal to rely on secondhand information, personas from secondhand data are usually better than not building personas at all.

Use a mix of methods, both surveys and interviews, and minimize opinions and guesses. You'll often notice a behavior in an interview or field study and then you can look to understand its prevalence by conducting a follow-up survey to a larger set of customers.

Avoid asking for opinions and concentrate on *motivators*. Many times, users do not know exactly what they need, but they do think about what they want.

While there is an art and science to writing good survey and interview questions, in general you don't want to lead customers down a predetermined path. Avoid questions that suggest an answer or have simple yes or no questions. For example, "Would you like this product to be easier to use?" is not the best question because in most cases customers will say yes. A better question would be, "If you could fix only one thing about the product, what would it be?"

Like building customer segments, just because you have data (like detailed demographics) doesn't mean it will be relevant to constructing a persona.

Step 2: Dividing data

After gathering data about your customers, look for themes and patterns that are relevant and based on behaviors and goals. Categorize open-ended comments or actions observed in field studies with other similar comments and actions to identify patterns. In particular, look for patterns around:

- ✔ What they expect to accomplish with your product
- ✔ How they go about achieving their goals
- ✔ What their technical background or product proficiency is

At this point, it is useful to brainstorm:

- ✔ Do you need more information?
- ✔ Can you group the data in other ways?

For example, we were conducting research on the major email providers such as Gmail, Yahoo!, and Hotmail. After surveying 1,000 users, we found repetitive comments about how Yahoo! changed its interface too often. This would be a good candidate for understanding how often Yahoo! actually changes its interface and what type of customer is averse to the changes.

Step 3: Identifying and refining personas

From the most important groups identified in Step 2, define an initial set of primary personas as described in the earlier automotive website example. These will constitute your "set of characters" the product or marketing teams should focus on.

For each persona, create a realistic portrait.

✔ Create an *identity* with details that make the persona more real:

- *Name*
- *Picture*
- *Personal history*

✔ Create a *portrait* with data that connects a persona to a customer segment:

- *Goals*
- *Habits*
- *Expectations*
- *Skills*
- *Attitudes*
- *Motivations*
- *Environment*

Some personas in your set of characters are not among your target customers. In fact, some of them could be examples of whom you are *not* designing or marketing for.

Don't overdo the persona process. Although personas provide many cost- and time-saving benefits, there is a diminishing return if you spend too much time and effort developing them. Don't get too bogged down in documenting every detail or spend too much time creating bloated documents. If development teams and marketers are faced with too much information, it will get ignored.

Creating a good persona requires composing both qualitative and quantitative research, but it should be presented in no more than about one or two pages. It is not a job description. Stay away from minutiae like tasks, duties, and responsibilities. Concentrate on *skills, attitudes, motivations, environment,* and *goals.*

Follow these guidelines as you develop a persona:

✔ **Use multiple sources of data: Segmentation, interviews, surveys, and observations.**

✔ **Get buy-in:** Interview stakeholders from sales, product development, product support, and marketing to look for agreement and insight.

✔ **Don't base it on one customer and his idiosyncrasies.**

> ✔ **Distinguish types of data:**
>
> - *Data that connects a persona to a customer segment (for example, proficiency level with your software)*
>
> - *Data that only makes the persona more real to you (for example, his name is Andy MacPherson)*

Creating a persona in three steps

Here's an example of using all three steps to build a persona. My company helped the National Multiple Sclerosis Society (NMSS) with the redesign of its website. As part of the effort, we needed to define who uses the website, and then build a set of personas to help the new development team design for this cast of characters.

This figure shows an example of a persona called "Vanessa." It was created as one of ten distinct personas representing archetypal members or people otherwise interacting with the website:

✔ We started with demographic data obtained from 1,000 visitors to the current website collected over a two-month period.

✔ We supplemented this demographic data with six stakeholder interviews to understand whom NMSS was targeting and to ensure the new website aligned with the organization's mission.

✔ We conducted 30 in-person interviews that matched the customer segments identified from the surveys and stakeholder interviews.

During the one-hour interviews, website users also showed us how they use the current website, the type of questions they have, and how they go about using the website to answer their questions.

Observing the portrait of Vanessa reveals several strategies you can use to build better personas:

✔ Vanessa is introduced not only by a name and a picture, but also by a defining quote.

✔ Although simple and conversational, the main body of the text reveals important information: how the disease of multiple sclerosis concretely affects her life, her attitude about it, and how she interacts with the Society. These are real pieces of information gathered through research and interviews about a certain segment of people living with MS.

✔ The text is written in the first person, like a testimony. This is another strategy to make Vanessa more true to life.

✔ Key information, both fictional and from research, is emphasized on the right side.

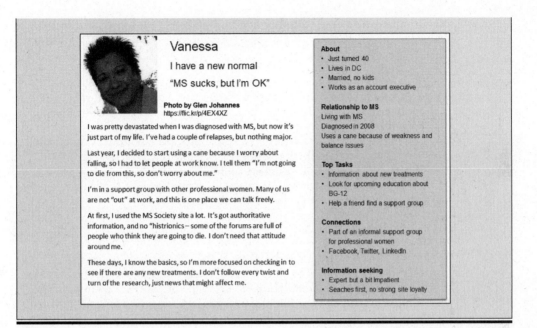

Vanessa

I have a new normal

"MS sucks, but I'm OK"

Photo by Glen Johannes
https://flic.kr/p/4EX4XZ

I was pretty devastated when I was diagnosed with MS, but now it's just part of my life. I've had a couple of relapses, but nothing major.

Last year, I decided to start using a cane because I worry about falling, so I had to let people at work know. I tell them "I'm not going to die from this, so don't worry about me."

I'm in a support group with other professional women. Many of us are not "out" at work, and this is one place we can talk freely.

At first, I used the MS Society site a lot. It's got authoritative information, and no "histrionics – some of the forums are full of people who think they are going to die. I don't need that attitude around me.

These days, I know the basics, so I'm more focused on checking in to see if there are any new treatments. I don't follow every twist and turn of the research, just news that might affect me.

About
- Just turned 40
- Lives in DC
- Married, no kids
- Works as an account executive

Relationship to MS
Living with MS
Diagnosed in 2008
Uses a cane because of weakness and balance issues

Top Tasks
- Information about new treatments
- Look for upcoming education about BG-12
- Help a friend find a support group

Connections
- Part of an informal support group for professional women
- Facebook, Twitter, LinkedIn

Information seeking
- Expert but a bit impatient
- Seaches first, no strong site loyalty

Answering Questions with Personas

Personas provide details to important questions that a customer cannot define:

- How can you make your product easier to use?
- What is your product's top task?
- What motivates customers to use this specific product over a competitor's?
- How do you develop a successful marketing strategy for the product?

By using a persona to answer these questions, design and marketing teams can actually be in the user's shoes, and can better meet a real user's needs and wants. The following scenario illustrates how personas make that possible.

Will Swanson is a 52-year-old civil engineer working for a consulting firm involved with multiple projects in China. He travels to Beijing or Shanghai at least once every two months, always flying from Chicago. Additionally, once a year, Will and his wife (Sarah) fly to Hawaii for a week to visit his parents.

Will routinely flies with United Airlines and usually pays for his flights online using his United credit card. He visits the United website about once every two weeks.

Laurie O'Reilly is a 30-year-old K-12 English teacher who lives in Albany, NY. Once a year, carrying coloring books and pencils, she flies to Florida with her husband (Ben) and their two young children. There, they enjoy some family time in the sun. Twice, Laurie found a special deal and they went to the Bahamas instead. Laurie has some flexibility around her traveling dates, which enables her to look for the best prices. She does not own an airline credit card, but she does buy tickets on the Internet. She does not have any special preferences for United Airlines; however, she visits the website about once every two months to check ticket prices.

Will and Laurie are very different personas; they will not answer questions in the same way. An example of a question could be, "What is the most important feature of the United Airlines website?" For Will, the website's most important feature is to allow him to quickly find the exact flight that he needs: right time, right destination, no layover. For Laurie, the most important feature is the ability to find the best possible deal: She is flexible with time and exact destination and does not mind layovers, but she wants to pay as little as possible. Therefore, if both of the customer segments represented by these personas are to be satisfied, both of these tasks need to be easy to perform (without getting in the way of one another).

United Airlines' marketing team can also use Will and Laurie's personas to segment the airlines' customers and reach them in different ways. Will is likely to be more responsive to emails promoting special frequent flyer benefits, while Laurie might appreciate time-sensitive emails from United, alerting her when there has been a price drop on family-friendly beach destinations, such as Florida or the Caribbean.

This is just a simple example of how personas enable you to efficiently and effectively understand, identify, and communicate what the user needs. Usability testing is another strategy to identify specific opportunities to improve, innovate on, and bridge the gaps to make sure you are delivering a fully functional and usable product. Usability testing is covered in detail in Chapter 14.

Another example of a product designed for one user that reached a surprisingly wide audience is the GoPro camera prototyped and developed by surfer Nicholas Woodman. Woodman designed a wrist strap with an attached video camera to record himself surfing. He hoped to produce professional quality footage of himself while on the water. For that task, he had very specific needs: a camera that had a very wide viewing angle, that was waterproof, that could be positioned in different ways, and that was not too expensive.

He soon realized that he would have to design not only the wrist strap, but also the camera. Focusing only on his own specific needs, Nicholas Woodman had created a product that was perfect for millions of other amateurs like him. It exceeded its original market, California's surf culture, and is now sold to snowboarders, skiers, social activists, and countless others all over the world.

While most products are not designed by the user, similar results can be obtained with a persona-centered perspective.

Chapter 6

Determining Customer Lifetime Value

*I*f you've ever signed up for a credit card that had a low introductory interest rate, or enjoyed a low cable subscription in the first year of signing up, then you've experienced marketing strategies informed by a company's analysis of customer lifetime value (CLV).

The CLV is the total profit that an individual customer generates for your business over his or her lifetime. The *customer lifetime* is the time period that starts when a customer first uses your business (in person or online) and ends when he buys his last service or product from you. The CLV covers the entire relationship you have with that specific customer, or segment of customers.

In Chapter 4, I discuss the importance of segmenting customers. One of the primary reasons for segmenting customers is that not all customers generate the same revenue or profits for an organization. Certain segments are more profitable than others. Now, the next step is to understand how segments of customers differ in the duration of their relationship with your business. The CLV is intimately linked to customer loyalty (see Chapter 12). Some customer segments are more prone to loyalty and are therefore more likely to cultivate a long-term relationship with your business, thus generating more revenue over their lifetime. Identifying the CLV of different segments enables you to balance the acquisition costs of a new customer with expected long-term revenue. This knowledge also helps you fine-tune your marketing strategy to acquire more high-CLV customers.

Why Your CLV Is Important

The CLV metric serves many purposes. The most obvious is that it gives you a good idea of how much total profit you can expect from a customer. It isn't a hard science, but solid calculations based on data yield a reasonably accurate estimate to work with. Knowing the total lifetime profit (or loss) created by a specific client can also help you determine which goods or services justify higher marketing costs or sales compensation. Moreover, calculating the CLV of different customer segments helps orient your marketing strategy.

Aside from gaining a holistic view of the client, CLV is a good tool for forecasting future sales and profits, using resources efficiently, and controlling costs. Cable companies are a good example of effectively utilizing the concept of CLV. The reason cable companies offer such low upfront fees is that they've calculated the lifetime value of their customers and therefore know they can afford to initially lose a certain amount of money in order to acquire long-term customers.

As another example, the financial services firm Charles Schwab has the lifetime revenue of individual customers ready for managers and employees when resolving problems customers encountered with their service. Employees have the ability to credit customers with free trades, and in some cases, even help offset the losses based on the lifetime value of a customer. It doesn't make sense to haggle over $100 with a customer who has spent $10,000 over 10 years with the firm. This philosophy has helped make Charles Schwab a financial firm with one of the highest customer loyalty levels.

Using CLV to acquire customers

Knowing how long the average customer who initially benefits from low fees does business with them, organizations can determine how much money they can lose to acquire new customers. Consider these examples:

- Eastman Kodak which used to take a loss on selling its cameras because it knew it could make the loss up with the sales of film.

- Razor blades are relatively cheap and, in some cases free, when you purchase them with a new shaver. It's the years (and therefore, the additional money) customers spend buying the refill blades that allows for the initial low prices.

- If your printer breaks, it doesn't make sense to repair it. You can buy a new color printer for under $50 now. The reason is that the printer companies are willing to sell you a printer at a loss in order to get the years of ink-toner purchases.

- Remember the old record/CD clubs like Columbia House? They'd charge a penny for ten CDs, because they knew they'd lock you in to purchasing ten overpriced ones even if you didn't want them over the next year.

All of these are examples of companies calculating the lifetime value of their customers and basing their customer acquisition strategy on that piece of information.

A daring customer acquisition strategy like those used by cable companies could be a financial catastrophe without appropriate data to back it and predict customer behavior. Although the CLV concept has been around for years, few companies have the technology to track each customer, know the usage on an individual basis, and implement this metric in order to quantify behavior. In the next section, I explain how to effectively calculate and use the CLV.

Applying CLV in Business

The CLV can be used to evaluate the amount of money that can reasonably be devoted to customer acquisition. In order for your business to be profitable and financially sustainable, it is essential that the CLV outweigh the customer acquisition costs. Otherwise, your business is bound to lose considerable amounts of money. If it costs $1,000 to acquire a new customer through marketing, sales, and production costs, but the customer generates only $75 over the typical lifetime, then that's a losing strategy.

To develop a marketing budget, you need to reflect on how much and where you will invest your money:

- ✔ **Explore allowable acquisition cost:** How much can you afford to spend to get a customer who will continue to return for repeat business?

- ✔ **Explore investment acquisition cost:** How much is it going to cost to acquire new customers?

Certain customer segments are more loyal and generate more profits than others over their lifetime. Focusing the customer acquisition strategy on those more profitable segments helps ensure that the customers you invest money to acquire are going to stay with you and keep generating revenue.

Calculating Lifetime Value

Calculating customer lifetime value can involve some complex math with many variables and equations that can be quite intimidating. There is even very expensive software to compute complicated CLVs for all different types of customers and products. Fortunately, you don't have to be a mathematician or computer scientist to compute a basic, helpful CLV estimate.

The analysts at KISSmetrics present a simple way to calculate the CLV using an infographic on its website, and I summarize a similar approach here. Remember that the more data you can gather about your customers' buying habits, the more accurate your results will be. However, the method is quite easy and you can get a good estimate of your CLV with relatively little data. It's a three-part process:

1. Estimate revenue.

2. Calculate the CLV.

3. Identify profitable customers.

Estimating revenue

I recommend this process to estimate a typical customer's revenue:

1. **Calculate how much money a typical customer (or a typical customer from a specific segment) generates per purchase.**

   One way to do that is to average the revenues from several customers (within a segment or from your market as a whole).

   For example, the typical revenue from a customer's purchase in a sandwich shop can be around $8. Figure 6-1 shows fictional purchase data from six different customers, as well as the average.

Revenue per purchase

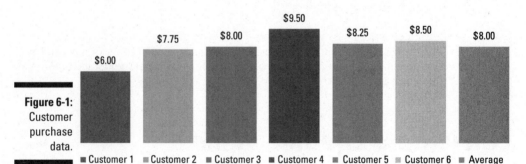

Figure 6-1:
Customer
purchase
data.

■ Customer 1   ■ Customer 2   ■ Customer 3   ■ Customer 4   ■ Customer 5   ■ Customer 6   ■ Average

The larger the customer sample, the more precise the results are. The CLV can't be more precise than the data it is calculated from. Therefore, look at "hard" data such as historical or current sales, to obtain accurate averages.

2. **Estimate the frequency of the customer's purchases.**

   The appropriate time frame, called the *purchase cycle,* depends on the industry. A sandwich shop may find that the most relevant time frame is one week, and that each customer purchases about three times per week (like some of my colleagues), as illustrated in Figure 6-2. For purchasing desktop and laptop computers, it's likely two to four years, and for rental cars and airline tickets it may be a few times per year, depending on the customer segment.

Frequency of purchase (per week)

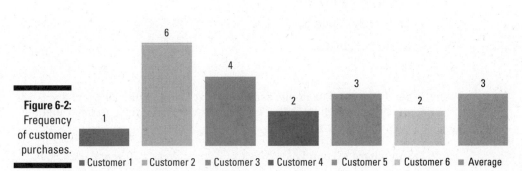

Figure 6-2: Frequency of customer purchases.

3. **Calculate the revenue per customer over a certain time period.**

Multiply the revenue per purchase by purchase frequency:

Revenue per purchase x Frequency of purchase = Revenue over a certain time period

In the sandwich shop example, the result would be expressed in dollars per week:

$8/purchase × 3 purchases/week = $24/week

Figure 6-3 shows the breakdown of this average for the same six customers.

Revenue per week per customer

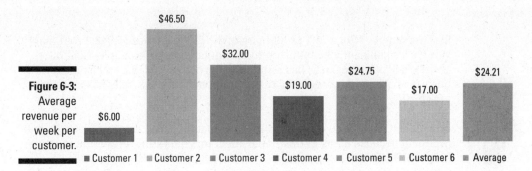

Figure 6-3: Average revenue per week per customer.

Calculating the CLV

The simplest way to compute the customer lifetime value is to evaluate how long the average customer does business with your company and to calculate how much revenue is generated during that period:

> Revenue per purchase
>
> x Frequency of purchase
>
> x Customer lifetime
> ———————————————
> CLV

In the sandwich shop example, assuming that the revenue per purchase is $8, the frequency of purchase is three times per week, and the customer lifetime is 20 years, the CLV is:

> $8/purchase x 3 purchases/week x 52 weeks/year x 20 years = $24,960

However, to make the result more precise, other factors should be taken into account if the data is available. Using the revenue generated from a customer will almost always overestimate the customer's true lifetime value because it doesn't factor in the costs of things like employees, building and/or equipment lease, and advertising. In fact, without factoring in costs, CLV is usually referred to as customer lifetime revenue (CLR).

It therefore makes sense to factor in the profit margin, which is the percentage of the revenue left over after subtracting all the company's expenses. A more realistic CLV can then be calculated using the following equation:

> Revenue per purchase
>
> x Frequency of purchase
>
> x Customer lifetime
>
> x Profit margin
> ———————————————
> CLV

In this example, with a 21% profit margin, the CLV becomes $5,242. Profit margins vary significantly by industry and product type. For example, General Electric's lighting business has profit margins of less than 5% and its industrial business has margins around 15%. Computer software typically has margins above 70%.

Do the best you can to compute a realistic margin based on your business and products because it has a substantial effect on computing an accurate lifetime value calculation.

Two values can be used to refine your CLV calculation:

- ✔ **Retention Rate:** The customer retention rate is the percentage of the customers who repurchase over a specific period of time.

  As a simple example, if 800 out of 1,000 customers are still customers after a year, the retention rate is 80%. If you have the data, look at multiple years to generate a more accurate rate of retention.

- ✔ **Discount Rate:** The discount rate is an economic notion that is used to calculate the present value of future revenues.

  The basic idea is that having money today is worth more than having that same amount of money at some distant point in the future. Would you rather have $10,000 today or $10,000 in ten years?

  The same principle applies to company profits. Future profits are discounted to account for their current value.

  If the lifetime of a customer is short (weeks, months, or a year or so), then the discount rate won't have as much of an effect as if the lifetime lasts years or decades.

The CLV equation becomes more accurate if retention rate and discount rate are taken into account:

> Revenue per purchase
>
> x Frequency of purchase
>
> x Customer lifetime
>
> x Profit margin
>
> x (retention rate) / (1 + discount rate – retention rate)
>
> CLV

If the retention rate is 75% and the discount rate is 10%, you obtain a CLV of $11,233 for the previous example. While the retention rate is always lower than 100% and therefore reduces the CLV, taking the value of future money into account using the rate of discount results in a higher yet more realistic CLV.

As with most of the customer analytics discussed in this book, the precision of the CLV depends on the quality of the data available and the number of variables that can be evaluated. However, even imperfect results can be used to compare different customer segments and identify the most profitable customers.

Identifying profitable customers

Calculating the lifetime value of different customer segments enables you to identify the segments that are worth the investment of large acquisition costs.

To find the most profitable customers, calculate the CLV for your different customer segments and compare with the average CLV. Differences in lifetime value between segments can be rather large and should help focus your customer acquisition strategy. It may be more expensive to gain the good customers' loyalty, but in the long run, they will generate more revenue.

If, for example, the sandwich shop's frequent customers generate about $3,000 more than the infrequent customers over their lifetime, then an investment of say $500 spent marketing to acquire these more frequent customers would pay off.

Marketing to Profitable Customers

Identifying the most profitable customer segments can be done in a sound, data-driven manner using the CLV. However, even increasing the number of your "good" customers may not be worth an expensive marketing campaign or costly incentives. To find out whether your efforts will pay off in the future, calculate your marketing campaign (or customer acquisition efforts) return on investment (ROI).

The CLV can be used to evaluate the success of a marketing campaign. Looking back at the money spent for customer acquisition during a certain time period and dividing by the number of customers acquired during that time, you obtain the average amount of money spent to acquire each individual new customer. You can then calculate the ROI of your marketing campaign to evaluate whether it was a financial success or failure.

To calculate the ROI of your marketing campaign to acquire new customers, use the following equation:

ROI = (CLV – Marketing cost per customer acquired) / Marketing cost per customer acquired

For example, if the sandwich shop spends $5000 on advertising and finds that it obtains 50 new customers, the cost to acquire a new customer is $100. The ROI of the advertising campaign will depend on the type of customer (frequent or infrequent) that's gained.

For example, using the CLV of $5,242 for the frequent customers from the previous example, the ROI of this campaign is:

($5,242 – $100) / $100 = $51

For every $1 spent on advertising, $51 is gained over the frequent customer lifetime.

However, if the advertising campaign attracts infrequent customers who may only purchase $6 once a month over 5 years, generating lifetime revenue of $360 and a CLV of $75.60 (after factoring in the profit margin of 21%). The ROI is then:

($75.60 – $100) / $100 = $-0.24

In other words, if the advertising campaign attracts infrequent customers, over a 5 year period, the campaign will result in a loss of 24 cents for every dollar spent. Not a good investment at all.

A negative ROI means that the marketing campaign was a money loser. CLV thus provides crucial information about just how much should be spent on a marketing campaign or how much you can afford to lose by offering incentives.

Just like acquiring new customers by creating attractive incentives and marketing specifically to them, increasing your existing customers' CLV by boosting their satisfaction helps your business grow:

- ✔ A higher satisfaction rate increases the frequency of purchases, the amount of revenue generated each time, and your customer lifetime. All those factors contribute to a higher CLV.

- ✔ Satisfied and loyal customers are more likely to recommend your products or services to their friends and colleagues (see Chapter 12), thus enlarging your customer base.

- ✔ The cost of acquisition of new customers is often much higher than what needs to be spent to retain existing customers and increase their purchases.

- ✔ Customers who are highly satisfied provide free word-of-mouth marketing!

Part III

Analytics for the Customer Journey

Visit http://www.dummies.com/extras/customeranalytics for great
Dummies content online.

In this part . . .

- ✔ Define the journey a customer undertakes with your company or product.
- ✔ Find out what customers think of your company and brand.
- ✔ Question customers about their attitude regarding a product or service experience.
- ✔ Quantify the customer decisions and conversion process.
- ✔ Track customer's post-purchase behavior.
- ✔ Measure customer loyalty and understand what drives it.
- ✔ Visit `http://www.dummies.com/extras/customeranalytics` for great Dummies content online.

Chapter 7

Mapping the Customer Journey

*I*n this chapter, I discuss the importance of mapping out customer journeys and walk you through an example showing how to create one for yourself. A customer journey map is a visualization of the stages customers go through as they become aware of, purchase, and use a product or service. It has clearly defined stages and details customer touchpoints and metrics that quantify each stage.

The goal of a customer journey map is to identify problem areas customers have while engaging a product or service and identify opportunities for improvement. It can also help unify often disparate and competing efforts within the same organization by providing different departments with a single document that maps the customer's entire experience with a product or service.

Working with the Traditional Marketing Funnel

For about as long as people have been selling products, they've been thinking about where to find customers and how to reach them. The classic sales and marketing funnels date back to the late 1800s and provide a simple metaphor to think about the path a customer takes on the way to purchase. The sales funnel in Figure 7-1 is a common example of how a funnel can map the journey a person takes from prospect to customer. It can also be used as a starting point in building a journey map.

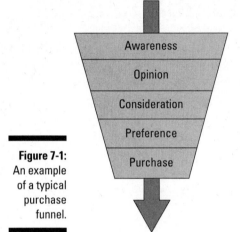

Figure 7-1:
An example
of a typical
purchase
funnel.

Funnels, like the one shown in Figure 7-1, show that people move from becoming aware of a product or company to becoming interested to eventually making a purchase. They provide some clear stages for understanding the customer journey and targeting marketing, advertising, and sales efforts accordingly. For example, it doesn't make much sense to talk about pricing when people don't want or haven't heard of your product.

Just about every marketing organization has or should have a funnel. In fact, the funnel concept of AIDA (Awareness, Interest, Desire, and Action) was at the center of a famous scene with Alec Baldwin in the movie *Glengarry Glenn Ross.*

Organizations likely have different names for each of the stages. Table 7-1 shows some popular examples of marketing and sales funnels your organization might use. Despite some minor differences, funnels generally share a similar pattern of customer behavior:

1. Contemplate a purchase.

2. Narrow down on a choice.

3. Purchase the chosen product.

4. Experience post-purchase effects.

It's a theme you'll use with the customer journey map you create as well. Table 7-1 compares different types of marketing funnels to illustrate their similarities.

Table 7-1	Similarities between Marketing Funnels		
Forrester Funnel	*Diffusion of Innovation*	*Principles of Marketing*	*Main Idea*
Awareness	Knowledge	Problem recognition: "Perceiving a need"	Contemplating a purchase
Consideration	Persuasion	Information search: "Seeking value"	Narrowing down a choice
Preference	Decision	Alternative evaluation: "Assessing value"	Purchasing that choice
Action	Implementation	Purchase decision: "Buying value"	Experiencing post-purchase effects
Loyalty	Confirmation	Post-purchase behavior: "Value in consumption or use"	Considering repurchases

The marketing funnel is a linear process as the metaphor suggests. People start at the large end of the funnel and then make their way through the stages. The narrowing of the funnel conveys the smaller percentage of people who make their way through. Linearity in mapping the customer journey can be limiting because it assumes every customer starts in the same spot, proceeds through the same steps, and finishes at the same end point. You can overcome this challenge by incorporating loops back through earlier stages.

Another adaptation to the model, like one from McKinsey in Figure 7-2, emphasizes that customers' loyalty is less of an end point, but the beginning of a loop where the customer goes back to the consideration phase before the next purchase point. This is especially the case with products and services that are purchased regularly, like rental cars, coffee, computers, or hotel reservations.

I always thought the funnel metaphor was a bit odd. After all, as any kindergartner will tell you, everything that goes in one end of the funnel comes out the other. That would be like every prospect turning into a purchaser. If that were true, all you'd need to do is make and advertise a product and you'd be the next Bill Gates!

So unless you're working for the IRS or have some sort of mandatory product, customers will drop out of the funnel at some stage. A better metaphor might be the marketing filter or marketing sieve.

Despite some recent criticism of the linearity of the marketing funnel (and the flaw with the metaphor), the marketing funnel will probably continue to endure. One reason is that modifications to the model are still generally linear, as you see with the customer journey map.

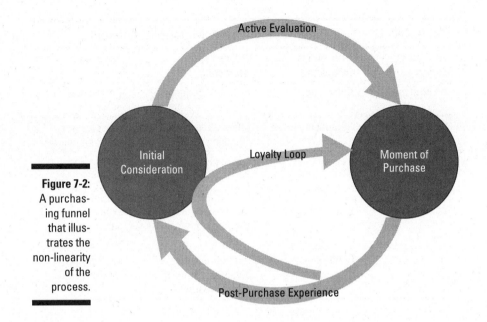

Active Evaluation

Initial Consideration

Loyalty Loop

Moment of Purchase

Post-Purchase Experience

Figure 7-2: A purchasing funnel that illustrates the non-linearity of the process.

What distinguishes a journey map?

The customer journey is a natural extension of the marketing funnel and shares many of the same components and goals. Both attempt to map the process a customer goes through with a product or service. Here are four main areas that differentiate a customer journey map from a marketing or sales funnel:

✔ **More detail:** A journey map is like Google Earth: You can go from a 30,000 foot view to get high-level insights but still zoom into the street-level view to understand the micro-interactions in each stage. The typical sales funnel focuses more on the macro view (say above 10,000 feet) and leaves the micro interactions to separate departments.

✔ **Focus on touchpoints:** The moments of friction or delight where companies can differentiate themselves are hallmarks of the journey map and aren't typically addressed by the sales funnel. Touchpoints happen well before, during, and after a sale and across media.

✔ **More emphasis on post-purchase behavior:** There isn't much direct selling going on when a customer is using most products, yet long-term usage, usability, and experience impacts a user's intent to repurchase and recommend the product to his or her networks. Journey maps provide this detail to identify opportunities for improvement.

✔ **Not just for the sales and marketing teams:** The customer journey may be one of the only documents that shows an organization how a customer interacts with it from beginning to end. Typically the marketing and sales teams are only the ones that care about converting leads into sales, while the product team is primarily concerned with fixing problems and adding new features. The customer journey map should, and can, act as a unifying document for disparate departments with different goals.

What Is a Customer Journey Map?

Like a marketing funnel, a customer journey map is a visualization of the phases a customer goes through when engaging with a product or service. Almost any experience can be mapped, including the following examples:

✔ The shopping experience at Whole Foods, from parking to unpacking

✔ The birthing experience: Admittance to the hospital to taking home baby

✔ New customer download experience: From software trial download to installation to long term customer

But unlike typical marketing funnels, a customer journey map illuminates stages in the journey with *touchpoints*. Touchpoints are moments when a customer comes in contact with things like a website, a physical store, a support representative, or an advertisement. The journey map should also have some way of quantifying the experience for each step in the journey.

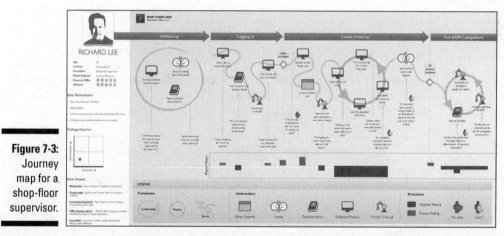

Figure 7-3:
Journey map for a shop-floor supervisor.

Photo courtesy of Alan Ho (https://www.behance.net/gallery/User-Journey-of-a-Shop-Floor-User/15650709)

Another example, shown in Figure 7-4, shows "Sarah's" journey as she selects a new Internet and phone service provider after moving into a new house.

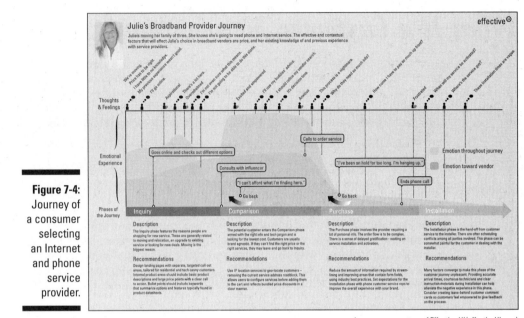

Journey map courtesy of Effective UI (effectiveUI.com)

Figure 7-4:
Journey of a consumer selecting an Internet and phone service provider.

Customer journeys can map an experience from minutes to years. An example of the journey a customer goes through when purchasing a laptop computer is shown in Figure 7-5. Notice how this journey starts before the customer has engaged with a company or product. You work on building this customer journey map throughout the rest of this chapter.

	Awareness		Consideration		Preference	Action		Loyalty	
	Define Need	Evaluate Need	Response Decision	Category Decision	Brand Decision	Purchase	Setup/Unbox	Initial Usage	Extended Usage
Quotes	"I answer most of my emails on my phone while waiting for my PC to load"	"I saw a commercial that said I could speed up my PC with some software"	"I need a new computer."	"I've always had a Dell and my Dad said they are the way to go."	"Dell Seems the most reliable and my friend recommended them."	"I found a coupon code but it took a long time to configure on the website."	"I had a problem installing software."	"Configuring two monitors was painful."	"I wish I knew the hard drive wouldn't be big enough when I was configuring it."
Touchpoints	Ads & Website		Ads & Website PC Magazine		Online User Reviews Expert Online Reviews	Website Phone Support Chat Support Retail Partner	Shipping	Website Forums Chat Support Retail Partner	Website Forums Chat Support
Metrics	Industry metrics, demographics	Brand Awareness Index		Brand Affinity Index		Usability Scores		Net Promoter	
Ownership	Marketing Team					Usability Team		Customer Insight Team	

Figure 7-5:
Journey of a consumer purchasing a laptop computer.

One of the core ideas behind mapping the customer journey is that it helps employees understand how their role has an impact on sales and revenue, even if they don't directly sell or market to customers. The map should provide ideas for stakeholders to develop ways of treating the customer more holistically, rather than perpetuating a fragmented experience where each department rules an isolated fiefdom. It's like telling your story to one person on a phone call, getting transferred to someone else (of course, being placed on hold first, for who knows how long — ugh!), waiting for the next person to talk to, and then having to restate your information all over again to that individual!

Define the Customer Journey

Building a customer journey can sound like something akin to writing Homer's *Odyssey* — a lengthy, complicated and time-consuming exercise. While it's important to do research and include the relevant stakeholders when mapping a customer's journey, it doesn't have to be overly complicated. In fact, it should be just detailed enough to communicate the stages, touchpoints, and influences that lead to actions.

Ernest Hemingway is attributed with writing a six-word story: "For Sale: baby shoes, never worn." He considered it his best work. If the Nobel Prize winning author of *The Old Man and the Sea* finds such value in only six words, then surely a customer journey doesn't have to be long, either. When mapping the customer journey, start simple and think Hemingway instead of Homer.

Finding the data

The customer journey should be based on data that describes reality, not any idealistic image or impression you might have. Here are approaches for gathering data to build the customer journey:

- **Look for existing data:** Before planning an extensive research campaign, look for existing sources of information.

  Surveys, customer interviews, and call logs to customer support usually have great insights into what the customer experiences. When the data's already collected, there's no reason not to use it.

- **Follow Me Home:** One technique for conducting your own primary research is a technique called Follow Me Home. As the name suggests, you follow customer volunteers to their house or workplace and observe them.

Intuit (maker of QuickBooks and TurboTax) used this extensively at one time. The idea is to immerse yourself into your customers' typical lives to understand how they use and perceive your products and company.

This is a great opportunity to get quotes and interview people face to face. Most importantly, it gives you an opportunity to observe what customers do rather than rely on what customers say.

✔ **Analytic thinking:** If you have a good idea about how the process works, you can start by putting yourself in the customer's shoes and walking through his journey.

This can be an easy way to get a journey map off the ground, but be prepared to validate your thinking and make room for corrections. You don't want the journey to be based just on what you think.

✔ **Stakeholder interviews:** Interview the sales team, the marketing team, accounting, a support person — anyone who has direct contact with customers at different stages.

Look for patterns but don't immediately dismiss one-off data points — look to corroborate them with later methods and data.

✔ **Survey customers:** Surveys are one of the most efficient ways for collecting data from customers. Find a way to survey current, former, and prospective customers, and have them describe their process for deciding, purchasing, and using a product.

Look for patterns and consider using third-party research firms that can present a more objective face to customers who may engage with your organization and its competition.

Sketching the journey

With some data at your disposal, it's time to sketch the journey. Start with a persona, or at least a specific customer segment, and then work from general to specific details. You can sketch out the journey using paper and pen, a whiteboard, or a charting program like Microsoft PowerPoint. You can follow along with the figures in this section by using PowerPoint.

1. Pick a persona or segment

With customers segmented by demographics and behavior, you have many of the important pieces of the customer journey ready. It helps to create a customer journey map for each of your personas. In many cases, some or all of your personas will share similar goals, touchpoints, and journeys, so you can consolidate later. (See Chapter 5 for more detail on creating personas.)

Let's start with a persona called Pragmatic Phil for a consumer electronics device like a laptop computer. Phil's computer takes a long time to boot up, crashes frequently, and has limited memory, causing Phil to delete files to make room for new software. The details of Phil's persona suggest that he's value-oriented (seeks out deals) and is not a technology laggard, but doesn't need cutting-edge technology, either. His goal is to have one PC that he can use for both work and personal use. It should be durable but also compact enough to take on airplanes and watch movies with his kids.

2. Determine the stages

As the name "journey" suggests, journey maps are usually constructed around a sequence of events that happen in a timeline. The timeline can then be broken into stages and then smaller steps.

For each stage, be sure to focus on the goals of your customers and what they are trying to accomplish.

If there are some existing stages from prior research, use those. It's likely they'll be similar to the five phases discussed in the sales funnels (Awareness, Consideration, Preference, Action and Loyalty); that's what we'll start with, as shown in Figure 7-6:

- ✔ **Awareness:** Phil's computer is getting slow and he's contemplating getting a new computer or perhaps just trying to get it fixed. He talks to his friends about their computers and what he should do. He eventually decides he needs a new laptop.

- ✔ **Consideration:** Next Phil starts doing research to see what new laptops cost and what the features are. He's price conscious but wants something that will last. At this stage, he's researching many different product models.

- ✔ **Preference:** Phil narrows his choices down to a few brands and products based on research and recommendations from his friends.

- ✔ **Action:** Phil makes his decision to purchase a new laptop from the Dell.com website. He receives it a few weeks later, takes it out of the box, sets it up, and begins to get used to the fast, new machine.

- ✔ **Loyalty:** Phil's been using his Dell computer for several months. He's taken it on trips, on airplanes, and back and forth from work and his home. There are parts of the hardware and software he likes and parts he wishes were better. He's mentioned to a friend that he wishes the hard drive had more space and that it was lighter, but he's already recommended it to two colleagues.

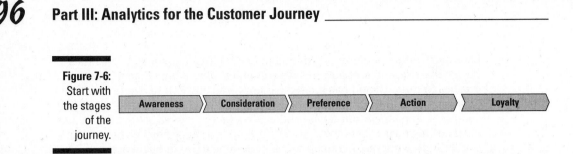

Figure 7-6:
Start with
the stages
of the
journey.

3. Define the steps

From the research, construct a sequence of major steps the customer takes from awareness to post-purchase. The steps are basically more finely grained segments to describe the sequences through the journey. The steps often, but don't always, align with the higher level stages.

Figure 7-7 shows the stages Phil goes through when considering a new laptop. I use a circle to differentiate the steps from the stages used in Step 2.

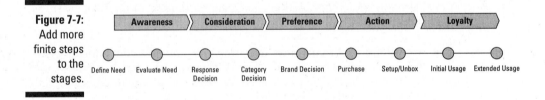

Figure 7-7:
Add more
finite steps
to the
stages.

4. Identify the touchpoints

A *touchpoint* is a physical or digital interaction your customers experience during their relationship life cycle with your product or service. Here are some examples of common touchpoints:

- ✔ Website
- ✔ Salesperson
- ✔ Store
- ✔ TV and radio advertisements
- ✔ Search engine results
- ✔ Direct mail
- ✔ Email
- ✔ Social media platforms such as Twitter and Facebook

The example PC purchasing journey identifies the touchpoints as advertisements, the product/company website, and different support channels like chat, phone, and forums, as shown in Figure 7-8.

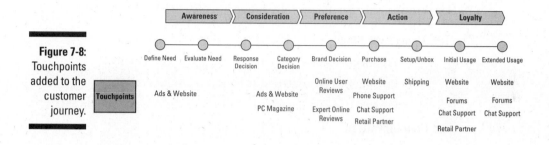

Figure 7-8:
Touchpoints added to the customer journey.

5. Identify customer questions at each stage

During the research stage, such as when conducting the "Follow Me Home" technique, ask your target customers what questions they have about the product or service. This helps craft branding messages, opportunities for product improvements, and the metrics to collect to determine how well you're addressing each stage. Figure 7-9 shows examples of representative customer quotes to capture the sentiments at each stage.

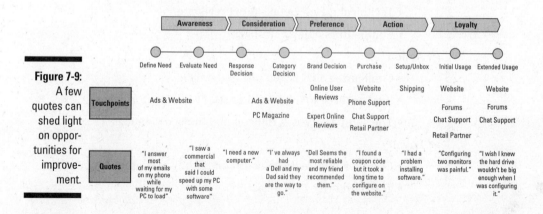

Figure 7-9:
A few quotes can shed light on opportunities for improvement.

It's good practice to use the most precise metrics available to quantify an experience. However, a single quotation from a user will often convince and compel more people to action than any metric ever could. Look for representative quotations that indicate the challenges and opportunities at each stage.

6. Find the pain points

At each step, understand where the customer, or prospective customer, encounters barriers or friction to making a purchase.

Here are several pain points you can identify through the PC journey for Phil:

✔ **Awareness Stage**

- Prospective customers aren't aware of the company.

- Prospective customers don't know a product exists.

- Prospective customers aren't aware of their need for a product.

✔ **Consideration**

- Customers misunderstand features and product offerings.

- The perception of quality is low.

- The perception of value is low.

- Customers are unable to find information about your company/product.

✔ **Preference**

- It's unclear what features differentiate the products.

- Technical review details don't resonate.

- Competitors appear stronger.

✔ **Action**

- Configuring a PC is complicated online.

- It takes three to five weeks to receive the laptop.

- The setup process is difficult and time-consuming.

✔ **Loyalty**

- Certain software downloads corrupt the operating system.

- The hard drive fills up fast.

7. Define metrics for each stage

It's likely that your organization collects at least a few metrics already. In defining the metrics for each stage, look for metrics that are already being collected in your organization or by a third party, or attempt to collect them yourself. I cover metrics for the different phases of the customer journey in detail throughout Part III.

Here are some examples of metrics for the stages in the PC journey.

☑ **Awareness Stage**

- *Annual Computer Sales:* Understand the current market of how many PCs are sold and the average sales amount.

- *Average Life Span of a Laptop Computer:* Knowing the typical churn rate helps to anticipate the need for existing customers.

- *Advertising Recall:* Understand if prospects recall your advertising message or associate your brand to features and products.

☑ **Consideration**

- *Product Market Share:* Track which models are sold the most and what the trends are. This information is often publicly available for many industries.

- *Feature Affinity:* Identify which features are driving sales and word-of-mouth.

☑ **Preference**

- *Brand Leaders & Laggards:* Quantify how often a brand is mentioned relative to its competition (see Chapter 9).

- *Social Media:* Find the number of mentions, especially positive ones, on social media platforms like Twitter and Facebook. Use a free version of a social analytics tool such as Topsy (`http://topsy.com/`) or Social Mention (`http://socialmention.com/`) to help you determine what customers are talking about and their sentiment toward your company or product.

☑ **Action**

- *Click-Through Rates (CTR):* The percent of visitors who are clicking on call-to-action buttons like "buy," "register," or "add to cart."

- *Shopping Cart Abandonment Rate:* The percent of visitors who had items in their carts but never purchased them.

- *Average Time on Site:* This is a measure of engagement. If users don't spend much time browsing a website, there's less opportunity to connect with them and convert browsers to buyers. Time on site and other engagement metrics can be measured with website analytics tools, including Google Analytics.

✔ **Loyalty**

- *Net Promoter Score (NPS):* Asking how likely customers are to recommend a product is a good way to measure word-of-mouth. For details about measuring customer loyalty, see Chapter 12.

- *Likelihood to Repurchase:* For products and services that are used repeatedly (for example, rental cars and hotel visits), you'll want to have as many customers with a high propensity to repurchase the product.

8. Identify who is accountable for each stage in the journey

A final step in completing your journey map is to be sure someone is accountable to each stage — and ideally, each step. Different disciplines, from product development to marketing to usability, know their domain and metrics best. These teams will likely be familiar with relevant third-party research on customer habits and demographics, and know how to measure the touchpoints.

One of the key goals behind the journey map is to identify opportunities for improvement. If you find problems and have some ideas but no one is accountable for implementing them, then the full potential of the journey map won't be realized.

9. Uncover the opportunities

One of the main goals of the journey map is to fix problems and propose solutions that aren't as readily noticeable when the journey is fragmented.

In a "Follow Me Home" conducted at Intuit (I describe this earlier in the chapter), small-business owners were observed at their location of business while checking out customers on their point-of-sale (POS) registers. At the end of the day, the merchants would then export their data from the POS machine and import it into QuickBooks. This was a clear pain point for the customers, even if some didn't directly articulate it. The design team wondered if they could eliminate that step and came up with QuickBooks POS — an integrated check-out and accounting solution. Be honest about identifying and mapping the pain points. From pain comes opportunity. Look at each of the pain points as an opportunity for innovation and improvement — not just as damage control.

10. Periodically validate

When you create your first journey map, you'll likely have made some assumptions and worked off data that will become stale over time. Plan on revisiting your journey map to see what information has changed and needs to be updated.

If critical pieces of information become invalid, like shifting customer demographics or new competition, an out-of-date journey map may be worse than no journey map at all.

Flag areas that change frequently and be sure people who are accountable for the stages have a way of getting the latest data and can update the journey map.

Making the map more useful

Here are three important guidelines to make your journey map more useful and effective.

✔ **Make the journey map interactive:** As more work goes into a journey map, it will inevitably get bigger and packed full of information. Trying to fit all that on one flat page may get unwieldy.

Consider having an HTML version of your journey map that allows your organization to drill into the stages. Some organizations even connect their internal sales and metrics systems right into the stages of their journey maps.

✔ **Make it interesting:** You don't have to stick with the typical flow-chart shapes of circles and squares.

If you need inspiration, look at a subway map with symbols and how a lot of information can be conveyed in a dense graphic.

✔ **You don't have to include everything:** The more dimensions you add, the more complex the journey map becomes. For some phases, you'll need to drill down to many details, such as in the online purchase process.

It may make more sense to include these details on an auxiliary map (hyperlinked from an electronic version) that allows the organization to access it without getting bogged down in the details.

Chapter 8

Determining Brand Awareness and Attitudes

▶ Valuing brand awareness and attitudes

▶ Measuring brand awareness

▶ Asking aided and unaided branding questions

*W*hen marketers talk about brands, familiar companies and products come to mind — think Coca-Cola, Nike, BMW, or Rolex. But think about the last time you purchased something in a category about which you were unfamiliar with the brands — perhaps ceiling fans, windshield wipers, or website hosts.

All things being equal, consumers prefer brands they know rather than brands they have not heard of.

Customers generally progress through stages of the hierarchy of effects: They become familiar with a brand, form an attitude about the brand through repeated usage, and finally, become loyal to that brand. (It's part of the customer journey; if you're unfamiliar with the customer journey, see Chapter 7.)

The hierarchy of effects provides a framework for you to measure. Customers' attitudes toward brands and products are constantly changing. In this chapter, I show you how to measure brand awareness, attitudes, and experiences.

Measuring Brand Awareness

You measure brand awareness using two approaches:

✔ **Unaided awareness:** Asking customers what their favorite brands are

✔ **Aided awareness:** Asking customers to rank brands from a list that you provide

You can ask aided and unaided brand questions in the same survey to current or prospective customers. When you do, ask the unaided questions first to minimize the suggestion bias and to discover which brands are top of mind. Then ask the aided branded questions by listing relevant brands and include an "Other" option so participants can provide any brands you might not have considered competition.

Unaided awareness

The best way to measure unaided brand awareness is to ask customers which brands come to mind when thinking about a particular product or service. Here are some examples:

- ✔ List mobile phone manufacturers.
- ✔ List three makes and models of family sedans.
- ✔ Name four rental car companies.

Keep your unaided awareness questions open ended so customers provide written responses. Categorize each response and then compute the frequency of each response. This number can constitute a benchmark from which you measure future improvements.

Finding a benchmark is helpful before key events, such as an advertising campaign or prior to a new product introduction. It also provides an idea about the competitive landscape by providing a relative rank of where your product falls relative to the others that participants mention.

Count the number of participants who mention a brand and convert that total to a percentage; then put confidence intervals around the percentage. (See Chapter 2 for a reminder on how to use confidence intervals). The confidence intervals provide the best estimate for how aware all prospective customers are about a brand from the sample of customers.

For example, in a survey of brand awareness for computers, 120 prospective customers were asked to list the brands they'd consider if they were to purchase a new laptop in the next six months. In total, participants listed ten brands; 60% of respondents mentioned Apple and 20% listed Sony (see Figure 8-1). According to the results, although Apple clearly has more top-of-mind share than Sony, this data suggests that sales can be increased by increasing prospective laptop buyers' awareness of Sony's laptop products. The confidence intervals indicate how much the mind share would change if more customers were sampled (these are shown as the small black lines in Figure 8-1). The lower and upper bounds of the Sony unaided awareness are 14% and 28%, respectively. This means we can be 95% confident that at least 14% and no more than 28% of prospective customers have Sony in mind when considering laptop purchases.

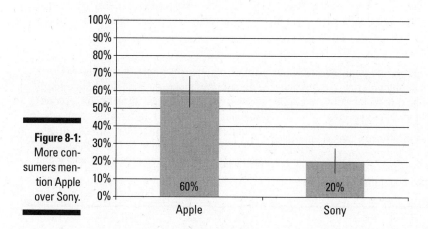

Figure 8-1: More consumers mention Apple over Sony.

Aided awareness

With aided awareness, you provide a list of brands to the customers and ask them to identify which ones they are familiar with. Your aided awareness questions are multiple-select questions, meaning customers can select as many companies or products that they recognize. For example:

Which of the following laptop manufacturers are you familiar with (select all that apply)?

Samsung

Acer

Dell

Gateway

Apple

Lenovo

Toshiba

Sony

Prionsonic

Zenith

Intel brand and product awareness

Intel wanted to determine how well consumers understood its class of laptops called Ultrabooks — lightweight laptops with solid-state hard drives and premium features.

The study involved asking unaided, and then aided, questions about features. Via an open-ended Comment box, participants were asked what they thought an Ultrabook was:

✔ Customers used phrases like "A very thin laptop" and "A laptop with superior features." Both responses exhibited knowledge about the new product category.

✔ Other comments, however, illustrated confusion — for example, "It's a laptop without any added features."

Then survey participants were asked to select from a number of alternatives features that defined Ultrabooks, such as solid-state hard-drives, to assess how strong their product knowledge was. This information was used to understand how effective marketing campaigns had been and identify the messages that needed to be reinforced on Intel's website and in its TV advertisements.

Aided awareness questions are less of an indication of top-of-mind awareness and more a measure of familiarity. Similar to a multiple-choice test, the mere suggestion of a brand may lead customers to select brands they aren't familiar with.

To get an idea about how suggesting brands may unintentionally prompt your customers, include some "distractor" brands to see which percentage of customer select it. For example, in the list of laptops from earlier, Prionsonic is fake and Zenith doesn't make laptops. You can use the percentage of customers who select these distractor brands as a way to gauge how reliable your aided brand results are.

Measuring product or service knowledge

Having awareness with a brand is one level of familiarity. But most brands have a range of products and services. For example, Apple has iTunes, iPad, and iCloud. Google has Gmail, Drive, and Search. Customers may be more or less familiar with different products, and it's often helpful to dig deeper into both product familiarity and knowledge.

You can better understand how effective your advertising campaigns are, and which channels (mobile, website, or TV, for example) are most effective when you follow up your unaided and aided awareness questions with specific questions about how participants heard about your specific brand. You can then attribute a higher or lower brand awareness to different campaigns. For example, if participants report higher awareness through a Facebook ad, you know how effective that ad was.

Always measure awareness separately for different customer segments. In the awareness survey, have participants select which customer segment best describes them and then analyze the awareness separately. You may find significant difference in awareness by geography, age, or gender, for example.

Measuring Brand Attitude

As you progress through the hierarchy of effects, it's important to measure the current ideas, beliefs, and associations that customers have toward a brand and product. Brand attitude is both what customers think and how strongly they feel. They may be completely familiar with your product, but may have an unfavorable — or at best, neutral — attitude.

To measure brand attitude and its strength, have a representative set of prospective customers rate how much they agree or disagree toward a number of statements that go from general to specific concepts, as shown in Figure 8-2.

Figure 8-2:
Customers
can rate
specific
features of a
brand.

	Strongly Disagree		Neutral		Strongly Agree
	1	2	3	4	5
I am satisfied with my experience working with [brand name]	○	○	○	○	○
[brand name] keeps its promises	○	○	○	○	○
I can rely on the [brand name] to deliver outstanding quality	○	○	○	○	○
Installing products from [brand name] are easy	○	○	○	○	○
I trust my data is secure with [brand name]	○	○	○	○	○
The features integrate well with my other products [brand name]	○	○	○	○	○
I am able to find answers to my questions on the [brand name] support website	○	○	○	○	○

A rating scale with 5, 7, or 11 points is common, but if your organization uses another scale with a different set of points, use that.

In most branding studies, you should ask about brand favorability for the product and a set of competitors. For example:

On a scale from 1 to 7, how would you describe your overall attitude toward the following airlines?

American Airlines

Delta

United Airlines

Southwest

Identifying brand pillars

After asking general questions about brand satisfaction, ask specific questions about characteristics associated with the brand, product, or experience. These are typically called *brand pillars* (think of pillars holding up a house). Brand pillars are the most important attributes and principles you want to communicate through your brand. While these differ depending on the industry and brand, they usually revolve around the following traits:

- **Value:** How much value customers feel for the amount of money they spend on the products.

- **Quality:** How well customers think a product is built, including the type of materials and process.

- **Trust:** Do customers feel like their data is safe, or that the company will deliver what it says?

After participants rate their satisfaction on brand attributes, have them also describe, in their own words, how they arrived at their rating. This is an excellent opportunity to collect insights both on the key drivers of satisfaction (see later in this chapter) and what you can do to improve the product attributes and brand perception.

Checking brand affinity

A brand affinity analysis identifies the words customers associate with your brand and experience. These attributes can be manipulated or neglected. It's usually the job of the marketing team to work on getting the right positive associations with the brand.

Think of the toothpaste you use. What words come to mind? Maybe it's something like

Good Attributes	*Bad Attributes*
Clean	Expensive
Fresh	Messy
White	Tastes Terrible
Healthy	Guilt

To measure what terms customers associate with your brand and product, use the same framework I describe throughout this chapter:

1. **Ask customers which words come to mind when they think of a product or brand.**

   Have them list as many as they can.

2. **Count the responses to see what terms are most common.**

3. **Provide a list of specific words you want or don't want associated with a brand and have customers pick from that list.**

For example, customers were presented with 24 terms — 12 positive and 12 negative — that represented the website experience for an automotive information brand. Figure 8-3 shows that 59% selected "Informative," and 35% selected "Valuable" and "Convenient." Fortunately, only a few participants selected negative words. However, approximately one out of every five customers selected "Hard to Navigate" and "Complicated." This suggests the website experience could use some improvements to make it easier to use.

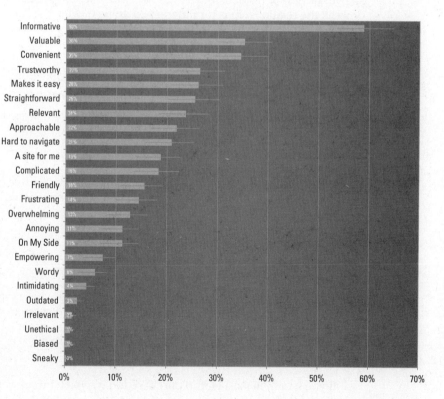

Figure 8-3: Words selected in a brand affinity exercise for an automotive information company's website.

When choosing phrases to present to customers, use terms that reflect the brand pillars to see how well these fundamental concepts resonate with customers.

Measuring Usage and Intent

The final stage of the hierarchy of effects is measuring usage — how much a customer has used the product in the past and what the customer plans to do in the future (intent).

Finding out past usage

You need to understand how frequently and how often customers purchase your products and your competitors' products or services. This provides an overall view of how customers interact with each brand and how strong or weak the relationship is for different customer segments. For example, in a study of airline and travel website usage, customers who recently booked flights online were asked the following questions:

> Which website have you used in the last year to book airfare?
>
> How frequently per year do you book tickets for business and pleasure?
>
> Do you belong to the airline loyalty program (for example, United MileagePlus or Southwest Rapid Rewards)?
>
> Do you own a rewards credit card for the airline?

Understanding how frequently these customers and prospective customers interact with your products allows you to understand how usage is affected by brand attitude, and to some extent, brand awareness.

Measuring future intent

Measuring customer usage with a brand helps describe what's happened in the past. But of equal importance is what's likely to happen in the future. Asking customers or prospective customers their future intent helps provide information about awareness and attitude to predict future sales. Examples of future intent questions include the following:

> If you had to make a laptop purchase today, which brand would you choose?
>
> How likely are you to continue flying on American Airlines?
>
> How likely are you to recommend Dell laptops to a friend or colleague?

Intent questions can be more sophisticated and combine brand and product questions with questions about pricing and features (see Chapter 13). Asking about customers' likelihood to recommend is such an important topic that I cover it in detail in Chapter 12.

Understanding the Key Drivers of Attitude

With all the data collected around awareness, attitude, and usage, you need to summarize each question type to understand the strengths and weaknesses of your brand or product. If your brand or product is not known, or only known by a small percentage of prospective consumers, then campaigns to increase awareness will improve customer awareness. See *Marketing For Dummies,* by Alexander Hiam (Wiley) for ideas on increasing awareness.

If your product and brand is known, you need to understand what's driving high or low satisfaction ratings. While any number of variables impact customers' attitudes toward your brand, usually only a few variables, called *key drivers,* have a disproportionate impact on attitudes. It may be that customers find the product is too expensive for what they get (value), or perhaps customers find the product difficult to use.

The first way to understand the drivers is to examine the comments customers provide in the survey (see Chapter 2 for categorizing verbatim comments). Look for patterns and concrete examples about what customers do and don't like.

A more sophisticated way of examining key drivers is using a statistical technique called multiple regression analysis (which I also discuss in the appendix). Customers' attitudes toward brand attributes are often correlated. That is, customers who are satisfied with the quality of a product are often also satisfied with the value and overall brand. Multiple regression analysis examines the correlation between the independent and dependent variables to determine which attributes contribute most to consumers' overall brand attitude. Seek the help of a statistician to assist you with running a multiple regression analysis. See Chapter 9 for an example using customer satisfaction as the dependent variable in a key driver analysis.

Structuring a Brand Assessment Survey

This chapter covers a lot of ways to measure consumers' ideas and beliefs about brands. Much of this data can be collected in the same survey, but be aware about how you arrange your questions. For example, by asking unaided questions before aided questions or asking participants to list adjectives before you have them pick from a selection. Also use a survey program that has branching and logic techniques that enable you to direct participants to different questions depending on their previous answer. Some platforms that use these techniques include UserZoom, Qualtrics, and SurveyAnalytics.

Here is one structure for a branding survey that works well.

- **Screening questions:** Ask qualifying questions ("Have you purchased a car in the last 6 months?") and key demographic questions (gender, age) to both screen and segment your responses. You only want qualified participants taking your survey.

- **Unaided branding:** Without prompting participants with any names, ask them to list products or brands that come to mind.

- **Aided branding:** Ask participants to select which brands they are familiar with among a list of alternatives. Consider adding some distractor brands.

- **Brand satisfaction:** For brands that participants select as being familiar with, ask them to rate their satisfaction on a rating scale.

- **Specific product knowledge:** Dig deeper into the product category by asking participants to list the features or attributes that distinguish your product from the competition's or from other categories. Start with an unaided question (open comments) and then move to an aided question (listing features to select from).

- **Brand affinity:** For a specific brand, have participants provide the words or concepts that come to mind when thinking about a brand or product. Start with an unaided question (open comments) and then move to an aided question (selecting from a set of positive and negative terms).

- **Product satisfaction:** Have participants rate how satisfied they are using the key attributes about a product (for example, quality, value, or features).

- **Future Intent:** Ask participants which product or brand they intend to purchase.

Chapter 9

Measuring Customer Attitudes

In This Chapter

▶ Recognizing the influence of customer attitudes on behavior

▶ Identifying the customer attitudes that should be quantified

▶ Measuring brand lift after a marketing campaign

Customers have a range of attitudes. But when measuring a product or service experience, you usually can only measure a certain number of attitudes, including satisfaction, usability, trust, loyalty, luxury, and delight.

In Chapter 8, I cover the hierarchy of effects, which includes awareness, attitudes, and usage from a broad brand perspective. In this chapter, I focus in more detail on customer attitudes: customers' ideas, sentiments, feelings, and beliefs toward a brand and product. I first cover the most common ways of measuring customer attitudes and then move on to constructing the right questions and scales.

Gauging Customer Satisfaction

By far the most common and fundamental measure of customer attitudes is customer satisfaction. Customer satisfaction is a measure of how well a product or service experience meets customer expectations. It's considered a staple of customer analytics scorecards as a barometer of how well a product or company is performing. You can measure satisfaction on everything from a brand, a product, a feature, or a website to a service experience.

Satisfaction measures how a particular customer is satisfied based on his or her expectations of a product or service. If you're selling a low-priced car, a budget-conscious consumer will be more satisfied with it than with a luxury, high-end car, even though the less expensive car might not have many features. Your customer's main satisfaction comes from the value (price for the features and quality offered).

Customer satisfaction is the first step of the customer journey. It leads to customer loyalty and recommendation. It's therefore a good idea to have some measure of customer satisfaction at each point in your customer journey. This includes everything from the product and its features, the buying process, service, and even how responsible you are toward your employees, shareholders, and the environment.

There are two levels of measuring customer satisfaction:

✔ General (or *relational*) satisfaction

✔ Attribute (or *transactional*) satisfaction

General satisfaction

Asking customers about their satisfaction toward a brand or organization is the broadest measure of customer satisfaction. It is often referred to as a relational measure because it speaks to customers' overall relationship with a brand. It encompasses repeated exposure, experiences, and often repeat purchases.

To measure general satisfaction, ask customers to rate how satisfied they are with your brand or company using a rating scale. Figure 9-1 shows an example where participants were asked to rate their level of satisfaction with their bank, US Bank.

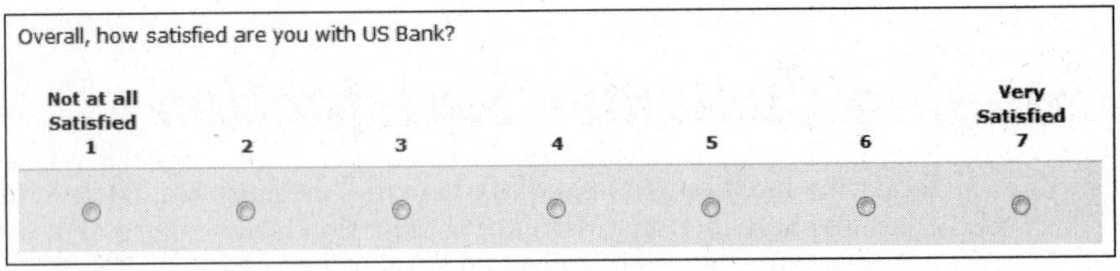

Figure 9-1:
Ask your customers about their level of satisfaction.

Overall, how satisfied are you with US Bank?						
Not at all Satisfied						Very Satisfied
1	2	3	4	5	6	7
◎	◎	◎	◎	◎	◎	◎

Because customer satisfaction is such a fundamental measure for gauging your company's performance with your customers, a number of firms offer a standardized set of satisfaction questionnaires and reports to allow you to compare your satisfaction scores with those of your competitors and industry. (This chapter outlines the benefits of using standardized questionnaires.)

One of the most common industry surveys of company satisfaction is the American Customer Satisfaction Index (ACSI; theacsi.org). ACSI uses a standard set of questions and surveys thousands of U.S. customers each year on products and services they've used. ACSI provides a series of benchmark reports across dozens of industries, including those for computer hardware, hotels, manufacturing, pet food, and life insurance, to name a few.

The ACSI reports enable you to see how satisfied U.S. customers are with your company. In some cases, satisfaction benchmarks are also provided at a more specific product level.

While you should always collect your own customer satisfaction data, data from third parties provides a more objective view of your brand and provides insights into former and prospective customers as well.

Attitude versus satisfaction

Although there is a slight difference between customer attitude and customer satisfaction, they are highly related and tend to predict customer loyalty (see Chapter 12).

Here's how to remember the difference:

- ✔ Potential customers have an *attitude* toward a brand or product they've never used.
- ✔ Actual customers rate their *satisfaction* after having experienced a brand or product.

Customer attitude and satisfaction are often used interchangeably in practice.

For example, customers can rate their opinions toward Apple before ever being a customer (attitude), their level of satisfaction with Apple after making a purchase (general satisfaction), their satisfaction with iTunes (product satisfaction), and with syncing iTunes with their iPhone (attribute satisfaction).

Attitude

If you're interested in the beliefs, ideas, and opinions of prospective customers, you have to measure attitudes.

For example, prior to evaluating customers on two rental car websites, participants were asked about their attitudes toward the most common U.S. rental car companies, as shown in Figure 9-2.

How would you describe your attitude toward the following Rental Car companies?							
	Very Unfavorable 1	2	3	4	5	6	Very Favorable 7
Thrifty	○	○	○	○	○	○	○
Hertz	○	○	○	○	○	○	○
National	○	○	○	○	○	○	○
Budget	○	○	○	○	○	○	○
Dollar	○	○	○	○	○	○	○
Enterprise	○	○	○	○	○	○	○
Avis	○	○	○	○	○	○	○

Figure 9-2: Have potential customers rate their opinions about your company.

One benefit of checking customer attitudes at the beginning of a survey is that you can screen out participants who have a very strong negative attitude toward your brand. While you don't want to ignore these customers — in fact, you'll want to follow up with them in the future — for this survey, you want to hear from prospective customers who are willing to use your product or service.

Attribute and product satisfaction

While customer satisfaction provides a broad view of a customer's attitude, you'll also want to find out whether or not your product or service is exceeding expectations.

To generate more specific and diagnostic measures of customer attitudes, ask about the satisfaction with features, or more specific parts of an experience. This is often referred to as attribute or transaction satisfaction because customers are rating attributes (features, quality, ease of use, price) of a product or the most recent transaction. Examples of attribute satisfaction include

- ✔ Check-in experience
- ✔ Registering
- ✔ Download speed
- ✔ Price
- ✔ Product (for brands with multiple products)
- ✔ Website
- ✔ In-store experience
- ✔ Online purchase process
- ✔ Product usability

To measure attribute satisfaction, use the same type of scale and questions as used to measure general satisfaction, but direct respondents to reflect on the specific attribute you're interested in (the check-in experience, the search results page, the download speed).

In addition to collecting closed-ended rating scale data from participants, offer a space for customers to add a comment about their attitude. You can use these comments to help understand what's driving high or low ratings. You can even turn these comments into quantifiable data (see Chapter 2 for how to do so).

Rating Usability with the SUS and SUPR-Q

Ease of use is usually one of the biggest differentiators in the customer experience: If people don't find your product easy to use, they aren't going to be very satisfied or loyal.

The process of measuring usability involves both observing customers using a product and their attitude toward it. You can get half the equation (customer attitude) through a survey. For the other half of the equation, turn to Chapter 14, where I cover usability testing in detail.

To measure attitudes toward usability, ask customers to rate how satisfied they are with the ease of use of a product or a more specific feature or experience (attribute satisfaction), or use one of two common industry questionnaires. These two questionnaires provide a reliable measure along with industry benchmarks (see "Writing Effective Customer Attitude Questions," later in this chapter, for tips about developing survey questions).

System Usability Scale (SUS)

The most common measure of customer attitude toward usability is the System Usability Scale (SUS). It was developed by John Brooke in 1986. It consists of ten items that customers rate from Strongly Disagree (1) to Strongly Agree (5).

- ✔ I think that I would like to use this system frequently.
- ✔ I found the system unnecessarily complex.

✔ I thought the system easy to use.

✔ I think that I would need the support of a technical person to be able to use this system.

✔ I found the various functions in this system well integrated.

✔ I thought there was too much inconsistency in this system.

✔ I would imagine that most people would learn to use this system very quickly.

✔ I found the system very cumbersome to use.

✔ I felt very confident using the system.

✔ I needed to learn a lot of things before I could get going with this system.

The word "system" in the SUS is replaced with the name of the product or website you are testing. Figure 9-3 shows the response option format of the SUS.

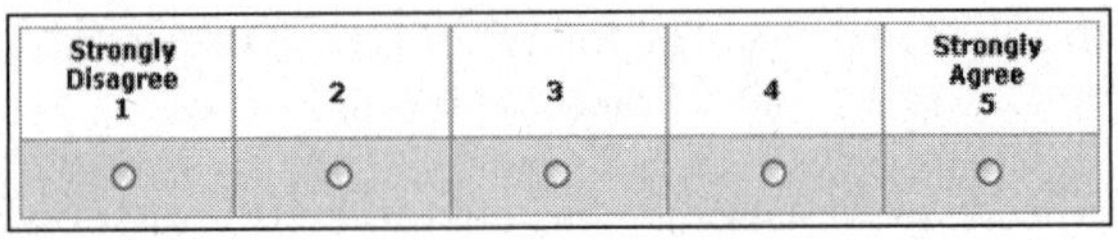

Figure 9-3:
The response option format for the System Usability Scale (SUS) questionnaire.

Strongly Disagree 1	2	3	4	Strongly Agree 5
○	○	○	○	○

To score the SUS, follow these steps:

1. **For odd items, subtract 1 from the user response.**

2. **For even-numbered items, subtract the user responses from 5.**

   This scales all values from 0 to 4 (with 4 being the most positive response).

3. **Add up the converted responses for each user and multiply that total by 2.5.**

   This converts the range of possible values from 0 to 100 instead of from 0 to 40.

4. **Average together the scores for all participants.**

What is a good SUS score?

A major benefit of using existing scales and questionnaires is to compare your score to a meaningful comparison (as discussed in Chapter 2). The average SUS score from over 500 studies is 68. That means a SUS score above 68 is considered above average and anything below 68 is below average.

The best way to interpret your score is to convert it to a percentile rank through a process called normalizing. The following figure shows how the percentile ranks associate with SUS scores and letter grades.

This process is similar to "grading on a curve" based on the distribution of all scores. For example, a raw SUS score of 74 converts to a percentile rank of 70%. A SUS score of 74 has higher perceived usability than 74% of all products tested. It can be interpreted as a B-.

You'd need to score above 80.3 to get an A (the top 10% of scores). This is also the point where users are more likely to recommend the product to a friend. Scoring at the mean score of 68 gets you a C and anything below a 51 is an F (putting you in the bottom 15%).

The SUS is considered a technology agnostic questionnaire, meaning the items aren't specific to any technology or platform. You can ask the SUS about physical products, software, mobile phones, websites, and even interactive voice response systems. For example, Intuit QuickBooks has a SUS score of 75 (above average usability), whereas Adobe Photoshop has a SUS score of 64 (below average usability).

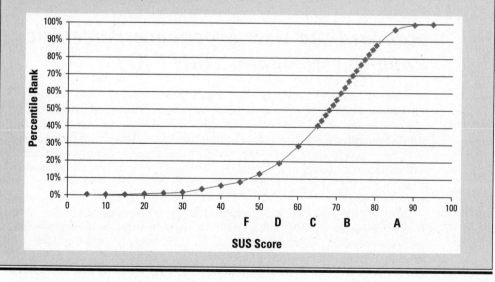

For example, if a participant in a survey responds with the following responses to the ten SUS items, his SUS score is 72.5.

Raw Response	Scaled Response
4	3
1	4
4	3
2	3
3	2
2	3
3	2
1	4
4	3
3	2
Total	29
SUS Score	72.5

Standardized User Experience Percentile Rank Questionnaire (SUPR-Q)

For measuring customers' attitudes toward your website quality, including usability, use an eight-item questionnaire called the Standardized User Experience Percentile Rank Questionnaire (SUPR-Q www.suprq.com). The SUPR-Q provides a reliable and valid measure of customer's attitude toward the quality of a website experience. While there are a number of variables that impact the quality of a website experience, previous research has identified four of the most common dimensions: usability, trust, loyalty, and appearance.

To administer the SUPR-Q, ask users to respond to seven of the eight items using a five-point Disagree to Agree scale (1 = Strongly Disagree and 5 = Strongly Agree). For one item ("How likely are you to recommend this website to a friend or colleague?"), users respond to an 11-point scale (0 = Not at All Likely and 10 = Extremely Likely). The following are the eight items in the SUPR-Q and what they measure:

✔ Usability

  • The website is easy to use.

  • It is easy to navigate within the website.

✔ Trust

- I feel comfortable purchasing from the website.
- I feel confident conducting business on the website.

✔ Loyalty

- How likely are you to recommend this website to a friend or colleague?
- I will likely return to the website in the future.

✔ Appearance

- I find the website to be attractive.
- The website has a clean and simple presentation.

A score is generated by taking half the score with the item with the 11-point scale and averaging it with the other seven items that use the 5-point scale.

Like the SUS, the SUPR-Q has a reference dataset that enables you to purchase access to industry data to understand how well a website scores. If you have a score of 50%, your website ranks as average. A score of 25% means your website ranks below average, while a score of 75% ranks above average.

For example, Figure 9-4 shows the overall SUPR-Q scores for airline and air travel aggregator websites. The average score for this industry is 83%. United Airlines had a below-average score of 65% compared to Southwest's above-average score of 91%.

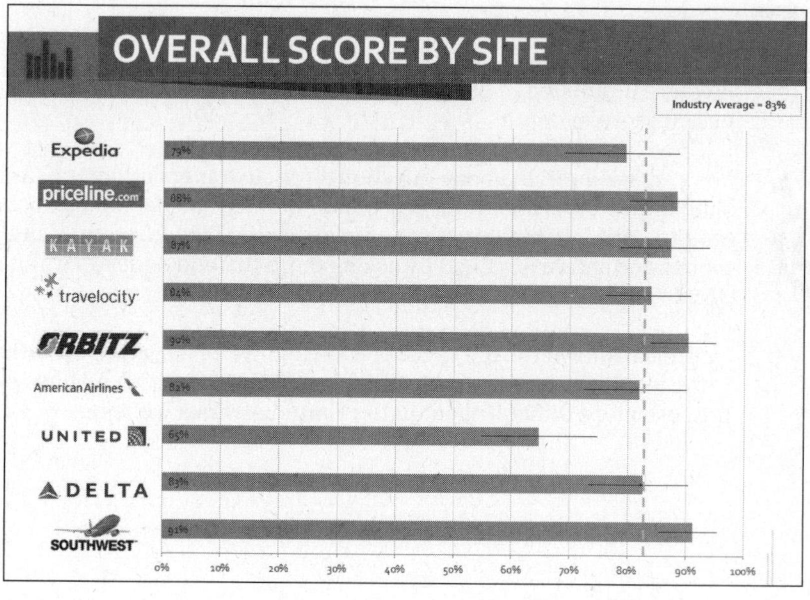

OVERALL SCORE BY SITE

Industry Average = 83%

Site	Score
Expedia	73%
priceline.com	88%
KAYAK	87%
travelocity	84%
ORBITZ	90%
American Airlines	82%
UNITED	65%
DELTA	83%
SOUTHWEST	91%

Figure 9-4: SUPR-Q scores for airline and travel websites.

You can also find similar questionnaires that include industry data for products from ForeSee (ForeSee.com) and WAMMI (wammi.com).

Measuring task difficulty with SEQ

Sometimes you need more specific data than the SUS and SUPR-Q provide you about a specific product.

Ask your customers how difficult they found a task, using the Single Ease Question (SEQ). It's a seven-point scale from Very Difficult (1) to Very Easy (7); scores above 5.1 translate into easier than average and scores below 5.1 indicate harder than average. Figure 9-5 shows a sample SEQ.

Figure 9-5:
The SEQ measures customers' attitudes about the difficulty of an experience or transaction.

Overall, how difficult or easy did you find this task?

Very Difficult 1	2	3	4	5	6	Very Easy 7
◯	◯	◯	◯	◯	◯	◯

If you're interested in using a SEQ, check out Chapters 14 and 15, where I discuss it more in-depth.

You can ask more than one question after customers attempt a task. However, similar questions about the perception of time, satisfaction, and confidence tend to correlate highly with the Single Ease Question, so typically only a bit more information is gained by asking more than one question. You need to decide if more is better — or just more.

Figure 9-6 shows the SEQ scores for making a reservation on three airline websites. Participants in the study found the American Airlines reservation process more difficult than on the United Airlines website.

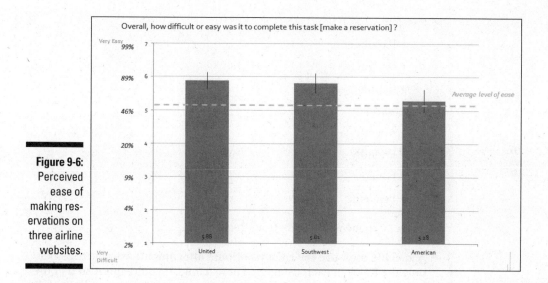

Overall, how difficult or easy was it to complete this task [make a reservation] ?

Very Easy

Average level of ease

Very
Difficult

United   Southwest   American

Figure 9-6:
Perceived
ease of
making res-
ervations on
three airline
websites.

Scoring Brand Affection

Emotions play an important role in how attached a customer feels toward
a brand. While emotions are harder to quantify than other attitudes about
experiences, there are some effective ways to measure these softer attitudes.

Emotions impact customer loyalty. See Chapter 12 for more about loyalty.

One way you gauge the emotional connection customers have toward your
brand or product is to ask questions around emotional attachment.

In the *Journal of Consumer Psychology,* Matthew Thompson suggests measures
of connection, affection, and passion.

Have participants rate their level of agreement to the following items on
a seven-point scale (1 = Strongly Disagree) and (7 = Strongly Agree) to ten
adjectives, including "attached," "delighted," and "affectionate."

✔ Connection
  • Connected
  • Bonded
  • Attached

✔ Passion

   • Passionate

   • Delighted

   • Captivated

✔ Affection

   • Affectionate

   • Friendly

   • Loved

   • Peaceful

You can get two measurements from these scales:

✔ **A specific measure for each emotional attachment:** Average together only the items in each category. For example, if you're interested in the passion category, average together the scores to Passionate, Delighted, and Captivated.

✔ **Overall connection measure:** Average together the scores in all categories.

Figure 9-7 shows the brand attachment toward airline and online travel websites. United Airlines customers had the lowest emotional connection (scoring around 4) compared with high scores for American Airlines (scoring around 5). The average for this group was 4.7 out of 7.

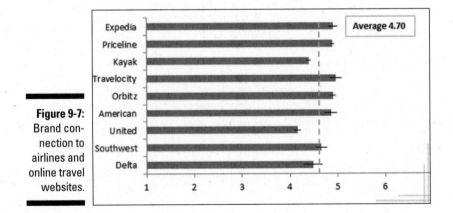

Figure 9-7: Brand connection to airlines and online travel websites.

Finding Expectations: Desirability and Luxury

Customer satisfaction in many respects is a measure of how well customers' expectations are met.

If a product does what it is supposed to, for a reasonable price, and is generally easy to use, customers are generally satisfied. When you exceed customers' expectations, they go from being satisfied to delighted. After delight comes desirability. Customers who are so delighted with your products or services will always come back to you.

Desirability

Researchers at Microsoft developed a way to test customer desirability. They identified a set of 118 positive and negative words that customers can select when describing their attitude toward a product, such as *advanced, annoying, appealing, difficult, innovative, predictable, simplistic, useful,* and *valuable.* Ask participants to select three to five adjectives they associate with a product or experience. Then calculate the ratio of positive (for example, appealing, clean) to negative words (for example, busy, dull, frustrating). There are no published benchmarks on the percentage of positive words or the ratio of negative to positive words. You'll want to compare performance over time or to other comparable products. At the very least, you'll want more positive than negative words.

You can find all the adjectives online at `http://en.wikipedia.org/wiki/Microsoft_Reaction_Card_Method_%28Desirability_Testing%29`

Chapter 13 covers the Kano model, which is another technique to help differentiate between features customers expect and those which delight them.

Luxury

Luxury products set themselves apart in the market through their capability to go above and beyond satisfaction — to *delighting* consumers. Delight is an emotional response, often described as a combination of surprise and joy.

This means that, especially in the luxury brand market, measurement tools need to aid in the differentiation between how consumers describe an experience cognitively and how they feel about it emotionally. One way of measuring customer attitude toward the perceived luxury is to have a set of representative customers rate a brand or product using a series of adjectives. This is part of a questionnaire called the Brand Luxury Index (BLI). Figure 9-8 shows a selection of the items in the BLI. Participants mark an "x" on the line between the adjectives when rating the luxury of an item or experience. More information about the BLI can be found in the *Journal of Brand Management*.

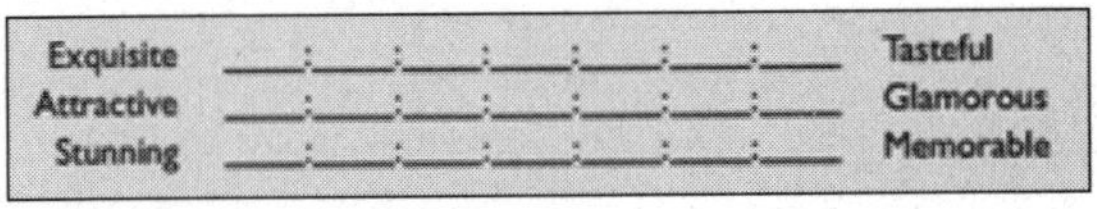

Figure 9-8:
A selection
from the
Brand
Luxury
Index (BLI).

Exquisite	Tasteful
Attractive	Glamorous
Stunning	Memorable

Measuring Attitude Lift

One way to understand how a product or service experience impacts customers' attitudes is to measure *lift* — the difference between attitudes before and after the experience.

Earlier in the chapter, I introduce the idea of customer attitude as a measure that's appropriate for both existing and new customers. To understand how an experience impacts attitude, you measure your customers' attitudes before they use your product and again after they use your product. The difference is the lift in attitude. The lift can be positive or negative, where a negative lift means the attitude declined after exposure.

For example, in a study of the Enterprise and Budget rental car websites, customers were asked to rate their attitude toward each brand prior to and after renting a car through each website.

Figure 9-9 shows the average brand favorability of Budget increased 12% after participants rented a car through its website (from 4.7 to 5.3). In contrast, the brand favorability declined 15% for participants after renting through Enterprise.com (from 5.3 to 4.5). More details about this study are discussed in Chapter 14.

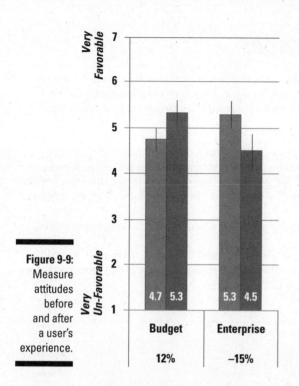

Figure 9-9:
Measure
attitudes
before
and after
a user's
experience.

Calculate your lift measures with these steps:

1. **Subtract the post measure from the pre measure, then change the order of the numbers.**

   For Enterprise, this was

   ```
   4.5 - 5.3 = -.8
   ```

2. **Divide the difference by the pre measure.**

   ```
   -.8 / 5.3 = -.15
   ```

3. **Multiple by 100 to get a percentage.**

   ```
   -.15 * 100 = -15%
   ```

   The result is a 15 percent decline in brand lift (a negative lift) for Enterprise.

Asking for Preferences

Customers inevitably make choices between competing brands. To understand how your products stack up against each of your competitors' products, have participants select which brand they prefer given a set of likely alternatives.

When measuring preference data, collect data on both choice and intensity. That is, you want to know which brand customers would pick if they had to, and how strongly they feel. You only need one question to get this data because the direction of the intensity (for or against one brand) includes the preference.

Collect preferences both before and after a product or service experience.

For example, in the rental car website study, 62 participants were asked to rate which rental car website they preferred (see Figure 9-10) after having a chance to rent a car through both websites.

Figure 9-10:
Which site did customers prefer?

Which rental car website did you prefer using?

Strongly Preferred Enterprise 1	2	3	Neutral 4	5	6	Strongly Preferred Budget 7
○	○	○	○	○	○	○

The distribution of the 62 responses is shown in the following table. For example, 20 participants selected seven (Strongly Preferred Budget). These participants showed both a preference for Budget and strong intensity toward it. Note that 7 other participants selected 5, meaning they preferred Budget, but only slightly.

Preference Rating	*# of Participants Selecting*	*Preference*
1	7	Enterprise
2	5	Enterprise
3	1	Enterprise
4	4	Neither
5	7	Budget
6	18	Budget
7	20	Budget

To compute the percentage of customers who preferred each brand, follow these three steps:

1. **Add all the customers who selected a 5, 6, or 7 as customers who preferred Budget (45 people).**

   Participants who selected 1, 2, or 3 preferred Enterprise (13 people).

2. **Exclude the four participants who preferred neither Enterprise nor Budget.**

   This step leaves a total of 58 participants.

3. **Compute the percentage preferring each brand.**

   45/58 = 78% prefer Budget and 13/58 = 22% prefer Enterprise.

4. **Test for statistical significance.**

   Don't forget to calculate the error rate. You can use the online calculator at www.measuringu.com/onep.php. There's less than a .01% chance this difference in preference is due to chance. See Figure 9-11.

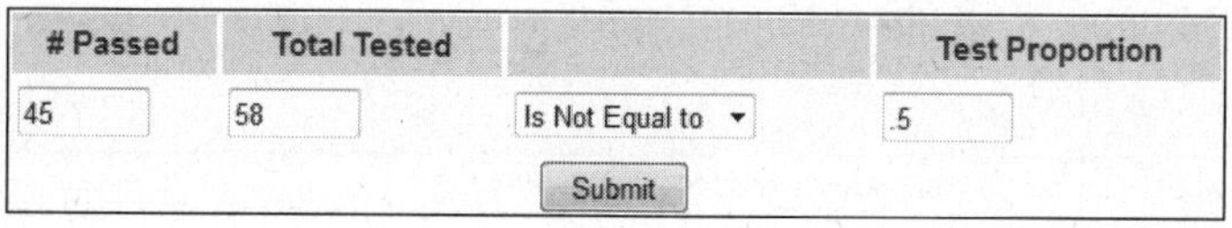

Figure 9-11: Test if the proportion of participants preferring Budget is statistically significant.

# Passed	Total Tested		Test Proportion
45	58	Is Not Equal to ▾	.5

Submit

Repeat the same process for customers who expressed the most intensity toward each brand. Twenty out of 58 (34%) strongly preferred Budget compared to only seven (12%) who strongly preferred Enterprise. This difference is also statistically significant.

Finding Your Key Drivers of Customer Attitudes

Having all the data on customer attitudes is one thing; you now have to take all that data and interpret it to know what to do in order to improve your customer attitudes. What you need to look at are your key drivers — the features and attributes of the product or experience that contribute the most to your brand reputation.

You can find your key drivers with two methods:

✔ **Open-ended questions:** Analyze the responses to your open-ended questions. These can give you a good idea of what customers think is most important.

   You can group these comments into categories and rank their importance by quantity.

   With fuzzy concepts like satisfaction, usability, and luxury, always give participants space to write their own comments.

✔ **Multiple regression analysis:** Multiple regression analysis examines the correlation between the independent and dependent variables to determine which attributes contributed most to consumers' overall brand attitude. I cover multiple regression analysis in the appendix, but you should plan on enlisting the help of a statistician to assist you with running a multiple regression analysis.

For example, customers' satisfaction with a web-based software product was measured by averaging customers' responses to a product satisfaction question and a loyalty question, as shown in Figure 9-12. Customer loyalty is covered in detail in Chapter 12.

How would you rate your overall satisfaction with the product?

Not at all Satisfied 1	2	3	4	5	6	Very Satisfied 7
○	○	○	○	○	○	○

Figure 9-12: Two questions to determine customer satisfaction.

How likely are you to continue using the product?

Highly Unlikely 1	2	3	Neutral 4	5	6	Highly Likely 7
○	○	○	○	○	○	○

Participants also rated their level of satisfaction on 14 product attributes, including trust, reliability, specific technical features of the product, and usability.

The results of the key driver analysis are shown in Figure 9-13. It shows only seven variables drive most customer satisfaction with the product. The vertical axis is how important each variable is in predicting customer satisfaction. The numbers refer to how much each of these variables will increase customer satisfaction. Improving customer attitude toward being "more productive" by 1 point would improve customer satisfaction by .14 point.

The horizontal axis is how satisfied customers are on the seven-point scale. The two biggest drivers of customer satisfaction are customers' attitude toward the software helping them do their job quicker, and their perceived quality of the product. Both drivers have relatively low ratings (below 5 on a seven-point scale) and suggest that improving these two aspects of the product would have the biggest impact on customer satisfaction.

The R-Square value describes how much the combination of independent variables predict the dependent variable — customer satisfaction. (See the appendix for more information on the R-Square value.) In this case, 55% of customer satisfaction is predicted using just seven variables.

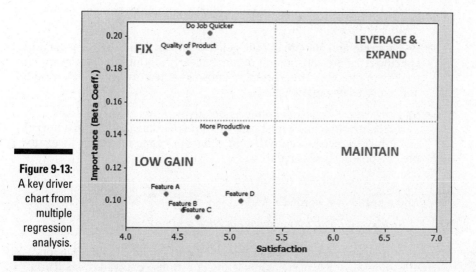

Figure 9-13: A key driver chart from multiple regression analysis.

Writing Effective Customer Attitude Questions

The process of measuring customers' attitudes involves asking the right questions in the right way with the right scales. It can seem daunting, but here are tips to make the process easier.

✔ **Look for existing questionnaires.** While you have to create your own questions that are specific to your product, look for questions that exist in published literature. Many existing questionnaires have gone through a process of standardization. This includes testing the reliability (how stable customers respond) and validity (whether the questions actually measure what they are supposed to). If possible, look for existing questionnaires (like the SUPR-Q and SUS) that have benchmark data you can compare your score to.

✔ **Don't obsess over scale steps.** Just pick a scale and stick with it. What matters, what makes a measure meaningful, is comparing the same responses to other products or over time.

Having more scale points is generally better (for example, seven versus five points); this matters most when you have only one or a few response scales. The more responses (for example, the SUS had ten 5-point scales), the less it matters.

✔ **Avoid double-barrel questions.** When writing questions, avoid using two concepts in one question (for example, "How satisfied are you with the price and quality of the product?") Is the customer rating quality or price? While the two concepts may illicit the same response, separate them into two questions.

✔ **Be concrete and specific.** While general satisfaction is high level, more specific attribute satisfaction requires clearly stating what you want customers to rate. Be sure customers know what feature you're referring to, and avoid using jargon.

✔ **Stay positive.** Phrase questions as positives rather than negatives. Participants often make mistakes when responding (usually in a hurry) and forget to reverse score the question. For example, here is an example of a positively worded item:

This website was easy to use.

And a negatively worded item:

It was difficult to find what I needed on this website.

Pretest your questions with a small sample of participants. Look for inconsistent responses or ask participants if any questions confused them. If you plan to use a set of questions repeatedly, hire a statistician to help validate the phrasing and scales.

Chapter 10

Quantifying the Consideration and Purchase Phases

Many times before customers make a purchase, they come across your company — they see your website, an advertisement, or read a review.

This is the awareness step. When you can get those potential customers interacting with your company — maybe they download a brochure from your website or sign up for your newsletter — those customers have moved into the consideration phases.

The places where potential customers interact with your company in the awareness and consideration steps are touchpoints (see Chapter 7). When you identify the touchpoints, you need to prioritize which touchpoints have the largest influence on your customers' decisions. You need to understand how each touchpoint impacts customers' decisions, then measure the strength of the impact and understand what can be improved.

Identifying the Consideration Touchpoints

Touchpoints are the places where customers find out about your company and products. (See Chapter 7.) Touchpoints can be media driven by your company — ads on TV, radio, or newspapers, for instance. But touchpoints can also be customer driven — reviews on websites and social media.

Before you can quantify the consideration phase, you have to know where customers are being influenced. To do so, you need to understand all the touchpoints that influence customers as they decide.

Company-driven touchpoints

Company-driven touchpoints are what you probably think of as advertising. It's generally paid for by the company and includes more than ads on TV.

- **Broadcast media:** Television, radio, newspapers, and magazines are still popular touchpoints for consumer brands with big marketing budgets.

- **Direct mail:** Postcards, catalogs, coupons, or anything that gets sent in traditional snail mail.

- **Email newsletters:** Your inbox is probably full of email communication from websites and companies that you've purchased from or signed up with, or that somehow just keeps showing up.

- **In person:** The in-store experience or interactions at places like a convention.

- **Company and product websites:** The company website is often one of the only touchpoints customers see. Product web pages are often linked directly from ads or directly from Google searches.

Customer-driven touchpoints

Customer-driven touchpoints are typically areas you don't have control over:

- **Friends and colleagues:** Few things have a bigger influence on customer behavior than the opinion of a trusted friend or colleague. It's this word-of-mouth marketing power that lies at the heart of the Net Promoter Score system (see Chapter 12).

- **Social media:** Sites like Twitter, Pinterest, Houzz, Facebook, and LinkedIn are electronic extensions of word-of-mouth from friends and colleagues. They have a way of taking one person's experience and making it viral — affecting an enormous number of potential customers with little control over the message or reach.

- **Bloggers and influencers:** The bigger the product or service, the more experts are writing about it, from airlines, technology, and restaurants to fashion.

- **Consumer reviews:** Potential customers rely heavily on customer reviews and will often use Amazon's reviews when considering a purchase (even on websites other than Amazon).

Measuring the Customer-Driven Touchpoints

The positive or negative experiences customers share about your brand and product potentially reach thousands of potential and existing customers on social media sites like Twitter and Facebook. Online services such as Brandwatch, Netvibes, Radian6, Sysomos, and Social Mention offer a service to measure and report on the positive and negative sentiments. You can track these positive and negative sentiments over time and associate changes with advertising campaigns, new product launches, or other events.

Even without these services, Twitter provides basic analytics on how many mentions or retweets or replies a company, brand, or product receives. More advanced software from products like Hootsuite will also tell you which links people are clicking on and growth in Twitter mentions over a period of time.

While these companies will aggregate the data for you, you can also compute it yourself by monitoring your own social media streams:

1. **Count all the times your product or brand was mentioned.**

   In Twitter, for example, you can search by hashtag #, @, or the name of the company or product.

2. **Categorize the comments into positive, neutral, and negative.**

   Negative comments can include everything from a bad purchase experience to a high price or failed product.

   For example, a positive tweet posted to Twitter for an airline might be "I can't wait for @ajaxair to launch nonstop service to @curacaotravel from JFK. Just in time to save the summer tan #ILuvAjaxAir."

   And a negative tweet might be "Very sad @ajaxair Shifted our Xmas travel flight 10 hours today. Forcing $ plan changes that will cut into family time."

3. **Compute the percentage of positive and negative sentiments by dividing the number of positive by the total number of mentions.**

   For example, if you count 10 positive comments out of 85 neutral and 5 negative, 10% of the total are positive mentions. Repeat this for the negative comments and graph the difference by week or month.

Figure 10-1 shows the proportion of positive and negative mentions of a hardware manufacturer over a six-month period. In January, the ratio was even at 14% positive to 14% negative, then it fluctuated a bit until June, when the negative percentage was more than 1.5 times the positive percentage (15% versus 9%).

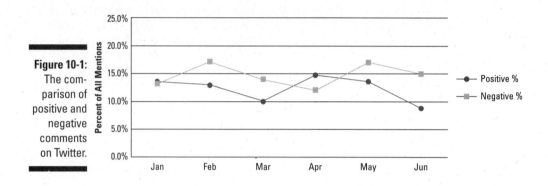

You can expect the changes to fluctuate due to random chance variation, so include confidence intervals (or run statistical comparisons) when making decisions. Figure 10-2 shows the graph updated to include 90% confidence intervals (see Chapter 2 for more about confidence intervals). When the intervals overlap, you can't be sure the difference isn't due to chance alone (for example, in Jan, Feb, and March). However, in June, the confidence interval error bars don't overlap (notice the small gap), meaning the percentage of negative comments exceeds the percentage of positive comments.

It's just as important to measure positive and negative comments via word of mouth. Turn to Chapter 12 to find out how to do that.

Figure 10-2:
Positive and negative comments on Twitter with a confidence interval added.

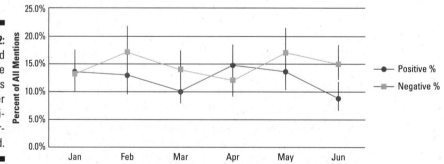

Measuring the Three R's of Company-Driven Touchpoints

To measure the effectiveness of company-driven touchpoints, including direct mail (postcards and coupons), email newsletters, TV and radio ads, and company websites, measure the three R's: reach, resonance, and reaction.

Reach

Understand the total number of customers your advertising is reaching:

- For TV and radio, this can be estimated by market share and is usually provided by the media outlet or companies like Nielsen.
- For newspapers, magazines, and trade journals, this can be estimated by circulation rates.
- For online advertisements, use page views that are recorded using website hosting log files or Google Analytics (see the section on website analytics, later in this chapter).

Resonance

It could be that prospective customers saw your ad, email, or postcard and even recall some of its details. It's important to understand how well the messages are resonating. Company websites are often the most seen forms of communication and branding opportunities and play a major role in shaping the customer decisions. Most websites convey important branding messages, benefits, and features of purchasing a product service.

Ask a series of open- and closed-ended questions to gauge customers' attitudes toward the message. See if customers can correctly list the benefits of what's being offered and understand the value proposition the company is offering.

For example, I worked with the website team at PayPal after a redesign of its home page. The new home page introduced a major design departure by highlighting new offerings, as shown in Figure 10-3.

Attribution modeling

To improve brand awareness, companies need to get the word out using marketing methods such as advertising and word of mouth. Advertising can be online, on television, on the radio, or a number of other forms.

You can better understand how effective advertising campaigns are by asking participants in the branding survey where participants heard

of the product or brand (on their mobile phones, a website, or on TV, for instance).

You can then attribute higher or lower brand awareness to various campaigns. For example, if participants report higher awareness and also report having seen a recent Facebook ad, then there's at least a tenuous link to this campaign.

Figure 10-3: Test how design changes resonate with customers.

To measure how the new PayPal home page design resonated with prospective and current customers, we had several participants answer questions about both the old and new website designs.

Reaction

After understanding how the message works, measure whether customers' attitudes and behaviors changed. Use the measures of customer attitude, satisfaction, and future intent to assess the reaction, as described in Chapter 9.

To measure behavior, measure customer purchases (if possible) by looking at revenue or the number of transactions at the stores or online (see the A/B discussion section later in this chapter).

Measuring resonance and reaction

You can test resonance and reaction before or in conjunction with a company-driven touchpoint. For example, I worked with computer manufacturer Lenovo to understand the resonance and reaction for its new convertible laptop advertisement. It was a new concept and the advertisement would cover TV and the web, so we wanted to see how well it resonated with customers, and how it impacted their attitudes and their potential reaction (to purchase). We used this process to measure resonance and reaction, and you can too:

1. **Measure existing attitudes, such as brand favorability or purchase intent, before showing a stimulus such as an advertisement or newsletter.**

2. **Show the stimulus (the advertisement or newsletter).**

3. **Measure the attitudes, comprehension, and intent to purchase after the exposure.**

   Look for changes in attitudes (see Chapter 9 for measuring lift) and how well participants' attitudes and sentiments match the intended attitude.

Tracking Conversions and Purchases

A purchase is a *conversion,* but a conversion is not always a purchase. Potential customers often engage with a company in multiple ways during the consideration phase. These actions, such as signing up for the company's email list or downloading a product brochure from the company website, can also be considered a type of conversion, or a *micro conversion.*

Like purchases, micro conversions that happen online can be tracked and quantified, giving you a clearer picture of the customer journey to purchase (see Chapter 7). These conversions also can be considered leads that can turn into customers. Giving potential customers in the consideration phase a way to engage with your business through micro conversions is one form of *lead generation:* the process of creating sales leads that might convert into sales. You can help nurture a lead that engages with your company through a micro conversion to make a purchase through additional communication, or touchpoints, along the customer's journey to purchase.

In order to turn a potential customer who engages with your company website via a micro conversion into a paying customer, you first have to create micro conversions and a way to record them.

Tracking micro conversions

To start measuring micro conversions and ultimately conversions on a website, you need to set up an analytics tool. A number of analytics tools allow you to track website interaction. The most popular solution (free) is Google Analytics (`http://www.google.com/analytics`).

Web analytics tools allow you to collect the following metrics on online interactions.

- ✔ **Page views:** One of the most fundamental measures of engagement on a website is which pages customers are viewing and how many times those pages are viewed. This will become a key metric for tracking conversion opportunities.

- ✔ **Average session duration:** *Average session duration* is simply the total duration of all sessions on your site divided by the number of sessions. In other words, it's how long, on average, visitors spend on your site. Sometimes also referred to as *time on site,* this metric can give you insight into whether visitors are spending a significant amount of time browsing your site or leaving quickly after arriving.

  This metric can be measured over time to compare how visitor behavior changes. For example, if you add additional page content, you can compare average session duration before and after the change was made to determine if the new content had an impact on how long visitors were interacting with the website.

- ✔ **Bounce rate:** Bounce rate is the percentage of single-page sessions. This means that site visitors immediately left the website from the page they first entered without interacting with the page.

  A high bounce rate, generally upwards of 60 percent, can be an indication that website visitors aren't finding what they anticipated when they clicked through to your site. On the flip side, it can also be an indication that website visitors found the information that they wanted quickly and had no need to view additional content. A low bounce rate, generally below 40 percent, means that most website visitors are engaging with multiple pages on your website.

- ✔ **Pages per session:** Related to session duration is the metric *pages per session,* which measures on average, how many pages on your website a visitor looks at during his or her visit. This can give you an indication of how visitors are spending their time on your website, not just for how long.

Like average session duration, pages per session can be compared over time to help determine if changes made to your website or marketing campaigns affect how much content visitors are interacting with.

✔ **New versus returning users:** This metric tells you what percentage of visitors to your site are visiting for the first time versus visiting for a second or subsequent time.

Looking at the new versus returning visitor metric can be helpful in analyzing user behavior and on-site engagement (as discussed in Chapter 4 on customer segmentation). You may find, for example, that visitors who have previously visited your website spend more time on-site and view more content than those who visit it for the first time. You may also find that returning visitors are more likely to move from the consideration phase to the purchase phase as they become more aware of your products and services and gain confidence in buying from you versus a competitor.

Creating micro-conversion opportunities

Even if your ultimate goal is to drive sales of your product, online or offline, think about what other actions your potential customers might take as they work their way through the consideration phase. Use your segments and personas to determine offers that resonate with customers' pain points and needs. (See Chapter 5 for the scoop on setting up personas.)

You may already have some micro conversions on your website, perhaps a form that allows visitors to sign up for an email newsletter, or a phone number at the top of the page that will allow them to contact customer service or the sales team.

Other examples you might consider adding include:

✔ Web form for the user to request prices or general information

✔ Web form that allows the visitor to send an email to the company

✔ White papers, case studies, e-books, or other downloadable assets

✔ Digital product catalogs or brochures that can be downloaded

✔ A form that allows a user to request a brochure or catalog by mail

✔ Video tutorials or product demonstration presentations

✔ Calculators and other useful utilities

✔ Capability to create a user account on your website

Setting up conversion tracking

Once you have created micro conversions on your website, be sure that you can track their behavior. Google Analytics allows you to track micro conversions and sales through the setup of Goals.

Google Analytics Goals can currently track four types of actions a visitor takes on your website:

- ✔ **Destination:** Visitor reaches a specific page
- ✔ **Duration:** Sessions that last for equal to or longer than a specified amount of time
- ✔ **Pages/screens per session:** Visitor views a specified number of pages or screens
- ✔ **Event:** Action specified as an event is triggered (for example, a video is played)

Say, for example, that you have created an email sign-up form and a brochure download as micro conversions on your site. In each case, the site is set up so that the visitor reaches a confirmation page, thanking her for taking the action. You can set up two separate destination goals in Google Analytics: one that records each email sign-up and another that records a brochure download as a type of goal completion.

In addition to tracking micro conversions, you need to track online purchases. Google Analytics also offers *e-commerce tracking* that passes information about the purchased product, including quantity purchased, associated revenue, and tax and shipping costs, as well as how many times a user visited your site before completing a transaction.

Google Analytics provides extensive documentation on how to set up a profile for your website and how to create goals on its support site (`https://support.google.com/analytics`).

Measuring conversion rates

Conversion rate is the number of website visitors taking a desired action divided by the total number of visitors. Conversion rates can be measured for your entire website, a single page, or even for individual marketing channels that drive traffic to your website, like search engine listings or social media platforms. You can also track conversion rates for individual conversion or micro-conversion types.

Say you want to determine what the overall conversion rate for your website is over the past year. Here's how you find your conversion rate:

1. **Look at the total number of users who visited your site during the last 12 months.**

2. **Add up the completed online conversions.**

3. **Divide the number of completed online conversions by the total number of users.**

   For example, if you had 350,000 visits to your site last year and 3,500 of those turned into a purchase, you would divide 3,500 by 350,000 for a resulting conversion rate of 1%.

   If those 350,000 visits had led to 7,000 conversions, your conversion rate would be 2%.

Determining what a "good" conversion rate is depends on the type of website, the industry, and what customers are being asked to do:

- For signing up for an online newsletter, the conversion may be between 1 percent and 20 percent.

- If you're asking people to make a purchase or donate money, expect the conversion rate to be small, usually less than 1 percent.

  When I helped Wikipedia measure and improve its online donations, the conversion rate was below 0.1 percent.

What makes a strong conversion rate for your site is best measured against your previous conversion rate.

Measuring Changes through A/B Testing

The true success of company-directed messages is to measure how changes to your message affect recipients' behavior. Here are two common methods:

- **Usability testing** is done ahead of time. It's ideal for testing major new concepts with qualified participants in a study before you launch to your full customer base. This provides an insight into how designs will affect conversion rates and is covered in Chapter 14.

- **Real-time testing** involves running a live experiment with your prospective and current customers on a specific touchpoint. Savvy direct marketers have used this technique for decades. It's used extensively on websites, online ads, email newsletters, and even email subject lines. It's best used when you aren't introducing major new concepts, but rather, want to tweak or optimize existing designs to improve conversions.

The approach is often referred to as A/B testing because there are usually two alternatives being tested: option A and option B.

You can test more than two alternatives (A/B/C testing). It's called *split testing* (because different alternatives are split between your customers).

The idea behind A/B testing is that customers are randomly presented with one of two alternatives and in real time, you measure which alternative generates a better outcome. Outcomes in this case are one of a number of metrics that measure engagement, consideration, and purchasing. Typically only one variable is changed for each design (for example, a color, picture, or price). That enables you to properly attribute responses to the respective variable. (See Chapter 2 for a reminder on variables.)

Offline A/B testing

One example of A/B testing is direct mailing two alternative promotions in two different color envelopes (white versus manila) to prospective customers. If the offer contained in these envelopes has customers follow through, you can compare the percentage of A versus B envelopes to tell you which promotion is more effective.

For example, I worked with a national advertising agency that placed ads in weekly newspapers. The goal was to understand the increase (or decrease) in revenue from a coupon for Pier 1 Imports, a U.S. retailer. Newspaper readers in a handful of U.S. cities received the coupon, and the sales that weekend in those specific cities were statistically compared to results for cities that did not receive the coupon. We also controlled for differences in the market by accounting for same-store sales the prior month and year. We were able to see that the discount from the coupon was offset by the increase in sales.

Online A/B testing

While A/B testing gives you a lot of insight, there is a hard cost in mailing and printing different design alternatives. It can take a long time to realize that a significant portion of people throw out one color envelope more than another color. If a significant portion of customers toss the envelopes in the trash, you've lost money. Not a good thing!

Online A/B testing has no printing or postage costs, and the feedback is immediate. For those reasons, it's very popular to optimize websites and online advertising.

By far, the most common type of A/B testing metric is the conversion rate described earlier in the chapter. As a reminder, a conversion can be anything from clicking a button, subscribing to email, or adding an item to a shopping cart, to making a purchase.

Here are the five steps to take to go from data to insights:

1. **Determine your metric.**

   The two most common metrics are conversion (or micro conversion) and average order value for a purchase.

2. **Find your variable.**

   Identify one salient element on the website: a button, headline, image, or layout. Choose two alternatives.

   For example, PayPal tested two alternative designs of its Check-out button. Small changes resulted in major differences in conversions and average order value.

3. **Randomize and test.**

   The secret to a successful A/B test is randomization. Alternate which design (A or B) the next customer coming to a web page receives.

   It isn't always possible to randomize designs; some companies run them sequentially (for example, Design A goes from Monday to Wednesday and Design B from Thursday to Sunday). Watch out for daily and weekly seasonality. You may have a different type of customer during the evening or weekends and running tests sequentially means you can't tell if different conversion rates are the result of the designs or just the different customers.

4. **Determine your sample size.**

   Differences in A/B test results are often very small, usually less than 5 percent or even 1 percent. For high-traffic websites, though, increasing conversion rates by even .1 percent can result in a substantial increase in sales.

   For example, I worked with Wikipedia to help measure the best banner ads to increase donations. The differences in conversion rates were often less than .05 percent. But because millions of people viewed each website monthly, differences this small translated into thousands of dollars.

   The sample size you need depends on the size of the difference you hope to detect (if one exists). The smaller the difference, the larger the sample size you need. Table 10-1 shows the number of customers you need for each design alternative.

Table 10-1		Finding a Sample Size		
Difference	*Each Group*	*Total*	*A*	*B*
0.1%	592,905	1,185,810	5%	5.1%
0.5%	24,604	49,208	5%	5.5%
1.0%	6,428	12,856	5%	6.0%
5.0%	344	688	5%	10.0%
10.0%	112	224	5%	15.0%
20.0%	40	80	5%	25.0%
30.0%	23	46	5%	35.0%
40.0%	15	30	5%	45.0%
50.0%	11	22	5%	55.0%

For example, to detect a 1% difference in conversion rates (5% compared to 6%), you should plan on randomly assigning 12,856 participants to Design A or Design B. One approach to sample size planning is to take the approximate "traffic" you expect on a website and split it so half receives treatment A and half receives treatment B. If you expect approximately 1,000 page views a day, then you need to test for about 13 days. At that sample size, if there was a difference of 1 percentage point or larger (for instance, 5% versus 6%), then that difference would be statistically significant.

If you want to determine if your new application has at least a 20 percent higher completion rate than the older application, plan to test 80 people (40 in each group).

5. **Compare the difference.**

Don't be fooled by randomness by eyeballing the results. A higher conversion rate could be from chance fluctuations. To determine if two conversion rates are statistically different, use an A/B test calculator, like this one (http://www.measuringu.com/ab-calc.php) (see figure 10-4).

For example, if 100 out of 5,000 users click through on an email (2% conversion rate) and 70 out of 4,800 click through on a different version (1.46% conversion rate), the probability of obtaining a difference this large or larger, if there really was no difference, is 4% (p-value = .04). That is to say, it's statistically significant — you just don't see differences this large very often from chance alone. The input and output of the A/B test are shown in Figure 10-4. See the appendix for how to compute the statistical difference between percentages.

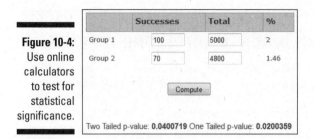

Figure 10-4:
Use online
calculators
to test for
statistical
significance.

Just because you get results that are statistically significant doesn't mean they are practically significant. *Practical significance* means the increase will have some practical meaning to the company or customers. For instance, a new design may increase the number of customers (statistically significant), but the increase might be so small (say, .01%) that it will have no noticeable impact on sales.

While your goal may be to optimize conversions (more click-throughs and purchases), don't forget to consider the total revenue. In some cases, more customers will click through a design, but if it results in a smaller average order value, then you're ultimately losing money even though more customers are converting!

The changing visitors of Wikipedia

I helped the Wikipedia team better understand the conversion rate data that they were monitoring during their donation period. Wikipedia is the online encyclopedia that is ad free and free to all. It raises money by having a donation drive a couple weeks each year. It's therefore important to have as many customers as possible donate during that short window of time.

A lot of A/B testing of banners is used to see which messages and images elicit the highest response. The test banner that performs better is kept in place.

Wikipedia traffic is enormous: Hundreds of millions view it every day. That means statistical significance is reached quickly, usually within hours instead of days, as on many other sites.

One perplexing result the Wikipedia analytics team noticed was that they'd reach statistical significance but then the conversion rate would no longer be significant as the day progressed. After double-checking their numbers, it turned out that as it got later in the day in the U.S., more international readers started coming online and they reacted differently to the banners than did U.S. visitors. The conclusion was to split out banners by region. This illustrates the importance of understanding how your customers may change, even throughout the day!

Multivariate testing leads to surprising results

Testing multiple variables at the same time saves time, and more importantly, provides the optimal combination of variables. For example, I was helping a credit card company understand which combination of elements on a registration form led to higher conversions (applying for a card was the conversion outcome). During early tests, the two variables used were asking participants their Social Security Number (SSN) and offering a 0% introductory interest rate. In separate A/B tests, we found that prospective customers, not surprisingly, were more likely to apply with a 0% introductory rate.

Also, we found that asking just the last four digits of customers' SSN also increased their likelihood to apply. Both options cost the company money (in lower interest and higher costs to validate someone's identity). However, we found that customers were actually slightly more likely to apply even when there wasn't a 0% introductory offer when they were asked just the last four digits of the SSN. In other words, the interaction of these two variables led to a different optimal result than testing them separately.

Testing multiple variables

A/B testing typically involves measuring only one variable at a time, like a website button size, placement, or color to increase conversion rates. But design elements have a way of interacting with each other in unpredictable ways. It can be that one type of image works well with only a certain color button. Or perhaps a headline, image, and location increase the conversion rate, while another combination decreases the conversion rate. Software from companies like Adobe can be used to test and implement multivariate tests.

 The Which Test Won website, https://whichtestwon.com/, provides plenty of examples of online A/B and multivariate testing. It's surprising how people's intuition can be a poor judge of what design combinations will actually increase conversions.

Making the Most of Website Analytics

Website analytics tools contain a wealth of data and metrics that can help you quantify your customers' behavior and improve user experience. As you dive into the wealth of information tools like those that Google Analytics provides about your users, here are some guidelines for making the most of them:

✔ **Start with a goal.** With so much information at your fingertips, it can be easy to get lost in the data. You may find that you're spending a lot of time looking at information without taking action on it. The best way to combat this and make the data useful is to use the tool with specific goals in mind.

Write down one to three goals and use them to guide your time spent in Google Analytics. If you find yourself wandering off in another direction, remind yourself of your purpose for the current session and refocus.

✔ **Use historical data to put current data in context.** You can find out whether your current methods are in line or significantly different than previous time periods, which is incredibly helpful to decide when you need to make changes. Choose the date range you're interested in — usually the previous period, previous year, or a custom date range.

✔ **Use annotations.** Annotations are an incredibly helpful tool for flagging unusual spikes or drops in website traffic and other metrics. You can note a higher number of conversions due to a limited time offer or a drop in conversion following a website change. When you review historical data, you can remember what may have caused the change in your data.

Set your annotations to allow others to see them. Shared annotations can save your team a lot of work while looking for the cause behind data irregularities.

Use annotations for any data irregularities that you are aware of, as well as for noting when marketing campaigns launch or your company receives earned media mentions, so that you and your team can easily tie performance changes back to your initiatives and other external forces.

✔ **Use advanced segments.** Advanced segments are a powerful way to isolate subsets of your website traffic for analysis. Google Analytics comes with predefined segments, as well as the option to build your own, in order to compare and contrast how different segments of visitors behave on your website.

For example, you may find that users who visit the site via organic search results stay longer on-site and view more pages per session than those who come through another channel, such as referral from a social media page.

✔ **Create dashboards and shortcuts for views you use often.** Dashboards are a way to quickly view data that you use frequently, such as bounce rate, user locations, and more. You can create up to 20 dashboards in your Analytics profile, with up to 12 widgets that display different metrics on each of them.

✔ **Use alerts to stay on top of performance changes.** If there is a sudden spike or drop in conversion rates, or bounce rate, you need to know so you can address it.

✔ **Examine your search data.** Search data can be incredibly valuable: It lends some insight into the minds of users and can sometimes even tell a bit about their intent as they interact with your content. If you're using pay-per-click (PPC), or paid search, to drive traffic to your website, you have a wealth of information about the keywords and related search queries that drove people to your site.

Chapter 11

Tracking Post-Purchase Behavior

*Y*ou probably think that once a potential customer becomes an *actual* customer, your job is done. Not so fast! You may have put a lot of effort into getting that customer to make a purchase, but it's just as important to put additional effort into turning that customer into a repeat and loyal customer. Not only can that customer make additional purchases from you, but he or she also just might recommend your business, which could lead to even more customers.

As soon as the transaction is complete, customers move into a phase in which you provide service, support, and fulfilling the promises made during the pre-purchase process. This phase of the customer journey can be one of the longest, especially for products or services that aren't purchased frequently. During this phase, customers can move toward being loyal or less loyal, reconsider the competition, and even be negative influencers. This can lead to an improvement in the perception of the brand or its degradation. This outcome of the post-purchase phase will influence the next purchase consideration for the current customer and for other potential customers as they become influenced by positive and negative word of mouth in person or on social media.

In the post-purchase phase, you continue to measure customers' attitudes, especially customer satisfaction, brand and product loyalty, and future intent.

In this chapter, I use many of the measures introduced in Chapter 9. The same techniques you use in the pre-purchase phase and consideration phases work in the post-purchase phase, too.

Dealing with Cognitive Dissonance

In the post-purchase phase, you either confirm or alter the ideas and beliefs customers have of you from the pre-purchase and consideration phases. The mismatch between customers' expectations and their actual experience leads to delight or disappointment and cognitive dissonance.

Cognitive dissonance describes the mental discomfort people feel when their actions and beliefs don't align. In this case, the beliefs or attitudes are that the product was not a good value and didn't do what they believed — in other words, buyer's remorse.

Three of the main causes of cognitive dissonance are

- ✔ **Value:** The price or total payment cost isn't worth what was paid.

- ✔ **Quality:** The product or service doesn't perform as expected, is missing features, or breaks.

- ✔ **Better alternatives:** Buyer's remorse is more intense when a customer has rejected a lot of alternative products.

Reducing dissonance

Customers with cognitive dissonance will take actions to reduce it, which can mean returning a product, spreading negative word of mouth, or not purchasing the product again. Look for evidence of cognitive dissonance, and where possible, correct and prevent it so positive emotions are associated with the purchase and brand.

Customers with high cognitive dissonance can do several things.

- ✔ **Take no action:** The consumer gets over her dissonance (but likely remembers for future purchases).

- ✔ **Cancel or return the product:** This results in a lost sale and cost of handling the return.

   For service agreements such as software maintenance contracts, mobile phone service, or cable TV, the cancellation of a customer represents a major loss because of the loss of recurring revenue (see Chapter 6 on calculating customer lifetime value). To keep this customer, offer future discounts or more channels to prevent a cancellation, and assuage dissonance.

   When customers return a product, you have to track the return rate. See the upcoming section on dealing with returns.

✔ **Purchase another product:** Although the sale is made, the relationship with the company and future purchases are in jeopardy.

✔ **Contact customer support or customer service representatives:** This costs your company money in terms of time spent listening to the customer and fixing the problem.

How you handle customers through customer service is vitally important. You have the opportunity to turn a dissatisfied customer into a satisfied one, which could lead to a loyal repeat customer.

✔ **Take legal action:** Probably the worst outcome, customers feeling like they need to sue to get out of a contract or get their money back.

Turning dissonance into satisfaction

Product warranties, free return policies, free shipping, and free return shipping help reduce the changes for dissonance.

To address customers' dissonance, each of these reasons can be addressed using the following approaches.

✔ **Offer a better value.** Change the price or increase the offerings for the same price.

✔ **Improve quality.** Improving quality is easier said than done. Identify the root cause of the quality concern, whether it be features or performance.

One way to diagnose the root causes of problems is a cause-and-effect diagram. Turn to the later section "Finding the Root Cause with Cause-and-Effect Diagrams" for more information.

✔ **Confirm the initial choice.** Messaging, in email newsletters, ads, and follow-up calls, reassures customers that they made the right choice and that the purchase does conform to their attitudes and beliefs.

More information about marketing options to reduce cognitive dissonance can be found in *Marketing For Dummies,* by Alexander Hiam (Wiley).

Tracking return rates

One of the actions customers can take is to return a product. A return guarantee is key to alleviating cognitive dissonance, but it can be expensive to maintain if you suffer a spate of returns.

When a product is returned, it not only represents a lost sale, but increased costs in repackaging (or an unsalable item) and the logistics to handle the returns.

Once a customer returns a product, there isn't much that can be done for that customer, but you can learn a lot to prevent future returns.

1. **Collect the return rates, dates, and details.**

2. **Look to other clues that can predict the root cause of returns.**

3. **Predict the return rates based on patterns in the root causes.**

For example, I worked with a U.S.-based cellular service provider that carried a number of phones from different manufacturers, including Apple, Samsung, and Motorola. The cellular service provider collected the return rates for each type of phone and then looked into the causes of the returns. One reason for the returns was that customers found certain phones harder to use. The company started collecting usability data on all its phones, then associated that with the return rates. Based on the data, the company stopped selling the phones that lacked a decent usability score. (See Chapter 9 to find out how to use the System Usability Scale, or SUS.)

Measuring the Post-Purchase Touchpoints

The data you collect in the post-purchase phase aids in understanding how well the experience is at each stage and also how to improve the experience for current and future customers. It could be that customers had great first impressions but had a poor service experience. Measuring at different post-purchase touchpoints helps identify opportunities for improvement.

To easily collect data, establish a feedback loop. Problems, frustrations, and improvements are properly channeled back to the product development teams.

One of the quickest ways to identify opportunities for improvement is to ask customers in a post-purchase survey their level of satisfaction with each of the touchpoints.

Keep the surveys short and ask a mix of open- and closed-ended questions. You should include:

✔ An overall measure of satisfaction about the product or experience, using a rating scale (see Chapter 9)

✔ More detailed questions about each touchpoint (also using a rating scale)

✔ Questions about future intent, such as likelihood to recommend or likelihood to repurchase

✔ Open-ended questions for customers to describe in their own words their feelings (both positive and negative) about the experience and specifically how they'd improve the product

Digging into the post-purchase touchpoints

You can deploy your surveys at different intervals to correspond with a touchpoint. It's often most efficient, and less of a burden on the customer, if you ask customers to complete only one survey at a key point in the post-purchase process — say, after the customer has used the product for some time.

Some common touchpoints include:

✔ Shipping and delivery

✔ Unboxing (opening the product)

✔ Installation and setup

✔ Customer support

✔ Feature usage

✔ Overall satisfaction

Shipping and delivery

When customers decide to purchase something, they want it right away. For an in-store purchase, this isn't much of an issue when the item is in stock. For catalog and Internet purchases, the delay of receiving the goods attenuates the impulsiveness of the purchase decisions. Customers set firm expectations about when they expect a product to arrive. Amazon.com's next-day (and even same-day) shipping helps alleviate the gap in time that otherwise causes cognitive dissonance to fester. Even if you can't deliver products the next day, you can measure and improve the customer's expectations.

For example, when looking at the customer satisfaction of the purchasing process with computer manufacturer Lenovo, the promised production and delivery time are paramount.

Unboxing

The experience of removing a product from its package is one of the first physical touchpoints you have to influence the emotional connection a customer has with the brand. For example, the unboxing experience of the iPhone helps reinforce Apple's branding as being cutting edge, clean, and easy to use; see Figure 11-1.

Figure 11-1:
iPhone unboxing experience helps reinforce the brand attributes of a clean, cutting-edge design.

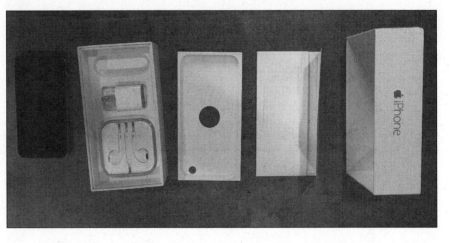

Installation and setup

For many products, after the unboxing experience, the setup and installation process defines the first moments of the post-purchase phase. A lot of customers lose enthusiasm for a product after unsuccessfully trying to get it to work. Asking about the installation and setup experience in your post-purchase surveys helps identify how much this step influences customers' overall attitudes and future intent. It also helps identify problems that can be addressed.

For example, in the mid-1980s, my friend Jim Lewis was helping the IBM printer division understand the impacts of the setup and installation phase of a new series of IBM printers. They discovered an error in the documentation that could potentially cause a problem in installation. This would lead to product returns, calls to customer support (see the next section), and a poor experience. But reprinting all the manuals to fix the problem would also be costly. So a team of IBM researchers wanted to see if adding a large "Read This First" paper with the correct instructions on top of the printer and original installation instructions would prevent the problem. After asking several customers to open and set up the printer, IBM researchers watched as most of these study participants completely ignored the "Read This First" paper and incorrectly set up the printer. IBM decided to reprint the manuals instead of risking high returns and a failed installation experience.

Customer support

Customer support is one of the most common post-purchase touchpoints. This usually consists of a call center, email support, or online chat feature. In many companies, the sales team is comprised of employees who have the charm and personality to make the sales process smooth. Unfortunately, that isn't necessarily the same experience the customer encounters when working with the support teams. Call centers and support teams are often outsourced, which may create a language, cultural, or physical distance barrier between the customer and this important company touchpoint.

Customer support is not just an opportunity to satisfy a current customer by addressing a question or complaint; it's also an opportunity to delight a customer by exceeding her expectations. This leads to more loyal customers.

The customer support touchpoint plays such an important role in post-purchase satisfaction that it often deserves its own (usually short) survey that's sent immediately after the interaction. Figure 11-2 shows an example customer support survey from Amazon.

If you find that most customers don't take your post-purchase survey, offer an incentive to do so, such as a discount off a future purchase.

Tell us how we're doing

Please rate the following:

Ease of working with Amazon on your issue	☆☆ ☆☆☆ Unrated
Quality of our service representative	☆☆ ☆☆☆ Unrated
Amazon's policy on this issue	☆☆ ☆☆☆ Unrated

Thank you for taking the time to give us feedback. We are unable to reply to the comments you have entered. If you need to contact Customer Service again, please click on the "Contact Us" button on any Help page.

More Comments: (optional)

Send Feedback

Figure 11-2: A survey invitation sent immediately from Amazon to measure the customer support experience.

Zappos . . . if the shoe fits (or doesn't)

Zappos.com is an online store that offers discounted shoes. Buying shoes online comes with some risk since customers can't try them on and may end up with a pair of shoes they don't want and the hassle of returning them. Prospective customers naturally want to minimize the chances of buying shoes that don't fit or that they don't like (avoiding cognitive dissonance). Zappos minimizes the risk to the customer by offering free returns and free return shipping.

What's more, Zappos provides one of the best customer service experiences. Zappos customer service reps are known for staying on calls for as long as it takes to resolve a customer's problems. (The longest call on record lasted seven hours!) The company's even been known to refund money, let customers keep the shoes, and even send a new pair, all to exceed expectations and keep customers coming back and telling friends about their experience.

Feature usage

It's often the case that customers will purchase a product for a set of features during the consideration phase, but use only a subset in the post-purchase phase. Collect data about which features of the product customers are actually using and those they are not using. Also ask what features are missing that they would like. (See Chapter 14 for ideas on measuring usability.)

Assessing post-purchase satisfaction ratings

You can create your own customer satisfaction questions, but remember that consumer-advocate organizations often also measure customer satisfaction for a variety of things: products, services, and websites:

- The magazine *Consumer Reports* publishes customers' complaints and ratings, including their opinions about repair service, for everything from appliances to electronics to automobiles. This information becomes valuable input for prospective customers in the consideration phase.

- Companies such as JD Power and the American Satisfaction Customer Index provide customer satisfaction rates on a number of products.

- The Amazon product rating system is an often cited reference for customers in the consideration phase.

You can use these published sources of customer satisfaction as a benchmark to your own efforts by seeing how competitors (and your product) compare with similar products.

Finding Problems Using Call Center Analysis

A number of analytics measure the customer call center experience. The point of these analytics shouldn't just be about finding ways to cut costs or improve your support staff's efficiency. Although it's important to control costs, it's equally important to meet customer expectations, which leads to higher levels of satisfaction and customers who are more likely to recommend and repurchase from you. Your metrics must be meaningful to the customer.

Here are six of the most common call center analytics to track, in addition to the satisfaction:

✔ **Customer satisfaction:** As with every post-purchase touchpoint, be sure your customer lets you know how well his expectations were met.

Use a simple rating scale, something like that from Amazon (refer to Figure 11-2).

✔ **Call resolution:** Was the reason for the call successfully addressed?

Don't rely exclusively on the customer support agent to provide this detail. Collect data from the customer, if possible. Many call centers pay attention to the percent of calls resolved, which can incentivize prematurely marking issues as resolved. Look at customer satisfaction along with call resolution to be sure expectations are met and problems are solved. See the nearby sidebar on request closed versus request resolved.

✔ **Hold time:** People don't like to listen to music or hear a recording about how valuable a customer they are while they are on hold. Long waits only increase the frustration of an already undesirable situation. It isn't an easy thing to fix, but it's an essential metric to track.

✔ **Call abandonment:** Long hold times lead to customers hanging up. These abandoned calls contribute to frustration and a degradation of the brand.

✔ **Reason for call:** Have customer support agents describe (using a categorization system or comments field) the reason and resolution for the call. All too often, I've worked with call-center data to address spikes in calls only to see data that has little information regarding the reason for the call.

✔ **Call duration:** A support call takes customers' time and call agents' time. While it's good to get to a resolution as quickly as possible, be careful that you aren't incentivizing agents to prematurely end calls. In general, no one likes to feel rushed when dealing with an issue. A rushed call might lead to another call, a return, or disloyal customer.

Customer ticket closed or customer request resolved?

The frontlines of the customer experience are often the customer support channels — phone and email. I had a problem with one of my online bank accounts. After trying several tweaks over a few months, I finally got around to submitting a problem ticket via email. Within 24 hours, I received a response (as promised).

Eight hours later, I was told that this sort of thing happens from time to time and is most likely a temporary issue, and that trying again in a day or so should work. I was then told the ticket was closed. Yikes! The next day, the temporary problem was still there. It was another six months before the "temporary issue" was resolved. So while the ticket was closed and closed quickly (both were positive metrics for the call center), my issue lingered.

Finding the Root Cause with Cause-and-Effect Diagrams

Many problems in the post-purchase phase are often symptoms of other problems:

- ✔ Customer complaints
- ✔ Returns
- ✔ Calls to customer support
- ✔ Low customer satisfaction ratings

One tool that is particularly handy at getting to root causes is the aptly named cause-and-effect diagram. It is also called the *fishbone* for its fishlike skeletal shape. An example is shown in Figure 11-3.

Cause-and-effect diagrams provide a visual display of possible causes of a problem. Most importantly, they remind you that there are usually multiple causes of problems that lead to low customer satisfaction. It would be nice if one reason always explained your complex problems — but that's rarely the case.

Fishbones are low-tech; you need only a piece of paper or a white board for team settings (no need to save the bones from dinner last night).

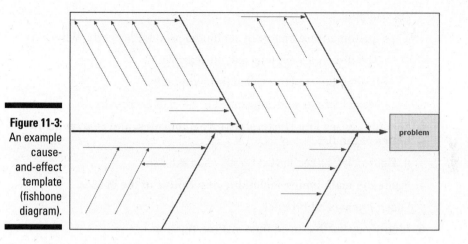

Figure 11-3:
An example
cause-
and-effect
template
(fishbone
diagram).

Creating a cause-and-effect diagram

Here's how to use a cause-and-effect diagram in five steps.

1. **Define the problem you want to avoid.**

   Ideally, you want this statement to be as specific as possible. So if you're dealing with customer returns, a problem statement would be

   "Customer return rates are higher than 10%."

   The problem statement goes at the head of the fish.

2. **Brainstorm possible causes for the problem.**

   For high customer return rates, this would be something like

   • Customers are unable to set up the product properly.

   • Shipping takes too long or is unclear.

   • Customers don't use the product after opening it.

   • The price is too high relative to what customers are getting.

   • The product breaks or stops working.

   These problems become the bones in the fish. You should think causally (for example, what causes customers to improperly set up the product?).

   Don't just use the fishbone to propose solutions. For each cause, ask "Why does this happen?" In fact, ask "why" as many times as you can (like a 3-year-old child does).

For example:

- Customers are unable to set up the product properly: Why?
- The directions are long and unclear: Why?
- It's complicated to explain the setup: Why?
- Many features and steps need to be explained: Why?

3. **Sort the causes into clusters, remove duplicates, and rearrange the bones of the fish.**

   In Figure 11-4, I filled in two branches of the fish.

4. **Name the main bones something descriptive of the causes.**

   I used Pricing and Product.

5. **Identify areas that need data or investigation.**

   Some causes are obvious (is there any indication of shipping?), whereas others need data (where are customers making mistakes in the setup?). You should get something that looks like Figure 11-4.

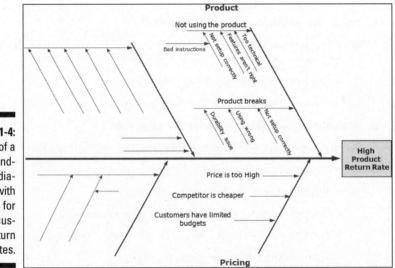

Figure 11-4:
A part of a cause-and-effect diagram with reasons for high customer return rates.

Now that the causes are in the fishbone, you'll likely see connections between the causes. Also use this opportunity to continue asking "why" to get at root causes.

Use the cause-and-effect diagram in all stages of the customer journey to brainstorm root causes for product and service problems. It becomes excellent input for finding design solutions and turning negative thinking into positive user experiences.

Chapter 12

Measuring Customer Loyalty

Do you find yourself buying the same products over and over again? Do you have a preferred airline? The last time you chose a new computer, did you ask a friend for a recommendation?

Consumer decisions are heavily based on prior experience and on the experience of friends and colleagues. A once happy customer is likely to be a customer again and to recommend a specific company to the people around him.

If a friend or family member helps you when in need, you are happy to reciprocate. You may feel a sense of duty, a sense of loyalty to people who have been there for you. The emotions that cement a customer's relationship with a company are similar. If the computer you purchased four years ago met or exceeded your expectations and customer service was outstanding, you'll purchase a similar model again. When a friend asks what computer you have, you're happy to recommend it. When you rent a car and the car is clean, the price is fair, and the pick-up and drop-off experiences are easy and quick, you're much more likely to use the same rental car company in the future.

In this chapter, I help you understand the importance of customer loyalty and explain common ways of measuring it. I also introduce methods for identifying what makes customers more likely to recommend a company's products or services.

Measuring Customer Loyalty

Understanding how to measure customer loyalty is an essential first step in predicting the potential future growth or decline of a product, service, or company.

The "best" metric for measuring customer loyalty depends on the industry, company, and type of product or service. Two that are applicable to most products and industries are the repurchase rate and the likelihood to recommend.

Repurchase rate

Probably the first way to gauge customer loyalty is to compute the percentage of customers who are repurchasing, reusing, or returning to a product or service. This data can be collected from past sales or from surveying customers about their past or future intent. Data can also be obtained from historical purchasing records, which are often captured in Customer Relationship Management (CRM) systems.

Valuing customer loyalty

Loyal customers are more likely to repurchase, reuse, and say good things about their experience to their friends and colleagues. Products, websites, software, and services that have more loyal customers therefore possess an advantage over competitors with less loyal customers.

Shareholders of companies care most about top-line revenue, profit, and growth. It's therefore important for company managers, employees, and owners to also strive for higher profits and growth. Crocs footwear, Lulu Lemon, Netflix, and the car service Uber are examples of companies that deliver a product or service that grew in popularity largely due to customers repurchasing and telling their friends. But Crocs, Lulu Lemon, and Netflix are examples of cases where the company's signature products fell in popularity: The same word of mouth that led to their rise contributed to their demise.

Stories of Crocs shoes being stuck in escalators spread, as did problems with the transparency of Lulu Lemon's yoga pants. As for Netflix, it split the company's products into two services and angered customers.

In all three cases, revenues took a hit, but even worse, the popularity of the products and brands suffered substantially. Therefore, what management, employees, and shareholders want to know is whether a product or company is going to grow or decline *before* it actually does.

Measuring customer loyalty is one way of estimating how well a company or product is positioned to grow or shrink. While not a perfect measure of actual future growth, there is some evidence that positive measures of customer loyalty correlate strongly with increasing earnings.

For example, a 2013 survey of smartphone users by the Yankee group found that 91 percent of iPhone owners indicated they will repurchase another iPhone.

In contrast, the repurchase rate for Android customers is a much lower 76 percent. Of the 24 percent of current Android customers who said they'd switch, 18 percent are considering purchasing an iPhone.

Repurchase habits are measured differently, depending on the type of product or service offered:

- ✔ For rental car companies, the repurchase rate is a good indicator of loyalty as certain customer segments rent multiple times per year and have many companies to choose from.

- ✔ For car dealerships, a variation on the repurchase rate as a measure of loyalty is repeat repair and maintenance visits.

- ✔ For software companies, a similar measure of repurchase loyalty is the maintenance contract renewal rates.

    At many software companies like the software giant Oracle where I worked, customers purchase new database, accounting, and human resource software packages about only once every decade, because the installation and the migration processes are costly and disruptive. The large time span between sales means the repurchase rate lags too much to gauge loyalty. While the original sales brought in revenue, the real value was having customers sign and resign service agreements. Such agreements typically bring in around 20 percent of the original sales price and were lucrative, as they are paid annually. One of the earliest indicators of the likelihood that a customer would purchase from a competitor was the canceling or non-renewal of service agreements. Consequently, this is one of the key measures of loyalty the company tracked.

Watch out for "false-profits." Customers who repeatedly purchase may be unsatisfied with their experience but feel they have no choice but to continue purchasing. Merge both purchase history and customer attitudes to help determine if the profits are from satisfied and truly loyal customers or customers who have no choice.

A *repurchasing matrix* takes the repurchase rate and displays the relative rates for a set of competitors or comparable products within the same company. To build one, compute the percentage of customers who repurchase a product or a competitor's product.

Table 12-1 is a repurchasing matrix for laptop computers using hypothetical data:

✔ The first cell indicates that 68 percent of customers who bought a Lenovo computer ended up buying a second one.

✔ The second cell indicates that 3 percent of the customers who first bought a Lenovo laptop chose Dell the second time around.

Table 12-1	Laptop repurchasing percentage (hypothetical data)				
	Lenovo	*Dell*	*HP*	*Apple*	*Asus*
Lenovo	68	3	4	2	3
Dell	14	43	4	2	5
HP	13	5	42	1	5
Apple	4	1	1	77	7
Asus	3	1	1	8	38

The values on the diagonal (the large numbers where each brand's column and row intersects) are the repurchase rates. The values off each diagonal are the competitors to which the customers are defecting.

The values often don't add up to 100%, because not all competitors are considered.

In looking at this example data, you can see that Apple customers are about twice as loyal as Asus's customers. Apple has a repurchase rate of 77% compared to 38% for Asus.

Given that actual repurchase rates can take years to collect, especially for products that aren't purchased frequently, building a repurchasing matrix can take years. To speed up the process and gauge your customers' loyalty before they defect, you can ask their intent to repurchase as well as their likelihood to refer a friend, which is the metric I discuss next.

Net Promoter Score

Word of mouth is a powerful and organic force that can't easily be controlled like an advertising campaign:

✔ On one hand, when customers continue to purchase and tell their friends about a positive experience, word of mouth can spread as fast as the norovirus in winter through social media and in-person conversations.

✔ However, ill will and customer defection spread like a virus, too, if customers have bad experiences.

The Net Promoter Score (NPS) is a popular way of measuring customer loyalty through understanding word-of-mouth marketing. It is based on a single question: "How likely are you to recommend [*product or service*] to a friend or colleague?" This type of question was found to be the best or second-best predictor of repeat purchases or referrals in 11 out of 14 industries. Net Promoter, NPS, and Net Promoter Score are trademarks of Satmetrix Systems, Inc., Bain & Company, and Fred Reicheld.

Most companies I work with use or have used the Net Promoter Score. Because of its popularity, I explain the scoring and its usage in more detail in the next section.

Computing the NPS

One of the most appreciated aspects of the Net Promoter Score is how it's presented as a percentage, which is appealing to executives.

Follow these steps to calculate the Net Promoter Score:

1. **Ask your customers how likely they are to recommend your product or service to a friend or colleague.**

   Use an 11-point scale: 0 = Not at all likely and 10 = Extremely likely. Figure 12-1 shows a layout example for this question.

	Not at all Likely										Extremely Likely
	0	1	2	3	4	5	6	7	8	9	10
How likely are you to recommend this website to a friend or colleague?	○	○	○	○	○	○	○	○	○	○	○

Figure 12-1: The Net Promoter Score.

2. **Compute the proportions of promoters, passives, and detractors.**

   Part of the research into building a Net Promoter Score is finding which numbers on the scale map to customers who are more likely to say good things, more likely to say bad things, or not say much of anything to friends about an experience.

They can be divided into three groups:

- *Promoters* are customers who rate a 9 or 10 on the response scale.

  These are the customers who were found to be most likely to speak favorably and recommend your product or service based on the research by Bain and Fred Reicheld. You want to have as many promoters as possible for your product or service.

- *Passives* are customers who rate a 7 or 8 on the response scale.

  Passive customers are generally satisfied with their experience and are loyal. However, they are less likely to recommend your product or service to friends. The goal is to turn passives into promoters.

- *Detractors* are customers who rate a 0 to 6 on the response scale.

  These customers are not only the least loyal, but also the most likely to actually discourage friends and colleagues from purchasing or using your product. Some detractors can be turned into passives or promoters by identifying their dissatisfaction and fixing it. Some detractors, however, are "lost" customers and no amount of product improvement will keep them.

Once you identify who the promoters, passives, and detractors are, convert them to percentages by dividing the number in each category by the total number of customers who answered the likelihood to recommend question. For example, if 100 customers answered the likelihood to recommend question and 10 responded with numbers between 0 and 6, then 10 percent of the sample are detractors.

3. Compute the NPS.

To compute the NPS, subtract the percentage of detractors from the percentage of promoters.

For example, if 50 out of 100 customers responded with 9's or 10's, then 50% of the sample are promoters. If 10 responded with numbers between 0 and 6, then 10% of the sample are detractors. The Net Promoter Score for this sample of data is then 50% – 10% = 40%. The NPS can range from –100% (all detractors) to 100% (indicating all promoters).

A sample of data from a 2014 survey of customers to the United Airlines website is displayed in Table 12-2. Customers were asked whether they would recommend using the United Airlines website to a friend or a colleague on the 11-point likelihood to recommend scale. Although more than 100 customers were surveyed, this example shows only the answers of the first 10 respondents.

Table 12-2	United Airlines Website NPS Data	
Respondent	*Response*	*Category*
1	6	Detractor
2	10	Promoter
3	8	Passive
4	7	Passive
5	9	Promoter
6	10	Promoter
7	8	Passive
8	10	Promoter
9	9	Promoter
10	9	Promoter

This data sample shows six promoters and one detractor out of the ten respondents. Therefore, the promoter percentage is 60% and the detractor percentage is 10%, making the NPS 50%.

Like all survey data, the Net Promoter Score has a sampling error and fluctuates from sample to sample. A very different Net Promoter Score could have been obtained in the preceding example if more (or less!) data had been used in Table 12-2. Sampling error depends primarily on the sample size, because most companies cannot survey their entire customer base. Only a small fraction of the customers, a *sample,* is considered. Usually, the larger the sample, the more its answers are representative of the whole customer base. Therefore, a larger sample translates into smaller sampling errors. Knowing the sampling error, confidence intervals can be calculated.

Due to the way the NPS is calculated, however, the confidence intervals are actually twice as wide as when using a simple proportion or computing the average score. Why? Because there is an uncertainty on both the percentage of promoters and the percentage of detractors.

The simplest thing to do is to compute a confidence interval around the mean score and calculate the confidence interval around that. Otherwise, contact your favorite statistician to help you compute the confidence intervals.

What's a good NPS?

As with any metric, you want to know what constitutes a good score and bad score. While a repurchase rate has its own intuitive appeal (people can understand that 48% means a bit less than half of customers are repurchasing), the NPS is less obvious because it involves two percentages.

In general, you want your NPS to be positive, which indicates there are more promoters than detractors. A negative NPS means there are more detractors than promoters, and consequently, a lot of negative word of mouth relative to positive word of mouth.

The best way to assess your NPS is to compare it to

✔ Other products or services in your company

✔ Published industry benchmarks

The average NPS varies quite substantially between industries and between business-to-consumer (B2C) and business-to-business (B2B) companies, so look to find the most relevant comparison. More NPS benchmarks for software can be found at `https://www.measuringu.com/blog/software-benchmarks14.php` or on the Satmetrix website (`http://www.satmetrix.com/net-promoter/industry-benchmarks`)

Table 12-3 shows the average NPS for some different classes of businesses and products from my company's internal data and publicly available benchmarks on `experiencematters.wordpress.com`.

Table 12-3	Example Net Promoter Scores for Industries and Specific Brands
Category	*NPS*
USAA Insurance	80%
Amazon.com	77%
Apple	76%
Airline Industry	23%
Consumer Software Industry	22%
Internet Service Providers	5%
Websites	-6%
Time Warner Cable	-10%
HSBC Banking	-42%

Tracking the NPS over time

Getting access to competitive data can be difficult for some industries and products. Even without competitive data, though, the best comparison is often measuring the same product, service, or company over time.

For example, in 2011, Netflix was one of the most recommended and poplar companies in the database of Net Promoter Scores my company tracked. In

February 2011, the Netflix NPS was a very high 73%. In the fall of 2011, the company decided to split off its home delivery of DVDs and the streaming service into two companies. While this switch might have made sense to the company, it angered customers, who took to the web and social media to air their complaints. We surveyed Netflix customers a month after the change and the found the NPS plummeted 70 points to –7%. Netflix at this point had more detractors than promoters.

Figure 12-2 shows the results of the NPS survey of customers over time. The lines on top of the bars in the graph show the 95% confidence intervals, which indicate how much to expect the NPS to fluctuate from sample to sample. See Chapter 2 on how to compute and interpret confidence intervals.

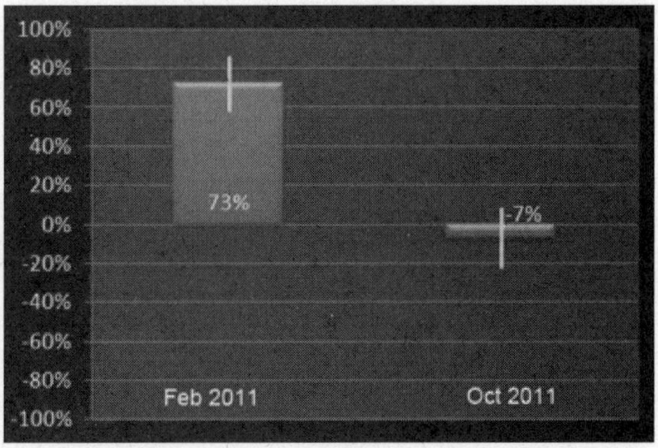

Figure 12-2:
The Net Promoter Score for Netflix measured in February and October 2011 after a major product delivery change.

Predicting with the NPS

The Netflix example shows that the NPS does track changes that occur in products or companies — in this case, for the worse. Netflix ultimately reversed its decisions based on word of mouth, and soon, data from another company showed the Netflix NPS hovering around 50%.

The value of measures like the NPS is that they help estimate what will happen to word of mouth while something still can be done to avoid disasters. One way to estimate the effect of splitting the company would have been for Netflix to test the idea on a subset of customers and then measure the Net Promoter Score. More than testing the idea, Netflix could have tested a small sample of users on its new website and product categories and then seen how that group's Net Promoter Score differed from the larger control group.

Perhaps Netflix did perform such testing and anticipate losing customers. The much larger loss is likely due to other factors and perhaps to untested customer correspondence and the geometric effect of negative word of mouth. But using the Net Promoter Score as a predictive analytic tool can help prevent disasters and identify winners early.

You use the NPS as a key measure to understand the effects of product changes before they are released to customers. You can test feature changes and user interface design changes, as well as changes in pricing and services. For example, I worked with a large mobile phone maker to determine which phones customers would like.

A key metric for this company was the return rate of the phones. Customers had up to 30 days to return their phone without incurring a fee. Naturally, returned phones cost the company money and in some cases, lost customers. The company wanted to predict which phones would have too high of a return rate before being released into thousands of stores in the U.S. We had a sample of customers use a series of phones they were considering and had them respond to a number of measures, including the Net Promoter Score (as well as the System Usability Scale; see Chapter 14 for measures of usability). We collected data for months and found that the Net Promoter Score had a high association with return rates. That is, phones with lower Net Promoter Scores in the testing had higher rates of customers returning them within 30 days.

Phones with average Net Promoter Scores below –25% had twice the return rate as phones with Net Promoter Scores above 30%. These Net Promoter Scores became a new benchmark for testing new phones, and the return rate and NPS score correlation continued to be monitored.

Finding the reason for the ratings

Collecting the NPS is the first step in measuring customer loyalty. But just knowing the NPS for your product or company is not enough. You immediately want to know *why* some customers are defecting and what about the experience makes others promote it.

One of the easiest and most effective ways to collect the "why" behind the numbers is to simply ask participants to provide some rationale for their ratings:

- At the very least, allow customers to tell you the reason for their rating using an open-ended question.

- A slightly more sophisticated approach is to customize the questions you ask to promoters, passives, and detractors:

   - *For promoters: What about their experience makes them most likely to recommend it to friends?*

   - *For passives: What can be done to get them to be more likely to recommend?*

   - *For detractors: What can be done, fixed, or improved to get them to recommend the product or service to a friend?*

You should spend time reading through the open-ended comments to look for patterns in each of the three categories. Look also to find some quick wins on how to fix problems with detractors. As datasets get larger, it can take longer to review each open-ended comment, so you may consider separating out the responses between multiple analysts.

One of the best ways to take action from Net Promoter Score data is to send those responsible for the product or specific functions the raw open-ended comments customers provide and their Net Promoter Scores. Even better, have a system in place so customers who have a problem are contacted to let them know you're trying to fix it.

Combining qualitative and quantitative data

A powerful way of making qualitative, open-ended comments more actionable is to combine them with a closed-ended rating scale response question, like the Net Promoter Score.

In addition to the open-ended reasons from the likelihood to recommend question, I often ask customers to name what could be improved. This way, I collect suggestions, even from promoters who are happy but still might have ideas to help improve the experience.

An example is shown in Figure 12-3. A survey on an automotive website netted 110 open-ended comments from customers. Customers were asked to name one thing they would improve on the website.

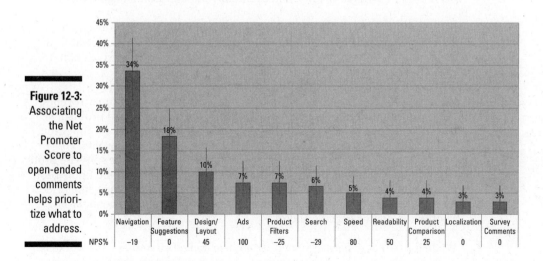

Figure 12-3: Associating the Net Promoter Score to open-ended comments helps prioritize what to address.

	Navigation	Feature Suggestions	Design/ Layout	Ads	Product Filters	Search	Speed	Readability	Product Comparison	Localization	Survey Comments
	34%	18%	10%	7%	7%	6%	5%	4%	4%	3%	3%
NPS%	−19	0	45	100	−25	−29	80	50	25	0	0

My team took the open-ended comments about what to improve and put them into categories. We then computed the Net Promoter Score for each of the suggestion categories.

To help prioritize what areas to focus on, we saw that comments related to website navigation and product filters are high in frequency and come from users who are likely generating negative word of mouth (notice the negative NPS). In contrast, design/layout comments and advertisements, while relatively high in frequency, appear to be minor issues for the users. This was an important finding for the company, as it had just introduced ads and wanted to know how much of a burden those ads would be for its customers. This analysis suggested that while customers didn't like the ads, they didn't seem to mind them based on the high Net Promoter Scores from customers who said they'd like them removed.

Bad profits

How does it feel to pay the check at the restaurant where you had terrible service and bad food? Or how do you feel when you pay your cable bill each month? And how about paying $150 to change your airline ticket reservation?

In all cases, the companies get your money. It's revenue in their books. But if you're like me, you aren't happy about the experience and will remember it next time you have a choice. Nobody likes to pay for a subpar or overpriced product or for bad service. *Bad profits* are made when companies financially benefit from these negative experiences.

Bad profits are a ticking time bomb. They lead to customer resentment and a decrease in customer loyalty, and eventually impact profits negatively.

Each company generates a certain share of bad profits and it is useful to know how much it represents to re-orient the company's strategy. But how are bad profits effectively and objectively measured? In the next section, I present two methods to do just that.

By combining Net Promoter Score data with customer-by-customer revenue data, you can estimate the amount of revenue derived from bad profits. Even if you don't have access to financial data for your company or a competitor, you usually can estimate the percentage of revenue from bad profits. For example, when my company measured customers of consumer software products a couple years ago, we found that about 17 percent of Adobe Photoshop users were detractors. Assuming that everyone pays around the same price for a Photoshop license, then around 17 percent of Adobe's revenue from Photoshop comes from detractors.

While it's bad to generate revenue from dissatisfied customers, it's worse if a large proportion of your revenue comes from detractors. With too much detractor revenue for a product or entire company, you are more susceptible to new competition, alternatives, or abandonment.

With cable companies, government services, or utilities, there often isn't much of a choice. So even though these industries have some of the lowest Net Promoter Scores, they continue to survive. However, competition from satellite, other cable providers, and now content delivered via the Internet (called OTT) threatens the revenue models of cable providers.

If a product is sold for one price, then it's easier to estimate the percentage of revenue that comes from detractors. When there are multiple products and prices, you need to match up customers' attitudes with their historical revenue. This isn't as easy as it sounds. Customer revenue data is often tightly controlled by companies' finance gurus, and other departments, usually marketing or customer experience, run the surveys. But even a sample of customers will give you some idea about revenue and how it relates to customer experience.

As another example, I helped analyze the survey data from a large software company. It has dozens of products, different pricing models, and sales channels. After merging the sales data for the prior year with the Net Promoter Scores, we found that around 17 percent of revenue came from detractors.

So how much revenue is too much from detractors? While that depends on the industry and the switching costs (more competition leaves less room for detractors), a common threshold is to obtain no more than 10 percent of revenue from detractors.

If more than 10 percent of company or product revenue comes from detractors, there are two things you can probably do:

- ✔ **Stop selling to these customers.** While that may seem crazy, in some cases, getting rid of mismatched customers may better your reputation and increase your profits in the long run.

- ✔ **Find out the reasons these customers are spreading negative word of mouth and attempt to fix it:**

  - *Start by analyzing the comments of these detractors in surveys to identify the low-hanging fruit.*

  - *Next, conduct a key driver analysis using multiple regression to understand what factors in their experience have the biggest effect on customers' likelihood to recommend.*

Understanding the reasons for detractors is the first step. Doing something about the information is usually a lot harder because it often involves adjusting the price, quality, and features to meet the customers' expectations. But that's usually what separates the best-in-class companies from the rest — their ability to make changes based on data.

Working with the NPS

The Net Promoter Score is a useful but imperfect tool. It is used in numerous companies. In fact, some companies take it so seriously that they pay bonuses based on how much they manage to increase their Net Promoter Scores. While it has often been referred to as the "only number you need," it has some drawbacks:

- **People are poor predictors of their own behavior.** The Net Promoter Score is meant to be a forward-looking indicator: Without looking at any actual facts, the score is solely based on what customers say they will do. However, just because people say they will do something doesn't mean they will.

  As a way to gauge how many customers who say they will actually recommend a product or website, you can also ask customers if they have in the last 12 months. This percentage most likely differs substantially from the percentage of customers saying they will recommend. But it's less important to nail down the exact number of customers who will actually recommend than to understand how that estimate, with its imperfections, differs across companies and products. As with most measures, scores make much more sense when compared.

- **The scoring inflates the margin of error:** By converting an 11-point scale into a 2-point scale of detractors and promoters (throwing out the passives), information is lost. What's more, this new binary scale doubles the margin of error around the net score (promoters minus detractors). Unfortunately, that means that if you want

to show an improvement in Net Promoter Scores over time, it takes a sample size that is around twice as large to calculate the difference; otherwise, the difference won't be distinguishable from the sampling error.

- Some organizations look at NPS dashboards and investigate why the NPS has gone up or down over a period of time. In too many cases, adding some error bars to the graphs shows that the changes are within the margin of error. The simple work-around is to use the raw mean and standard deviation when running statistical comparisons. The mean likelihood to recommend responses can predict the Net Promoter Score quite well. You can use the net scoring system for the executives, but use the raw data for the statistics.

- **Use other ways of measuring customer loyalty.** While the NPS is sold as the "only" measure you need, there are other ways of measuring customer loyalty and customers' likelihood to recommend.

  For example, if you're interested in estimating how many customers are likely to positively or negatively talk about your company, take a look at another way to measure word of mouth, called the word of mouth index (WoMI) from Larry Freed. It distinguishes between positive and negative word of mouth by asking customers both the likelihood to recommend question and if they would discourage others from doing business with a company. Top 100 U.S. brands, the WoMI index score, and the Net Promoter Scores have a high average correlation of $r = .8$.

Finding Key Drivers of Loyalty

One of the most effective ways to understand what drives customer loyalty is to conduct a key driver analysis. A key driver analysis uses a statistical technique employing multiple regression analysis. It tells you which features or aspects of a product or service have the largest statistical impact on customer loyalty. It can be conducted for all customers but also for each of your different customer segments (see Chapter 2 for more on finding customer segments).

Here are three steps to conducting a key driver analysis:

1. **Obtain a baseline set of Net Promoter Scores (or whatever measure of loyalty you use).**

   If you aren't doing so already, survey your customers to get a current baseline of how likely customers are to recommend the product to a friend. Ask the 11-point LTR (short for "likely to recommend") question about both the brand and the product. In fact, you can extend the LTR question down to feature and functional areas if you have a lot of functionalities. Include an open-ended question to ask what's driving users to give the ratings they gave. These surveys should be conducted monthly or quarterly or set to collect data in some systematic way. You can email customers, use a pop-up window on the website, or use a third party to gain perspective. Ideally, use all three approaches — they all provide different perceptions of the experience.

   Ask a handful of key questions about features and functions: Many products and websites have vast amounts of features and functions. While you can't expect to obtain detailed metrics for every one of these, you should be able to collect data at a level that allows you to narrow your focus. For example, are poor quality reviews, advertisements, check-out forms, or shipping costs driving detractors?

2. **Conduct a multiple regression analysis.**

   With the NPS scores and items about features and the experience, you likely can identify the pool of candidates who are driving word of mouth for better or worse.

   To determine which are having the biggest impact, you can use a multivariate technique called multiple regression analysis. It can determine statistically what aspects are having the biggest impact on NPS and allow you to prioritize. More details on conducting a key driver analysis are provided in the appendix.

   The chart in Figure 12-4 shows an output of a key driver analysis for a publishing company's educational software product. Over 3,000 customers were asked to rate their satisfaction on 20 features and aspects of the product, including its speed, accuracy, and usability. Customers' impressions of usability had the largest impact on their likelihood to recommend this software product to friends and colleagues. What's more, their overall satisfaction with the usability was relatively low (at about 75%), indicating that poor usability is reducing the probability that customers will recommend the product.

3. **Identify the most popular or unpopular features or aspects of your product or service and have customers rate that experience as well.**

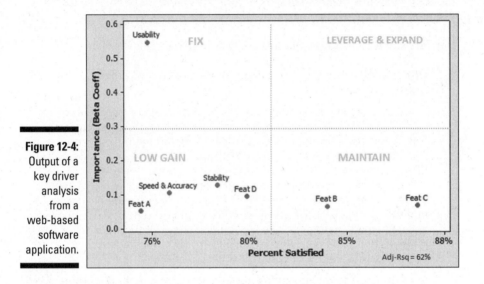

Figure 12-4:
Output of a key driver analysis from a web-based software application.

By understanding both the value of positive word of mouth and the cost of negative word of mouth, you can estimate the net value of word of mouth for a product or services for a group, or for all customers.

Valuing positive word of mouth

While companies should strive to obtain as many promoters as possible, it's often helpful to understand how valuable a promoter is, both in terms of revenue and in how many new customers a promoter brings to a company. With the lifetime value of a customer understood (see Chapter 6), money and effort can be spent to turn detractors and passives into promoters if it makes financial sense.

The best way to understand how much revenue a promoter generates is to tie actual sales to survey responses to see how many promoters actually recommended someone, and how many of those people who heard the recommendation actually became customers.

TIP

Reading a key-driver chart

Here's how to read a key-driver chart, such as the one shown in Figure 12-4. In this case, it's a chart showing the relationship between two variables, customer satisfaction with a feature, and how much the feature contributes to customer loyalty:

✔ The vertical (*y*-axis) in Figure 12-4 shows the relative importance of each item, using the beta coefficient from the multiple regression analysis.

This is a standard output that your statistician and most statistical programs provide. It tells you how much each item contributes to the users' likelihood to recommend. For example, the customers' satisfaction with the usability of the software was the biggest driver (highest on the *y*-axis). A one-point increase in satisfaction with usability results in a .55-increase in customers' likelihood to recommend.

Usability is about five times as important as the next most important driver, stability, which increases likelihood to recommend by .12 points for every point increase in customer satisfaction.

✔ The horizontal axis (*x*-axis) shows the relative customer satisfaction with each feature.

For example, a particular feature of the software (Feature C) has the highest relative satisfaction of the drivers, at around 87 percent compared to the other features. It has a smaller impact on customer loyalty, likely driving positive word of mouth.

Common key drivers of customer loyalty

What customers value in your company may vary widely. Results of NPS surveys across multiple industries reveal that four main areas affect customer loyalty:

✔ **Quality:** Are you products and services of a high quality or are they unreliable and don't work as expected?

✔ **Value:** Customers don't like to feel ripped off and like a bargain (some segments more than others). The total cost and the price relative to what customers receive for their money can generate a lot of detractors or promoters, especially for business-to-consumer products and services.

✔ **Utility:** Do your products offer all the essential features your customers need and value? A product doesn't have to do everything, but it should do the right things for your customers.

✔ **Ease of Use:** A product or website can have all the bells and whistles, but if it's hard to use, or an otherwise frustrating experience, the features might as well not work.

However, the databases in many companies can be so fragmented that connecting customer survey data to sales data is too difficult. It isn't that it's technically difficult; it's usually because the data and initiatives are owned by different teams (usually marketing and IT) who work on different projects. But Owen and Brooks, in their book *Answering the Ultimate Question* (published by Jossey-Bass), provide a good way to estimate the value of a promoter from survey data alone.

Here are six steps to estimate the value of a promoter from customer survey data.

1. **Positively Referred:** Ask all customers in a survey if they recall actually referring anyone to consider using a product or service in the past year. People have notoriously inaccurate memories but this can give you a rough idea of a historic referral rate.

   As shown in the upper-left corner of Figure 12-5, it was 61% from a sample of TurboTax customers (2011 data).

Estimating the Value of a Promoter (Turbo Tax Example)

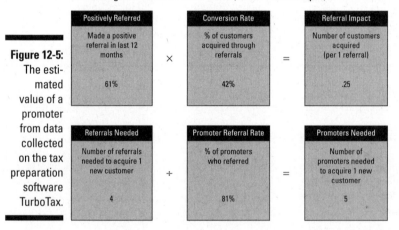

Figure 12-5: The estimated value of a promoter from data collected on the tax preparation software TurboTax.

2. **Conversion Rate:** Ask each customer if a friend or colleague referred him/her to the product. Again, memories are faulty, but this gives you some idea about the percentage of current customers who visited the website or purchased the product or service based on a referral.

   For TurboTax, it was 42%.

3. **Referral Impact:** By multiplying the percentage that made a positive referral by the percent of current customers who were referred, you have an idea about the number of customers you get through each referral.

   0.61 x 0.42 = 0.2562

Note: The slight difference from 25% shown in Figure 12-5 to 25.62% is due to rounding.

4. **Referrals Needed:** Because there aren't quarters of people walking around, it helps to get a whole number of customers you need to generate a referral.

   Dividing 1 by the referral impact gets you the total number of referrals you need to generate one new customer, like this:

   1/0.25 = 4

5. **Promoter Referral Rate:** Keep in mind that despite the guidance that answers of 9's and 10's are more likely to recommend a website or product, it doesn't necessarily mean all the respondents actually will recommend.

   While people's ability to recall past behavior can be poor, their ability to predict future behavior is even worse. To help account for that uncertainty, look at which promoters say they referred someone else in the last year and use that as a proxy for those who are more likely to refer someone in the future.

   I also call this the Promoter Efficiency Rate.

   For TurboTax, 81% of the sample of promoters said they referred someone else to the product in the last year.

6. **Promoters Needed:** By dividing the Referral Impact Rate by the Promoter Referral Rate, you get the number of promoters needed to gain a new customer.

   This works out to be five new promoters needed to generate one new TurboTax customer.

With some estimate of the number of promoters you need to gain a new customer, you can then weigh the cost of new programs, features, pricing, and promotions to determine if the benefit from new customers outweighs the cost. For websites, a new "customer" might just be a new visitor or subscriber, so the cost of gaining new promoters can be important.

The estimates used in the preceding TurboTax example are based on survey data and, therefore, aren't as reliable as actual internal numbers. If actual referral rates or conversion rates are available from historical data, then those can be used to supplement or supplant the survey data. Keep in mind that past behavior is no guarantee of future success, so having data on the past and potential future is a prudent approach.

With any survey data comes a margin of error because you almost always are dealing with a small fraction of the customer population. As an added step, I also like to compute a conservative estimate of the value of the promoter. For the boxes labeled "Positively Referred," "Conversion Rate," and "Promoter Referral Rate," I also use the lower boundary of the confidence interval.

For example, from the sample of 117 TurboTax customers surveyed, while 61% said they referred someone in the past year, the 90% confidence interval is 52% to 68%. So the more conservative estimate is to use the lower end of 52% instead of the average of 61%.

Valuing negative word of mouth

While companies should strive for more promoters, it's often the customers who are least satisfied with their experience who have a much larger impact on referrals and the brand. Research supports that customers who are dissatisfied with a product or service experience are actually more likely to be vocal and tell more friends and colleagues about their bad experience than generally satisfied customers.

For example, I have been an avid user of the online personal finance website Mint.com for years. Its website allows you to see your personal and small-business finances, expenses, and investments all in one place. Unfortunately, the product team recently turned off the small-business categorization feature with no notice to customers. This meant hundreds of hours of logging small-business expenses were lost and unrecoverable. Understandably, a lot of loyal customers were upset and let the company know. While it's unclear what will happen to the product, the experience has been so frustrating that I've shared it with at least a dozen close friends who manage small businesses and track their personal finances with Mint.com. This one change turned a promoter into a detractor.

The negative effects of detractors can outweigh the positive effects of promoters. You can estimate this negative effect by using a similar procedure for estimating the value of promoters.

1. **Negative Word of Mouth Rate:** Ask all customers in a survey if they recall actually discouraging anyone from using or purchasing the product. Convert this to a percentage.

   For example, if 20 out of 100 people discouraged someone else from using the product, the rate is 20%.

2. **Number Discouraged:** Ask customers to estimate approximately how many people they discouraged from purchasing.

   If you don't have this information from customers, use the number 4 as a placeholder. There's some evidence that dissatisfied customers tell on average four friends and colleagues about their poor experience.

3. **Conversion Rate:** Use the same conversion rate used in estimating the value of a promoter. This is calculated as the percent of respondents (from a survey) that were referred to a product by a friend or colleague.

   In the TurboTax example, it is 42%.

4. **Cost of Discouragement:** Multiply these values to compute the cost of a discouragement:

   - Negative word of mouth rate
   - Number discouraged
   - Conversion rate

   For this example, the negative word of mouth rate (20%), the number discouraged (4), and the conversion rate (.42) work out to be 34%.

   You can divide 1 by this number to get the number of discouragements that result in one lost customer. In this case, it's 3.

5. **Detractor Discouragement Rate:** Not all detractors will discourage customers from using a company's product, especially those detractors who score higher, such as 5's and 6's on the LTR question. Find the percentage of detractors who also negatively referred to friends from the survey data.

   Use as an example that roughly 50% of detractors actually discouraged others. Divide 3 by 50%, and you get 6. That means for every six detractors, on average one customer is lost. The calculations are shown in Figure 12-6.

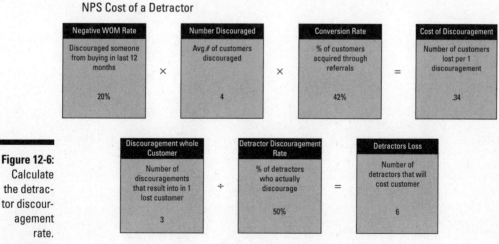

Figure 12-6:
Calculate the detractor discouragement rate.

Part IV
Analytics for Product Development

In this part . . .

✔ Find out what customers expect in your company's products.

✔ Test product features to find out how usable they are.

✔ Improve the navigation and findability of your website and products.

✔ Visit `http://www.dummies.com/extras/ customeranalytics` for great Dummies content online.

Chapter 13

Developing Products That Customers Want

*I*f you build it, they will come. At least you hope so! Understanding what customers want and what they will purchase is one of the holy grails of product development and is rife with analytics to help improve the process. Your product must meet customer needs (or perceived needs) better than your competition's and at a comparable or better price.

One of the most effective ways to produce products and experiences that customers want is to first understand what customers want to accomplish. For software products, that can be tasks such as accurately filing taxes, creating professional looking movies from raw clips, or organizing and sharing photos. For physical products, this can be tasks such as recording a show to a DVR, drilling a hole in concrete, or painting a room faster. For websites, customers are usually looking to answer questions or to accomplish tasks like purchasing a product or paying a bill online.

Some of the most innovative products don't come from what customers are asking for, but instead fixing problems with existing products and services.

In this chapter, I cover several methods to help you define and prioritize what features to include in your products.

Gathering Input on Product Features

Even if you already have a list of tasks and features ready to prioritize, here are four additional sources to come up with data (also see Chapter 7).

✔ **Stakeholder interviews:** Start with the people who know the product and customers the best. Sales and support teams hear complaints and probably have a lot of ideas about what customers want. In fact, there are probably already long lists of feature requests, bug fixes, enhancements, and wish lists. Combine and mine these to generate a list of requirements.

✔ **Follow me home:** A technique I learned while working at the software company Intuit was "follow me home." You literally follow a customer home or to his workplace and then spend the day watching him do his job. Look for pain points and problems in how he does his job to look for opportunities of improvement.

During one such follow-me-home, a team of researchers noticed that retail customers were exporting their transactions from their point-of-sale cash registers into QuickBooks to manage their books. This extra step took time and could cause problems if done incorrectly. The developers came up with the idea of integrating QuickBooks with a cash register that eliminated a step for customers.

✔ **Customer interviews:** Ask customers directly about the types of problems they have and the features they think they need. Customers can be notoriously bad at articulating what they want. A skilled facilitator can ask questions in a way that gets at the underlying root of the problem. Have customers describe a typical day as they encounter your product (or any type of product).

Use the 5 Why's technique when interviewing customers. It's a question-asking technique that explores the cause-and-effect relationship that underlies a problem. See `www.isixsigma.com/tools-templates/cause-effect/determine-root-cause-5-whys/` for more information on the 5 Why's technique.

✔ **Voice of customer survey:** A voice of customer survey allows customers to provide direct feedback about existing products by answering a few survey questions. These surveys are one of the most cost-effective ways of gathering feedback about customers' experiences with your products and services.

Finding Customers' Top Tasks

While there are hundreds to thousands of things users can accomplish on websites and software interfaces, there are a critical few tasks that drive users to visit a website or use a software or product.

Think of all the features Microsoft Word provides. It supports document editing, mail merging, desktop publishing, and a full range of HTML. By one estimate, it has around 1,200 features. Now think of the most important features that you need when you create or edit a document — the features you couldn't live without. These features likely support your top tasks.

Prioritizing tasks is not a new concept. Having users rank what's important is a technique that's been used extensively in marketing and conjoint analysis (I cover this topic later in this chapter). But having users force-rank hundreds or thousands of features individually would be too tedious for even the most diligent of users (or even the most sophisticated, choice-based conjoint software).

In the following sections, I outline the steps on how to prioritize your top tasks.

Listing the tasks

Identify the features, content, and functionality you want people to consider. The tasks can be specific to a website or to a class of websites. For example, here are a few things you can do on a healthcare insurance company website:

- ✔ Look up the address of a doctor.
- ✔ Find the office hours of a doctor.
- ✔ See if a healthcare provider accepts your insurance.

Avoid internal jargon as much as possible and make sure tasks are phrased as something a person can relate to and that are actionable.

The total number of tasks you need depends on how focused and extensive the functionality you are testing is. A broader experience (an entire e-commerce website) will have more tasks compared to a more focused experience (for example, on-demand videos for a cable provider). You might have as few as 20 or as many as 150.

Finding customers

Recruit a representative set of customers to determine the top tasks. As with all sampling methods, be sure the participants who take your study share the same characteristics as the larger customer base you are making inferences about.

The following table shows the sample size you'd need to have a desired margin of error (plus or minus around each percentage). For example, to achieve a margin of error of approximately plus or minus 7%, you should plan on a sample size of around 136. This percentage is based on the assumption that the percentage will fall at around 50%, at a 90% level of confidence (see Chapter 2 for details about confidence levels).

In top-tasks analysis, most items will actually only be selected by a small percentage of users, making the sample sizes shown on the high side for most of the items. In other words, this is a worst-case scenario sample size and means that sample sizes as low as ten customers still provide insights.

Sample Size	Margin of Error (+/-)
1,689	2%
749	3%
421	4%
268	5%
186	6%
136	7%
103	8%
81	9%
65	10%

Selecting five tasks

Present the enumerated list of tasks in random order to representative customers using software. You want to randomize because customers don't consider tasks individually, but scan your list for recognizable key words. With a randomized list, tasks have an equal chance of being near the top or bottom of the list.

You can use software to randomize the order of your tasks. UserZoom and SurveyMonkey are two that allow you to randomize.

Have users pick their top five tasks from the list.

It's hard to know every task a customer would like to accomplish. Therefore, include an "Other" option so customers can provide their own top task.

There's nothing sacred about picking 5; it's just a good number that works when you have 50 or more tasks. With fewer tasks, say 20 to 30, you can adjust the number down to 3 for users to select. This ensures users are forced to pick the really important tasks from the nice-to-have tasks.

Graphing and analyzing

After you collect the results of your survey, follow these steps to compute the customers' top tasks:

1. **Count the votes each task received.**

2. **Divide the vote total by the number of participants who voted.**

   This gives you the percent of times a task was selected.

3. **Sort the tasks by percentage in descending order.**

The characteristic shape of the top-task graph is the "long neck" of the vital few tasks your customers care about. Figure 13-1 shows four examples. Notice the handful of tasks that really stand out near the left side of each graph? They are the top tasks.

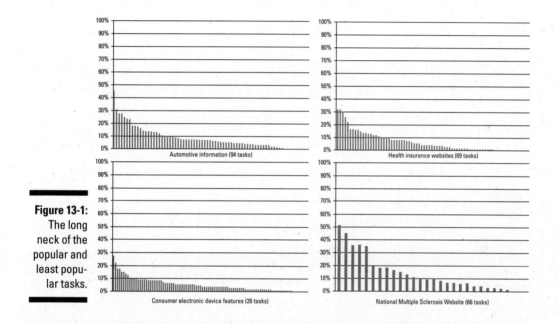

Figure 13-1: The long neck of the popular and least popular tasks.

You also see the long tail of the trivial tasks that are less important. Of course, you can't just stop supporting your less important tasks, but you should be sure that customers can complete top tasks effectively and efficiently. These top tasks should become the core tasks you conduct benchmark tests around and the basis for design efforts.

You can also add confidence intervals around top-tasks graphs to help stakeholders understand the margin of error around each item. This way, if there are strong opinions about how important or trivial a task is, one or two votes in general won't matter statistically. Figure 13-2 shows a larger version of the graph from Figure 13-1, with 90% confidence intervals. The gap after the fifth task (and the non-overlap in the confidence intervals) provides a good breaking point for prioritization. This particular top-tasks study was around what features consumers look for when researching consumer electronic devices on their smartphone.

Taking an internal view

Have the internal team working on the product also take the top-tasks analysis. This can be product managers, executives, designers, and developers. Compare these results with the customers' top tasks. Identify areas where there is agreement or disagreement. Where the two groups agree are the areas you should focus your attention.

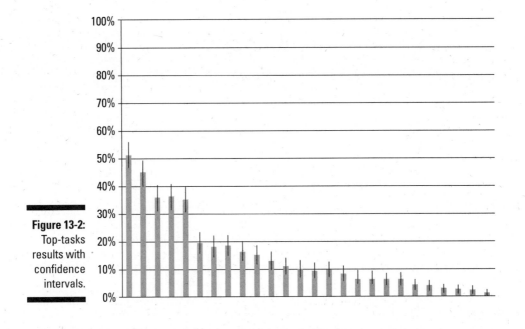

Figure 13-2:
Top-tasks
results with
confidence
intervals.

But can't I just look at Google Analytics?

For websites and even software products, log files record the pages and screens where customers visit and spend the most time. It would seem that this would eliminate the need for conducting a top-tasks analysis. And although resources like Google Analytics (see Chapter 10) will tell where customers are going, they don't do a good job of telling you why. This is best illustrated in an example with an automotive information company I worked with.

When we collected the tasks to prioritize in a top-tasks analysis for the website, a product manager said that he knew what customers wanted and were doing. In looking at the log files, most page views and time were spent on the Car Details page. The problem was that while customers did go to the Car Details page, we didn't know why they were going there or even which, if any, of the dozens of car details customers were driven to.

Using the top-tasks analysis, we found that the top task that customers wanted was information about each car's fuel efficiency. The only place that information existed was on the Car Details page! This top-tasks analysis led the design team to place the Miles per Gallon information on the Car Summary page.

Conducting a Gap Analysis

A complementary approach to the top-tasks analysis is a gap analysis. With a gap analysis, you understand how important customers find a feature and how satisfied they are with it in completing their tasks. If you have an existing customer base of people who have experience with a product (or competitive product), a gap analysis is what you need.

A gap analysis is a survey using two sets of items to be rated: importance and satisfaction.

Keep it to a smaller set of features or tasks than the top-tasks analysis, because you're asking participants to rate each item twice.

To conduct a gap analysis, follow these steps.

1. **Have customers rate how important a particular function or task is, using a numbered scale anchored with Not at all important to Very important.**

   A 7-point scale is popular, but almost any number from 5 to 11 will work.

2. **Ask customers to rate how satisfied they are with the same features using the current product.**

   Use the same numbered scale from Not at all satisfied (1) to Very satisfied (7).

3. **Use the following formula on each participant's task/feature scores: Importance + (Importance – Satisfaction).**

   This will reveal the "gap" or opportunity for improvement. This formula provides both a prioritization of features and also gives a higher score to features that are rated higher in importance.

An example of tasks and functionality for a web-based email system and some sample data are shown in the following table. Notice how the feature "Add contacts to an address book easily" and "Search for messages older than 6 months" both have the same "gap" in the Importance – Satisfaction column. But because adding contacts was rated as more important than searching for older messages (a 7 versus a 4), it gets a higher priority score (a 10 compared to a 7).

Task/Feature	Importance	Satisfaction	Importance - Satisfaction	Importance + (Importance - Satisfaction)
Add contacts to an address book easily	7	4	3	10
Create HTML messages and newsletters	4	3	1	5
Organize contacts by group	3	4	-1	2
Search for messages older than 6 months	4	1	3	7

Mapping Business Needs to Customer Requirements

Techniques like the gap analysis help prioritize the features from the customers' perspective. But it's also important to consider the organization's priorities. One such technique is Quality Function Deployment (QFD). QFD is a structured way to prioritize features, functions, or even website content by taking into account both business priorities (the voice of the company) and the customer/user priorities (the voice of the customer).

QFD separates what you do from the how you do it. In the rush to complete long lists of feature requests, it's easy to lose sight of what customers need.

The QFD's main output is a decision matrix, which looks like a house (see Figure 13-3). You might hear "house of quality" used interchangeably with QFD.

The following sections show you how to build a QFD, using an example of a website redesign for a multinational electronics company that sells through channel partners.

This is a simple QFD that balances the internal need to build and improve with a clear prioritized top-tasks list of customers. It helps narrow the scope and improve the quality of redesign.

You can build a more advanced QFD by incorporating competitive information, specifications, and positive and negative relationships between the "How's." Adding each of these parts to the house takes extra time, but it can be worth it depending on the complexity and consequences of the project.

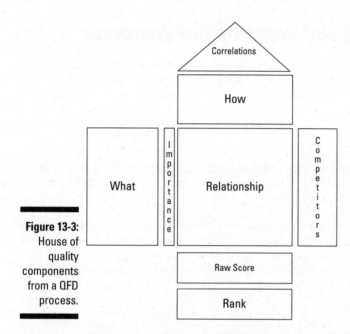

Figure 13-3:
House of
quality
components
from a QFD
process.

Identifying customers' wants and needs

Brainstorm as many possible features, functions, and task-based activities that customers would want to do. Look at the competition, survey and interview existing and former customers, review call center data, and interview stakeholders. These are your "What's."

For an informational-based website, most customer requirements are the tasks that users attempt, so a good task analysis can help identify these.

Here's a selection of some tasks from the B2B electronics website:

- ✔ Find detailed technical specifications (like CPU and power consumption).
- ✔ Find and download drivers.
- ✔ Contact a salesperson.
- ✔ Have a personalized profile to save products I'm interested in.
- ✔ View products for an industry (for example, entertainment or medical).
- ✔ Share my purchase with others.

Identifying the voice of the customer

Ask customers to tell you what they think is important, not what you want them to think is important. An essential part of this step is realizing that everything can't be important. If you ask customers and users what's important, they will often tell you everything is important. You need a way to force users to choose which tasks are really important and which features are nice to have.

You can get sophisticated with conjoint analysis, but the fastest and easiest way to get a forced rank is to run a top-tasks analysis or a gap analysis, as explained in the previous sections.

Use the average importance rating or the percent of users who pick each task as the weights in the QFD. Use higher numbers to indicate higher importance, so if you use ranks, reverse them so a "1" represents the least important. The following table shows the relative rank and the percent of users who picked the task as one of their top five (out of 35 possible tasks) in a top-tasks survey.

Rank	% Who Picked	Tasks (the What)
1	80%	Find detailed technical specifications (like CPU and power consumption).
2	73%	Find and download drivers.
9	27%	Contact a salesperson.
19	1%	Save products I'm interested in to an account page.
12	13%	View products for an industry (for example, entertainment or medical).
25	1%	Share my purchases with others.

Identifying the How's (the voice of the company)

Either use existing lists of enhancements and fixes or generate a new list based on the customer rankings.

The following are some example "How's" for the electronics website:

- ✔ Integrate Facebook and Twitter into the product pages to promote sharing.
- ✔ Improve the search function and search results.

> ✔ Integrate product videos.
>
> ✔ Provide 3D rotation of products.
>
> ✔ Add a customization feature.
>
> ✔ Add a Filter by Location.
>
> ✔ Integrate detailed product specs and drivers from the main product page.

Building the relationship between the customer and company voices

Next determine how each "How" impacts each customer "What," using the following scale:

    9 = Direct and strong relationship

    3 = Moderate relationship

    1 = Weak/Indirect relationship

    Blank = no relationship

The 1's, 3's, and 9's are mostly a convention and help accentuate the differences when you prioritize. Place each value in the cell where the "What" and the "How" meet, and leave the cell blank if there's no relationship.

In the example, "Integrate Facebook and Twitter buttons into the product pages" has a strong association with "Share my purchases with others." Something like product videos will probably have a modest impact on detailed specifications because users could view the products to get a better sense of size and even see what external ports are supported.

Figure 13-4 shows the "What's" and the "How's" and the relationships between the two in the cells, with higher numbers indicating a stronger relationship, and blank cells meaning no relationship.

Generating priorities

Multiply the importance by the relationship and add up each sum in the "How" columns. The sum of each column represents the overall magnitude that each feature/function will have on the customer. Higher numbers represent more of an impact.

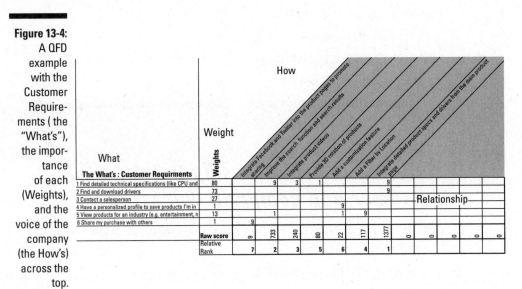

Figure 13-4: A QFD example with the Customer Requirements (the "What's"), the importance of each (Weights), and the voice of the company (the How's) across the top.

The actual value of each of the totaled columns is less important than the relative ranking, which the tool also calculates. For example, "Find detailed technical specifications" (a "what") has a weight of 80 and "Improve the search functionality and results" (a "how") has a strong relationship of a 9. This cell generates a score of $9 \times 80 = 720$. "View products for an industry" (a "what") has a weight of 13 and has a weak relationship with "Improve the search function and results." This cell has a score of $13 \times 1 = 13$. The search feature raw score is found by adding these two cell scores, $720 + 13 = 733$, which is the second-highest score relative to the other features considered.

Examining priorities

You should see gaps between features. The two highest ranked features (integrating the product specs and improving search) are well above the next five. A blank row means that a customer want isn't supported. That isn't necessarily a bad thing if it's a low priority task. In this example, none of the new features supported "Contact a salesperson." Assuming adding the contact information doesn't introduce new problems, it would also be a good addition to the redesign.

Measuring Customer Delight with the Kano Model

Differentiating a product from the competition often isn't about just meeting customer needs — it's about exceeding those needs and expectations.

Beyond a set of expected features, some features so exceed expectations that they "delight" customers into purchasing, repurchasing, and recommending a product. The Kano model helps differentiate between features customers expect and features that delight customers. For example, customers expect cars to be reliable and include features like power steering, radios, and air-conditioning. Up until the early 1980's, cup holders in vehicles were after-market add-ons. Cup holders, and the total number of cup holders, became a feature that delighted customers, so they were integrated into minivans and then to every type of car.

Named after Japanese professor Noriaki Kano, the Kano model is based on asking customers two questions about features. Features are categorized into one of six groupings.

- ✔ **Delighting:** The feature provides extra satisfaction when present but does not harm when absent.

- ✔ **One-dimensional:** The more of the feature the better.

- ✔ **Must-Haves:** Lack of the feature would lead to dissatisfaction.

- ✔ **Indifferent Attribute:** Customers don't care about the feature and it neither increases nor decreases customer satisfaction.

- ✔ **Reverse:** Including this feature leads to dissatisfaction.

- ✔ **Questionable:** Conflicting customer responses make it unclear whether this feature adds or detracts from satisfaction.

Here are the steps to take to understand what customers expect and what delights them:

1. **Aggregate the features in a similar way as you do for a gap analysis and top-tasks analysis.**

   The features should be articulated in a way that is meaningful to a customer, so avoid using internal company jargon and acronyms unless customers also use them.

2. **For each feature, ask participants two questions.**

   The first is called the functional question: What are your feelings when the feature is included?

The second is called the dysfunctional question: What are your feelings when this feature is NOT included?

For both questions use the following 5-point response scale:

  1 = I like it that way.

  2 = It must be that way.

  3 = I am neutral.

  4 = I can live with it that way.

  5 = I dislike it that way.

3. **Tabulate the responses.**

Table 13-1 shows how to score the responses to assign them one of the six categories. For example, if a customer responds to the functional question toward a feature as "I like it" and responds "I can live with it that way" for the dysfunctional question, the feature is a delighter. In comparison, if a customer responds to the functional question toward a feature as "Neutral" and responds "I like it" for the dysfunctional question, the feature is a reverse (less of it in the product).

Table 13-1	Scoring responses			
	Dysfunctional Question Response			
	Like it	Must be	Neutral	Can live with it	Dislike it
	Questionable	Delighting	Delighting	Delighting	One-dimensional
	Reverse	Indifferent	Indifferent	Indifferent	Must be
Functional	Reverse	Indifferent	Indifferent	Indifferent	Must be
Question	Reverse	Indifferent	Indifferent	Indifferent	Must be
Response	Reverse	Reverse	Reverse	Reverse	Questionable

Assessing the Value of Each Combination of Features

A more advanced method that identifies both the value (called the *utility*) and the optimal combination of individual features is called conjoint analysis. Where the Kano analysis identifies which features delight or dissatisfy customers individually, conjoint analysis identifies how the addition and reduction of features presented in more realistic combinations will lead to more or less interest in purchasing a product.

A conjoint analysis uses more advanced statistics and is usually done with software from companies like Survey Analytics (`www.surveyanalytics.com`), QuestionPro (`www.questionpro.com`), or Sawtooth Software (`www.sawtoothsoftware.com`).

To conduct a choice-based conjoint, you enter all the features, including price, into the software. These features are presented to customers in a survey format and the pairing of features helps identify how much each feature contributes to likelihood to purchase.

Kano airline analysis

My company recently ran a Kano analysis on how customers feel about the airline travel experience and features. One hundred participants who flew in the last year completed the survey. They rated the following items, using the two Kano questions:

Wi-Fi onboard	Full meal service
Free drinks (Non-alcoholic)	Purchase snacks on board
Extra legroom	Duty-free items for sale
Free carry-ons	Pillows and blankets
Free checked bag	Reclining seats
Early boarding	No change fees on tickets
In-seat TVs	Pick seat when booking online

We tabulated the responses by feature; two examples are shown in the following table. For example, for having Wi-Fi Internet access onboard the airplane, 22% found that feature delighting and 35% were indifferent toward it. In contrast, 33% of participants rated the Free Checked Bag as one-dimensional, meaning more free checked bags the better. Eighteen percent rated a free checked bag as a must-have and 14% would be delighted by that feature.

	Wi-Fi Onboard	*Free Checked Bag*
Delighting	22%	14%
Indifferent	35%	22%
Must Have	9%	18%
One-Dimensional	29%	33%
Questionable	4%	8%
Reverse	1%	5%

Here are two examples of possible conjoint screens:

- ✔ **How likely would you be to purchase a laptop with the following features (0 = not at all likely and 10= extremely likely)?**
  - Brand: Dell
  - 2GB RAM
  - 15-Inch Display
  - $999

- ✔ **How likely would you be to purchase a laptop with the following features (0 = not at all likely and 10= extremely likely)?**
  - Brand: Lenovo
  - 3GB RAM
  - 13-Inch Display
  - $1,199

Through a mathematical combination of features presented to the customer, the software identifies which features have the biggest impact on likelihood-to-purchase scores. This uses a similar statistical approach as the key drivers analysis described in Chapters 9 and 12.

Finding Out Why Problems Occur

Sometimes the best improvement that you can make to a product is not adding more features but instead, fixing features that don't work well or other problems with the experience that lead to undesirable outcomes.

A technique that works well for understanding the negative impacts of undesirable actions is the Failure Mode Effects Analysis (FMEA).

Things go wrong quite frequently in the customer experience, both online and elsewhere. Customers forget their passwords, install printers incorrectly, and experience long wait times on customer support. They are unable to find products, they take too long to make a purchase, and their information can be stolen. While you ultimately want a great customer experience, measuring poor experiences helps you understand how to prevent things from going wrong and generate better experiences. The following case study walks through an example of using an FMEA to identify problems with an online experience. It can be applied to offline experiences, too.

Imagine you're interested in buying a new car. Should you trade yours in or try and sell it yourself? Either way, you want the most money for your car, and knowing its true value is essential information. Many websites (for example, Edmunds, Kelley Blue Book, Autotrader, and Cars.com) offer a tool that tells you how much your car is worth.

The task seems simple: Enter your make and model, condition, and mileage, and like the Magic 8 ball, you get a value. Of course, a number of details complicate the process and things can go wrong. You can pick the wrong make, be unable to accurately describe the condition or understand automotive jargon, or leave off features — or the entire process can take so long that you finally give up.

Applying the FMEA in finding the value of your car can help the designers of these websites prevent nuisances and failures (such as taking longer to find the value of your car, or getting the incorrect value altogether).

To conduct an FMEA, follow these steps:

1. **Identify the steps in the process.**

   Break down a typical scenario into small steps to identify failure points or bottlenecks. Ideally, you can do this by watching the path users go down from a usability test (see Chapter 14) or from existing data.

2. **Identify what can go wrong.**

   Here's where recording poor experiences comes in handy. Are users taking too long, getting the wrong car value, making errors, or not recommending the website or product because of pricing or policies? Usability problem lists with severity ratings can be especially helpful in identifying the sort of failures you want to avoid. Are users entering the wrong make, picking the wrong condition, getting slowed down by too many pages or intrusive ads, or are they stopping at a preliminary estimate before getting the right value? Use any and all data sources to get a good picture about problems. These sources include call center data, surveys, third-party reports, former customers, and competitive data.

3. **Determine how common the problems are.**

   Not all problems affect all users. Watch just a handful of users in a usability test and you'll see that some users struggle with one step while others breeze through all of them. For example, in a test of the Enterprise Rental Car website, most users had a problem finding the total price for their rental car, while only a few users had difficulty picking the correct car type. For the FMEA, rank problems from least common (assigned a 1) to most common (assigned a 10). Even if a problem isn't terribly harmful, if most users encounter it, it can be worth addressing.

4. **Determine how severe the problems are.**

   Just because a problem affects a small percentage of users doesn't mean that it isn't a big deal. If a few users are getting the wrong car value and losing money on their trade-in, the negative experience can snowball after the dissatisfied customers tell their friends. In the FMEA, prioritize the severity of the problem from cosmetic/minor (assigned a 1) to leading to task failure, loss of money, or loss of life as a 10. The rankings are largely context dependent, so don't get bent out of shape arguing over whether a problem is a 4 or 5.

5. **Identify how hard the problems are to detect.**

   Some of the most pernicious problems are the ones that are hard to detect. If a problem is harder to detect, it's harder to diagnose and prevent. It's like when you take your car to the mechanic because of the noise it's making, but when the mechanic goes to listen, it's fine.

   For example, the wording of a condition of a car might confuse users trading in a certain model and year as well as those who have never traded a car in before. Or, the layout of an interface might only affect users on old versions of Internet Explorer with low resolution screens. Like the previous two steps, assign problems that are easiest to detect as 1's and the hardest to detect as 10's.

   TIP

   When in doubt, use a 5, and then change the rating when you feel more confident about how easy or difficult it is to detect. Using a 5 has the effect of neutralizing the detection aspect of the FMEA, and this gives more weight to frequency and severity.

6. **Calculate the Risk Priority Number (RPN).**

   The RPN is found by multiplying the ranking of occurrence by severity by detection (RPN = F × S × D). The higher the RPN, the higher the priority the feature has to be addressed.

   Figure 13-5 shows three examples of possible problems in the car appraisal and purchasing process. Like the QFD discussed earlier in this chapter, the raw value is less important than the relative rank or the magnitude of the difference. In the example data, the "Estimated Car Value" function has a higher problem possibility than the "Finding if a car is available in a zip code" function.

Measuring Usability

FMEA Worksheet

Item / function	Potential failure mode	Potential effects of failure	S (severity rating)	Potential cause(s)	O (occurrence rating)	D (detection rating)	RPN (risk priority	Recommended actions
Estimated Car Value	User gets the wrong (lower) value	Less money at trade in or sale	9	Users are getting prelim. Values, not scrolling down (see QFD)	3	5	135	Redesign UI to minimize the number of steps to arrive at a real car value
What is a good price	Users are not selecting the right package for a car	The incorrect prices are shown for models	5	The feature packages are not noticed	5	5	125	Test alternate designed to find a more salient package element
Finding if a car is available in a zip code	Inventory is incorrect	Users contact dealers who don't have the car and lose trust in the brand	3	Data feeds to website are delayed and updated every 48 hours.	5	5	75	Explore real time inventory options and call major delaers

Figure 13-5: Three example problems identified in the FMEA.

7. **Identify the root causes of the failures.**

Ranking what problems to address is one thing; finding ways to avoid them is another. For each of the undesirable outcomes, think of the root causes of the problem.

Sometimes the causes are obvious, while other times it can be helpful to use the 5 Why's technique. Ask "Why?" until you uncover root causes instead of symptoms:

- *Why are users getting the wrong car value?*

  They don't scroll down to see the additional features section.

- *Why don't they scroll?*

  The options take up more than a single page.

- *Why do they take up more than a page?*

  The screens are smaller to allow for more ads.

- *Why so many ads?*

  These pages are among the highest visited on the site and ads generate a significant portion of revenue.

Chapter 14

Gaining Insights through a Usability Study

*I*f you've ever struggled to change the time on an alarm clock, couldn't figure out how to work a remote control, or failed to successfully apply for insurance on a website, you have some idea about how important the ease of use of a product or experience is.

Your product can have all the features a user wants, but if it's too difficult to use, then the user will move on to another product.

Recognizing the Principles of Usability

If you make your products too difficult to purchase online, or make a form too difficult to fill out, customers will leave or call your customer support line. Both of these are expensive, undesirable outcomes.

Good usability can lead customers to recommend your product; poor usability leads customers to discourage their friends and colleagues from purchasing a product. (See Chapter 12 to find out how important customer loyalty is.)

Usability is different than other data collected from market research in that it measures both customer *attitudes* and customer *actions*. Usability is as much about what customers do as what they say.

A product or website is usable if

- ✔ Customers can complete what they want to do (effectiveness)
- ✔ Customers can complete their task quickly (efficiency)
- ✔ Customers don't find the experience frustrating (satisfaction)

There isn't a usability thermometer that tells you how usable an experience is. Instead you have to rely on the outcome of experiences by measuring the effectiveness, efficiency, and satisfaction of the experience.

A usability problem is anything in the interface, buttons, labels, designs, or layout that prevents users from completing their task, makes the task difficult, or leads to longer task times. In this chapter, I show you how to run a usability test so you can discover and fix your usability problems and provide a quantified better customer experience.

Conducting a Usability Test

One of the best ways to identify usability problems is to conduct a usability test. The basic idea behind a usability test is that you watch users complete (or fail at) tasks with software, hardware, or a website and see what problems they run into.

You might be tempted to help participants or just ask if they like software or a website. But the point of a usability test is to observe your participants and not interfere with their process.

Here are the steps to conduct a usability test:

1. **Determine what you want to test.**
2. **Identify your goals.**
3. **Outline your task scenarios.**
4. **Recruit users.**
5. **Test your users.**
6. **Collect as many metrics as possible.**
7. **Code your data and analyze it.**
8. **Summarize and present the results.**

The following sections provide the details to complete each of these steps.

Determining what you want to test

You can rarely test everything about a product or website that you want to at once. That would simply overwhelm your participants.

Narrow the scope of your study by focusing on known problem areas, high usage areas, or some combination of the two. See Chapter 13 for ideas on prioritizing features for testing.

Eye-tracking usability tests involve special equipment that track where participants look as they use websites and software. Eye-tracking studies are more involved and require special equipment, but can help answer questions about whether customers' eyes are attracted to features or content.

If you're developing a new product, you don't have to wait to test its usability. You can conduct usability tests on sketches or partially completed products. The earlier you find problems in the development process, the easier they are to fix. Test early and often to get the most of your usability testing.

Identifying the goals

While a usability test is primarily about observing customers and uncovering the problems they have, the approach you take depends on your goal.

Identify what the main goals of your study are:

- ✔ Are you trying to find and fix as many usability problems as possible?
- ✔ Do you want a benchmark of usability and performance?
- ✔ Are you comparing an application with a competing product or alternative design?

Each of these three testing goals requires slightly different testing parameters and sample size requirements (see Chapter 2). Many studies will also combine the goals. For example, you can have a study to compare your product to a competitor, and find out which tasks take longer to complete.

Outlining task scenarios

The task scenario is the hallmark of the usability test.

A task is made up of the steps a user has to perform to accomplish a goal. A task scenario describes what you want the participant to achieve. Crafting task scenarios is a balance between providing enough information so users aren't guessing about what they're supposed to do and not providing too much information (which could overwhelm them). Your goal is to simulate the discovery and nonlinearity of real-world application usage.

Follow these guidelines for creating task scenarios for your usability test:

- ✔ **Be specific.** Give participants a reason or purpose for performing the task. Instead of giving generalities like "find a new kitchen appliance," ask them to find a blender for under $75 that has high customer ratings.

  In the real world, users usually start searching with general ideas of what they want, and then quickly narrow their selection based on price, quality, and recommendations. In the artificial world of usability testing, users encounter problems if what you provide is too vague, and they will look to a moderator (if there is one) for what they should do. Don't be so vague in your task that users have to guess what you want them to do.

  For example, "You need to rent a mid-sized car on July 21 at 10 a.m. and return it on July 23 at noon from Boston's Logan Airport" is specific.

- ✔ **Don't tell the user where to click and what to do.** While providing specific details is important, don't walk the users through every step. Such hand-holding will provide biased and less useful results.

  For example, instead of saying "Click the small check box at the bottom of the screen to add GPS," just say "Add GPS to your rental car."

- ✔ **Use the customer's language, not the company's language.** It's a common mistake to mirror the internal structure of a company on a website's navigation or on software screens. It's also bad practice to ask participants to do things based on internal company jargon or terms.

  False positive test results or outright confusion may result if users don't understand the terms used in a scenario. Do users really use the term "asset" when referring to their kids' college funds? Will a user know what a product "configurator" is or an "item-page" or even the "mega menu"?

- ✔ **Have a correct solution.** If you ask a user to find a rental car location nearest to a hotel address, there should be a correct choice. This makes the task more straightforward for the user and allows you to more easily know if a task was or wasn't successfully completed.

  The problem with "Find a product that's right for you" tasks is that participants are in the state of mind of finding information to solve problems. At the time, there probably isn't a product that's right for them; they're more interested in getting the test done and collecting their honorarium. This can lead to a sense that any product selection is correct and inflate basic metrics like task completion rates.

✔ **Avoid making tasks dependent on each other.** It is important to alternate the presentation order of tasks so not all tasks are presented in the same sequence. Participants get "warmed-up" during a usability test and this can make earlier tasks seem harder and later tasks seem easier. When your tasks have dependencies (for example, create a file in one task, then delete the same file in another task), if a user fails one task, he or she fails the other.

Avoiding dependent scenarios isn't always possible if you're testing something like an installation process, but be cognizant of both the bias and complications introduced by adding dependencies.

✔ **Provide context but keep the scenario short.** Get the users thinking as if they actually need to perform the task, but don't go overboard with details.

For example, "You will be attending a conference in Boston in July and need to rent a car."

While there isn't a "right" number of tasks for a usability test, try to identify three to five tasks for your test participants to accomplish.

Make the tasks realistic and representative of what users actually do. Don't just ask participants if they like or will use an application or website. Have them register, log in, fill out a form, search for information, answer a question, or purchase a product. See Chapter 13 for more ideas on identifying the top tasks.

Write the task scenario in a way that gives participants enough information to complete a task but not too much that leads them step-by-step down a path. For instance, provide product names, specific price ranges, and brands.

Here's an example:

Task Example: Update a saved expense report.

Earlier you started to create an expense report but ran out of time. You saved your work with the description, "Industry Conference." You want to add an expense for sending a FedEx package to the report. Find the report and add the FedEx package as a new expense for $26. Submit the report for approval when you are done.

If you're testing different types of customers or users, you may need to set up a different set of test scenarios based on

✔ **User needs.** For example, software that both teachers and students use (like Blackboard) has different tasks.

✔ **User skills and experience.** For example, international non-English speaking users often have a different perspective than domestic U.S. users when browsing a website.

Recruiting users

You need customers in order to do usability testing. It can be a small-scale, do-it-yourself usability test or a large sample corporate usability test, but finding available (and willing) participants can be difficult. In fact, it's often cited as one of the reasons usability testing isn't done more often.

The process by which you find your users will vary depending on what you are testing, the types of users you need, and the stage of testing (early versus late).

Here are six sources to help find users.

✔ **Hallway testing:** Grab anyone who is unfamiliar with the application or website you're testing. These can be coworkers, friends, family, or folks at the local coffee shop.

Hallway testing works well for general purpose websites or apps and when you're looking to uncover the more obvious problems with the interactions (problems, of course, always seem obvious after you find them).

Don't rely too heavily on this method, especially when the design is more refined or users have specialized skills. When users don't have an interest in a product or service, they will be happy to give you an opinion on matters — but relying on them may generate false positive results and overlook issues that actual users will encounter.

✔ **Existing users:** Your existing users are an obvious wellspring for testing. If you're offering a brand-new product, you won't have this source, of course. But, if your company makes similar products, then it makes sense to leverage those customers:

   • *Finding existing users off your website is an easy place to start.* You can use pop-ups (offered by UserZoom and Ethnio) or fixed opt-in boxes to solicit volunteers. Marketing and sales departments usually have customer contact information you can tap.

   • *You can work with the customer support department and ask customers if they'd be interested in participating in follow-up studies.* While existing customers sound like a panacea for finding users, volunteers may not have the time or availability to commit to an hour-long study, so you often have to rely on other sources.

✔ **Usertesting.com:** This website not only delivers audio and video of users using a website or mobile app, but it also has a large panel of users. www.Usertesting.com allows you to recruit based on age, gender, and geography. You can also ask participants to self-select by asking them to participate only if they've used a certain website, own a particular product, have health insurance, or have a 401(k) account, among other things. Although it isn't a solution when you need hundreds of responses or very specific recruiting criteria, or to test software and hardware, getting a source of users and a 15- to 20-minute usability testing for under $40 per participant is often very effective.

Similar services are offered by the websites www.TryMyUI.com and www.YouEye.com.

- ✔ **Craigslist and Facebook:** When your recruiting requirements become more specific, you can post ads on Craigslist or Facebook. Marketing agencies have posted ads for focus groups for years in classifieds, so you should have no problem finding willing participants (usability testing is, of course, not a focus group, so be prepared to set expectations). Craigslist works for in-person and remote usability testing. In addition to the cost of the posting, be prepared to spend between $50 and $200, depending on the commitment and type of user you need.

Don't count on Craigslist for finding participants with highly specialized skills or who are high-income earners. You tend to get people who have time on their hands and are looking to make some extra cash. With the right posting and honorarium, you can usually find a great pool of participants for most usability tests.

- ✔ **Panel agencies:** For unmoderated usability testing or surveys where you need hundreds to thousands of respondents, consider using a panel agency. Panels have huge databases of people from around the world. They keep track of all the usual demographic variables but allow you to find people like small-business owners, IT managers, Costco shoppers, or tablet owners.

Opinions for Good (Op4G; op4g.com) helps non-profits raise money by having its members participate in the studies. The participants keep a portion of the honorarium and a portion gets donated. This model allows them to reach many people with specialized job skills and high-income individuals who normally wouldn't be interested in taking an online survey for a few dollars. You can also try Toluna (toluna.com) and Research Now (researchnow.com). Plan on paying between $15 and $55 per completed response.

- ✔ **Market research recruiters:** Looking for hardware engineers, lawyers, medical professionals, chief financial officers, or people with $100K+ in two investment accounts? When you need to find very specific skills for in-person testing, you'll likely need the help of professional recruitment firms. Firms like Fieldwork (fieldwork.com) and Plaza Research (plazaresearch.com) maintain huge local and international databases to match almost any recruitment need you may have.

Plan on paying a recruiting company between $150 and $300 per recruited participant plus an honorarium of between $100 and $250 per participant. This approach can get expensive, so be sure you put as much effort into creating effective tasks and asking the right questions as you do in finding the right test participants. Don't obsess over perfectly matching every demographic variable.

Find a sample of participants who represent the larger customer base you are interested in understanding. The total number of users you'll need to test will largely depend on your testing goals (see the earlier section "Identifying the goals").

- ✔ If your goal is to find and fix problems, then aim for between five and ten participants for each round of testing. See the later sidebar, "Sample sizes for a usability test."

- ✔ If your goal is to find a benchmark of usability performance, you need a sample size that achieves a tolerable margin of error around your metrics. See Chapter 2 for a table of sample sizes.

  For example, if you had 32 participants and 50% of them successfully completed the task, you can be 90% confident the percentage of all customers completing the same task would be between 36% and 64%.

- ✔ If your goal is to compare products, the sample size is affected by a number of variables (including the confidence, power, and type of metric).

  You can usually approximate the needed sample size based on two factors:

  - *How large a difference you want to detect (if one exists)*
  - *Whether the same users will attempt tasks on both products (called within-subjects) or if a different set will attempt tasks on each product (called between-subjects)*

  The following table shows the approximate difference you can detect in metrics, such as the completion rate or any other binary measure (at a 50% completion rate).

Difference to Detect 90% Confidence & 80% Power	*Sample Size Within*	*Sample Size Between*
50%	17	22
40%	20	34
30%	29	64
20%	50	150
12%	93	426
10%	115	614
9%	130	760
8%	148	962

Difference to Detect 90% Confidence & 80% Power	Sample Size Within	Sample Size Between
7%	171	1,258
6%	202	1,714
5%	246	2,468
4%	312	3,860
3%	421	6,866
2%	640	15,452
1%	1,297	61,822

For example, at a sample size of 426 (213 in each group), you can detect a 12% difference for a between-subjects design (see the row that starts with 12%). So if 50% complete a task on one product and 62% on a competitive product, the difference would be statistically significant.

These estimates are conservative but recommended when planning a study without prior data. For continuous measures like perceived difficulty and task time, you can detect smaller differences at the same sample size.

If you have the time and budget to test 15 users, it's more effective to test 5 users, fix the problems you see, then test another 5 users, fix those problems, and then test with a final 5 users.

Testing your users

When you're ready to test, plan on 60 to 90 minutes per participant. Participants start to get fatigued after 90 minutes. Aim for most tasks to take 10 minutes or less. This leaves time for an introduction, pre-study questions, three to seven tasks, post-study questions, debriefing, and to solve any technical problems that pop up.

To uncover problems during a usability test, have your participants think out loud. Tell them to articulate their thoughts: what doesn't make sense and what confuses them as they attempt the tasks. Don't stop participants while they are working through details. Instead, wait until they get stuck or after a task to have them explain something they didn't understand. See the later section, "Finding and Reporting Usability Problems," for more information.

Collecting metrics

In addition to usability problems, you should collect three core usability metrics when you want to understand the experience a customer has with your product. The following task-based metrics correspond to the three areas of usability: effectiveness, efficiency, and satisfaction.

- ✔ **Completion Rate:** If a participant completed the task, code it Success (1); if the participant didn't complete the task, code it as Fail (0). Figure 14-1 shows the completion rate for two tasks on two different websites.

- ✔ **Task Time:** Measure how long a user took to complete a task.

- ✔ **Perceived Difficulty:** After a participant attempts a task, ask her to rate how difficult it was. A 7-point scale with 1 being Very Difficult and 7 being Very Easy is common.

Record the errors users make, such as clicking on the wrong link, making typos, or not seeing the search results on a page. Keep this data for a findability study (see Chapter 15).

In addition to these task-based measures, capture at least one overall study measure that has participants rate their satisfaction with the overall experience with the product or website. Good questionnaires include the SUS and SUPR-Q (see Chapter 9).

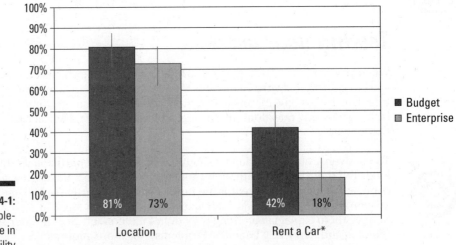

Task Completion Rates

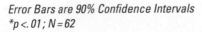

Figure 14-1: The completion rate in a usability test.

Error Bars are 90% Confidence Intervals
*$p < .01$; N = 62

Sample sizes for a usability test

Finding the right sample size is a trade-off between the cost of running participants and the capability to detect usability problems. The larger the sample size, the more usability problems that get uncovered. There is, however, a diminishing return as fewer new usability problems get uncovered with each additional user. Not all usability problems uniformly affect all customers. Some problems only affect 30% or 5%. The fewer *customers* a problem impacts, the larger the sample size you will need to have a good chance of observing the problems in a test.

The recommended way to make a sample size decision is to follow these three steps:

1. Pick a problem occurrence percentage that you want to detect.

    For example, 5%, 10%, or 20% of customers will have a problem with a task or element of a design.

2. Pick a percent of these problems you want to observe.

    For example, you might decide you want to observe 80%, 85%, or 90% of customers.

3. Use the binomial probability formula to determine the sample size needed.

For example, if you want to identify problems that impact 10% or more of your customers and you want to have an 85% chance of seeing them (if they exist) in a usability test, then you need to plan on observing 18 users. See `http://www.measuringu.com/problem_discovery.php` for calculations and background.

At the sample size of ten, most problems that affect 20% or more of customers will be observed. A sample size of five (for example, using a "new customer" versus an "existing customer" subset) will still uncover 68% of the issues impacting as few as 20% of users. At both sample sizes, virtually all issues experienced by 40% or more of users will be observed (given the tasks performed and type of user recruited).

The following figure shows the percent of usability problems uncovered by testing five and ten customers. For example, around 90% of problems that impact 20% or more of users will likely be seen after testing ten users. That is, if a problem exists that would affect 20% of all users, there's about a 90% chance of seeing it at least once in a usability testing with ten users.

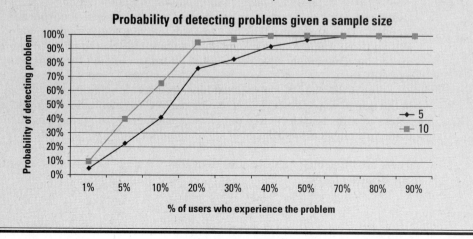

Probability of detecting problems given a sample size

Coding and analyzing your data

After you observe users attempting tasks, summarize the task and test metrics and include confidence intervals (see Chapter 2). Look for high and low performance across the metrics, and then look to understand "why" by summarizing what problems users encountered and what comments they made.

Summarizing and presenting the results

Correlate your results with graphs and a report or briefing. Report the results of the usability metrics, the usability problems found, and overall findings from the study. Conclude with actionable items that you can accomplish to make the tasks easier for customers to complete.

For example, in a usability test of Enterprise.com, the site lacked a total price for the rental car. A clear action item would be to add a total to the confirmation page. If a total can't be added because of variation in taxes or prices per state, for example, then provide a clear estimate in a prominent location on the page and an explanation of why a precise total can't be provided.

Considering the Different Types of Usability Tests

Usability testing originally was conducted only in expensive corporate facilities. These usability labs had two-way mirrors and expensive video and audio equipment. Participants had to take the time to come to the lab for testing. Only big-budget firms could afford to conduct these types of usability tests.

In the last 15 years, however, technological improvements have allowed marketers to collect task-oriented data from customers without needing them to come to a physical location.

There are three major approaches to usability testing. Each has its advantages and disadvantages:

✔ **Lab-based:** This is the classic approach to usability testing. Customers physically come to a lab, often with a two-way mirror, and are observed by a team of product developers or researchers. This is still the primary method for testing physical products, like remote controls or mobile applications. A facilitator moderates the session, so it's often referred to as moderated in-person testing.

While many companies may have a dedicated lab for testing customers (our company has two) and specialized software, you don't need much to conduct a usability test. You just need a conference room, office, or some other space where your product can be used by a customer. You also need adequate time to set up the study.

✔ **Remote moderated:** Customers log into screen-sharing software like GoTo Meeting (gotomeeting.com) or WebEx (webex.com) and attempt the same tasks as if they were in a lab. The software allows customers from anywhere in the world to share their screen and even control your computer. You can even have them turn on their webcam to see their faces. A facilitator still guides the participant through the tasks, but the customer and facilitator can be in different cities or countries.

✔ **Remote unmoderated:** Software from companies like UserZoom (userzoom.com) and Loop11 (loop11.com) walk customers through tasks and questions. It's particularly well suited for testing websites or web applications. Everything about the interaction can be recorded, including a recording of what testers did on-screen, and their facial expressions captured by their web cam. This technology also works for mobile devices so you can have testers from anywhere in the world.

This method can give you stats that you might not be able to replicate in a moderated or lab-based environment. Figure 14-2 shows how UserZoom offers a heat map, showing where testers first start to complete a task.

A variation on this method is a service from usertesting.com. Usertesting.com has a panel of users who are trained to think out loud as they walk through tasks. You can get feedback from five users the same day you launch a study. It's called remote unmoderated because you don't need a test facilitator to walk participants through each task. This allows you to collect a lot of data quicker and with less cost than with other methods.

Combine multiple methods to fully understand a customer's experience with a website or software. For example, you can have 300 users complete tasks using the remote unmoderated method and then have 10 to 15 users come into a lab so you can follow up on interesting interactions or problems.

Table 14-1 shows the pros and cons of each of the three usability testing methods.

Table 14-1	Usability Testing Method		
Attribute	**Lab-Based**	**Remote Moderated**	**Remote Unmoderated**
Geographic Diversity	Con: Limited to one location.	Pro: Users from anywhere in the world can participate.	Pro: Users can participate when it's convenient.
		Con: Time zone difference can limit participation.	

Attribute	Lab-Based	Remote Moderated	Remote Unmoderated
Recruiting	Con: More difficult because the geographic pool is limited.	Pro: No geographic limitation. Con: Sessions tend to run long.	Pro: No geographic limitation and short sessions.
Sample Quality	Pro: Limited to people willing to take time out of day. Tight control over user activity.	Pro: Able to recruit specialized users at minor inconvenience and can view all interactions.	Con: Often attracts people who are in it for the honorarium.
Qualitative Insights	Pro: Direct observation of both interface and user reactions. Facilitator can easily probe issues.	Pro: Direct observation of interface and limited user reactions. Facilitator can ask follow-up questions and engage in a dialogue.	Pro: If session is recorded, then direct observation of interface. Con: If no recording, insights are gleaned from answers to specific questions.
Sample Size	Con: More restricted due to geographic limitation and time.	Pro: Restricted by time to run studies but more flexible hours of scheduling.	Pro: Easy to run large sample sizes (100+).
Costs	Con: Higher compensation costs for users and facilitator time.	Pro: User compensation is lower and requires less facilitation time.	Pro: Compensation is cheap, and doesn't require facilitation or lab costs.

Finding and Reporting Usability Problems

When you have a usability test, one of your primary goals will be to find and fix as many usability problems as you can.

Follow these steps to uncover usability problems:

1. **Record the undesirable outcome.**

   Did users make a mistake, not notice an element, take a long time to complete a task, or fail to complete the task altogether? These actions are symptoms, but not guarantees of usability problems. Errors are undesirable, but they aren't necessarily caused by a problem with the interface (think typos). Both first-time and experienced users commit errors.

2. **Identify what in the interface is causing the problem.**

   Sometimes it's obvious (maybe users don't know what an icon means), but other times, knowing the context, what the user was doing, and what he was asked to do is essential for extracting a usability problem.

3. **Determine if the issue is global or local.**

   It can often be helpful to identify whether a problem affects the entire interface or just a section of it. For example, if users have problems turning on filters on a mobile TV app, it's likely local to the filtering functionality. However, if users don't understand what a name in the global navigation on a website means, it'll affect the entire website experience.

   Just because an issue is local doesn't make it less important. Rather, it helps you and the design team understand both the scope of the problem and the potential impact of the change.

4. **Assign a severity rating.**

   You want to separate the catastrophic problems from the cosmetic ones. One of the best ways is to assign a severity rating, from minor (1) to major (3). Most usability studies will reveal a lot of problems, many of which can't be addressed. The severity ratings help prioritize what to fix first.

5. **Recommend possible solutions, if appropriate.**

   Every usability issue doesn't have to have a proposed solution, but if there is an obvious fix, then suggest it or implement it if you're in charge of the development. You can often recommend solutions when a new design can fix multiple issues. Usability problem descriptions should be usable and useful. Often just a well-described usability problem can help developers generate ideas for design alternatives.

6. **Present usability problems.**

   While the "right" way to find and present usability problems will depend on the purpose of the study (finding and fixing versus comparing to previously identified problems), it's ultimately about balancing priorities, design, and business constraints to determine what to fix. Providing a list of usability problems is the simplest and most straightforward approach to presenting usability problems. Include the percent of users who encountered each problem and the assigned severity.

For example, in a usability test of a new email program that tested six users, here are four problems found, with the percent of users who encountered the issues, and the interpretation of each issue's severity (on a 3-point scale: 1 = Minor, 2 = Moderate, 3 = Severe).

Percentage of Users	*Severity*	*Description*
67	2: Moderate	Participants were confused that you can only drag and drop after clicking a check box, not by clicking anywhere within the email cell.
67	2: Moderate	Participants had trouble locating the "Add Contact" button.
67	2: Moderate	It was not immediately clear that the envelope icon means send an email.
50	1: Minor	Participants expected the email to show full screen instead of split screen.

Add screen shots, videos, and additional descriptions to help everyone understand the issues — especially if the usability issues are controversial. To aid comprehension, include a simplified problem list at the beginning of a report and a more detailed follow-up section with screen shots to provide the necessary context.

You can also chart your users and problems. In Figure 14-3, the users are numbered on the *y*-axis (1 to 30) and the issues have each been given a number (1 to 28) and sorted from most to least frequent. Each black square represents which user encountered which problem. You can compute such matrices by task or across tasks for the whole usability test.

Displaying problems in a type of matrix allows you to see three problems from three perspectives:

- ✔ **Frequency by problem:** For example, the most common problem (far left) involved users having trouble adding a GPS navigation to their rental (they had to do it after they entered their personal details). This problem impacted 24 out of 30 users (80%). You can be 95% confident between 62% and 91% of all users would also have this problem. (See Chapter 2 for a refresher on confidence intervals.)

- ✔ **Frequency by user:** The first user in the matrix encountered 9 of the 28 problems (32%), while user 28 encountered only 1 problem (3%), and users 29 and 30 encountered no problems while renting the car.

- ✔ **Problems that affected only one user (the long tail of usability problems):** The last nine problems were encountered by only a single user (3%).

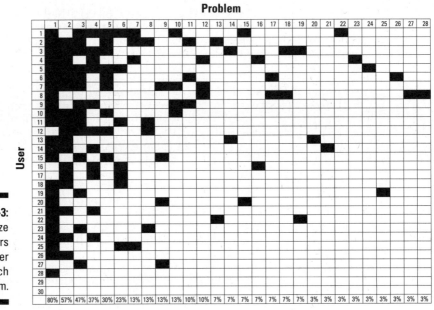

Figure 14-3:
Visualize
which users
encounter
which
problem.

What 3 users can tell you that 3,000 cannot

Just because you have a small sample size doesn't mean you can't identify major problems with a customer's experience. Software company Autodesk had a problem with a software download. The company noticed a large spike in customer support calls related to a trial version of AutoCAD. A usability study was set up to observe how customers downloaded the software from the website.

During the study, 3 out of 11 customers unknowingly downloaded the wrong version of the software. Not until several minutes into the installation did they encounter a problem — a bizarre error message telling them their operating system wasn't supported.

This message led customers to call the support line. It turns out that these users were confused about which version of software to choose from the layout of the trial download page.

Using confidence intervals, the company could be 90% confident that somewhere between 11% and 52% of all customers would be also struggling with this design element. In other words, with just 11 users, it could virtually be certain at least 1 out of 10 customers would have a problem and that many of them would call support.

Remember: It's easier to detect that a product experience is unusable with a small sample size than it is to conclude that the product experience is usable. More common problems will come up in a test with just a few participants, indicating an unusable experience. However, just because you don't observe a problem with a small sample doesn't mean that the product is usable. There can be problems but they may affect a smaller percentage of users. You can't be as confident the product experience is usable with a small sample size.

Facilitating a Usability Study

Facilitating a usability test takes practice, interpersonal skills, and the ability to juggle many things at once in order to collect data from a test participant. Here are some guidelines for facilitating a moderated usability test:

✔ **Be prepared to listen.** You need to talk to moderate a session, but don't let the talking get in the way of discovering.

Like in any relationship, you've got to know

- When to talk

- When to listen

- When to move on

✔ **Don't lead the user.** Even if a user asks if she "did it right" or is going down the wrong path and asks, "Is this the right way?" try and deflect such questions by asking back, "What would your inclination be?" or "Where would you go to look for that?"

✔ **Don't put the participant on the defensive.** One of your goals as a facilitator is to get into the heads of your customers as they use the product. You need to know why users are clicking in different areas or not understanding a term or concept, for instance. It's only natural to ask users why they did something. Instead of directly asking, "Why did you click that link?" ask "What about the link led you to click on it?" This will get the participant thinking about her motivations and mental models and not feeling defensive and respond with less helpful "because I thought I was supposed to go there." Balancing question asking without putting the user on the defensive takes some practice.

✔ **Probe users about interaction problems between tasks.** If you wait until after a participant is done, then you get an accurate reading of how long a task takes and you don't interrupt the user or inadvertently suggest ideas on how to complete a task.

✔ **Have a note taker and separate facilitator, if possible.** The facilitator is often kept busy asking follow-up questions, troubleshooting technical issues, answering user questions, and keeping the study on track. It's easy to miss valuable insights if one person is performing both functions.

✔ **Review the observations and problems after each user.** Review the issues when they're fresh — with another person, such as a note taker or stakeholder. It helps get the problem list out faster and allows you confirm or deny hypotheses about what's causing problems and what might fix them with your next set of users.

✔ **Record positive issues, suggestions, and usability problems.** Don't just collect the bad news. Collect those suggestions and positive comments and features that go smoothly. Although a development team will often want to get right to the problems, most will also appreciate that users and usability professionals aren't all gloom and doom.

✔ **Illustrate issues using screen shots and categorize problems.** Sorting problems into logical groups such as "buttons," "navigation," and "labels," along with a good picture, can really help with digesting long lists. Figure 14-4 shows responses to open-ended questions about what problems users had while renting a car. The open-ended comments were categorized and then charted. The vertical lines show the 90% confidence intervals around each percentage of comments (See Chapter 2 for a reminder on converting qualitative data to quantitative data and adding confidence intervals). The two biggest issues uncovered in the comments are from participants having problems finding the total price of the rental car ("Totaling") or finding the GPS and car seat to add on to the rental ("Finding Extras").

✔ **Use highlight videos.** Small clips of the most common usability problems or illustrative examples are helpful for stakeholders who rarely have time to view videos in their entirety.

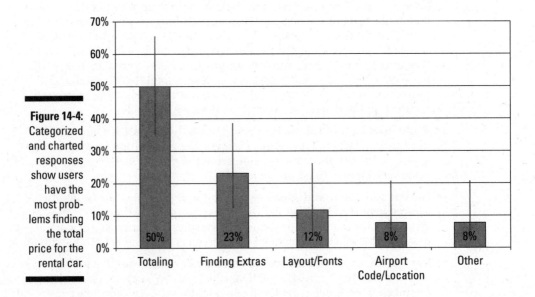

Figure 14-4: Categorized and charted responses show users have the most problems finding the total price for the rental car.

Comparative usability test of Enterprise and Budget.com

Here's how a comparative usability study between two rental car companies, Budget and Enterprise, was conducted.

Study Goals

How well prospective and current customers can use the websites, which websites customers preferred, and what problems customers encountered while trying to find the price of a rental car.

Participants

Asked 62 qualified participants (people who had rented a car online in the last year) to complete two tasks on both websites. Half the participants attempted the tasks on Budget first and the other half on Enterprise first.

Method

Unmoderated remote testing setup using software from UserZoom, with audio and video recordings.

Tasks

Two tasks were created.

✔ Find the nearest location.

Find the address of the nearest rental office to the Hilton Hotel located at 921 SW Sixth Avenue, Portland, Oregon, United States 97204. Write down or copy the name of the street of the nearest location.

✔ Rent a car.

Location: Logan Airport, Boston, MA

Rental Period: Friday, April, 13, 2012, at 11:00 a.m. to Sunday, April 15, at 5:00 p.m.

Class: Intermediate (No SUVs)

Extras: GPS navigation and car seat for a 2-year-old

If asked, use the following identification:

Name: John Smith

Email: john112233@mailinator.com

Phone: 303-555-1212

Credit Card: Visa

The total price for the rental determines if participants were successful in picking the right class of car, for the right dates and the add-ons.

Study Metrics

Brand attitude and usage were collected before the study and perceptions of website quality were collected at the end of the study.

Task Metrics

Completion Rate: The participants provided the correct price of the rental car from a list of options. If participants selected the correct price, it was coded as a 1; incorrect answers were coded as a 0.

Task Time: How long participants spent on each website.

Task Difficulty: Participants rated how easy or difficult the experience was; 1 = Very Difficult to 7 = Very Easy.

Results

Task-Based Metrics Results

Completion Rate: If users can't complete a task successfully, then not much else matters. In both cases, Budget had higher completion rates. The completion rate on finding the price of a rental car was statistically higher with a completion rate over twice as high as Enterprise. (Refer to Figure 14-4.)

(continued)

(continued)

Task Time: The data shows that customers took statistically longer to complete both tasks on Enterprise than on Budget.

Task Difficulty: Users found it easier to find a location and to rent a car on Budget. The difference was also statistically significant.

These three task-based metrics were combined into a Single Usability Metrics (SUM), which averages together each attribute of usability, as shown in the following figure. It provides a single view that shows Budget had a more usable experience.

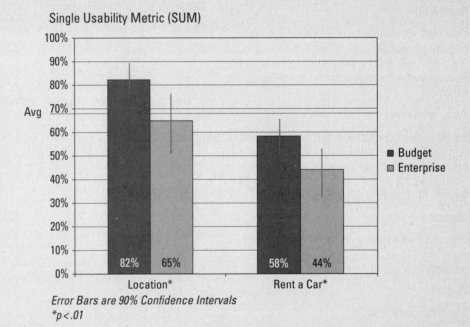

Single Usability Metric (SUM)

Error Bars are 90% Confidence Intervals
*p<.01

Click Maps

UserZoom provided a heat map showing where users clicked first. The heat map for Enterprise (refer to Figure 14-2) showed only a small fraction of users looked in the correct place — in the Rent a Car menu in the upper-left corner, suggesting problems with labels and navigation. (See Chapter 15 for more on findability.)

The heat map for the Budget website showed a substantial portion of participants correctly clicked the Location tab and most participants (84%) successfully found the nearest location.

Study-Based Metrics Results

SUPR-Q scores summarizing the participants' perception of the quality of the experience are shown in the following figure. Scores were overwhelmingly more favorable for Budget than for Enterprise. This was also reflected in the Net Promoter Score (NPS). Not surprisingly, participants preferred Budget over Enterprise by more than a 3:1 ratio.

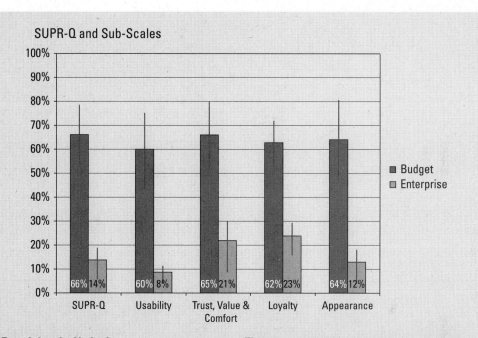

SUPR-Q and Sub-Scales

Examining the Verbatims

Here are a few comments users made during this study while on the Enterprise website.

It didn't give the whole total with the extras; I had to add that myself.

*Took the price of the car and manually added on 3-day price of car seat ($10.99*3) and same for GPS but still unsure of total because unsure if these items are taxed.*

I saw no area to add the extras.

I saw no way to add GPS or child seat.

These open-ended comments were categorized into groups and charted in Figure 14-4. The two biggest issues, and areas for improvement, are fixing the total price of the rental and finding the GPS and car seat to add on to the rental. Correcting both problems will likely improve the metrics and the customers' experience with the website.

For more details of this study, read the online article at www.measuringu.com/blog/benchmark-website-usability.php

Chapter 15

Measuring Findability and Navigation

*I*f customers can't find what they're looking for on your website — say your navigation is poor or your search function isn't working — customers will move on and find what they're looking for with another company. All your effort in regards to pricing, features, marketing, and packaging won't matter; the end result will be a lost opportunity. Your customers have to be able to find things quickly and easily.

In this chapter, I show you how to determine what customers are trying to find, then how to measure their capability to find the items (findability). I also give you ways to improve your findability and then measure whether changes you've made actually improve your findability.

 While this chapter mostly talks about websites, findability is more that just your website. It pertains to wherever customers interact with your company. That could be software or mobile apps they're navigating, or how you display products in your bricks-and-mortar store. You can apply the information in this chapter to every area of your company.

Finding Your Areas of Findability

If you've ever looked for a product on a website, tried to change the settings on your iPhone, hunted for food in a supermarket, or searched for a movie on cable TV, you have some idea about findability.

Findability is the percent of items that a customer can find successfully, how quickly items are found, and how much difficulty customers have in locating an item.

Customers expect quick and easy access to products and information. How do customers find items on your website? Take a critical eye to these areas of your website:

- ✔ **Search boxes:** Search functions are vital to visitors finding what they want.

- ✔ **Categories:** If you categorize your items and label each category appropriately, then visitors can find what they're looking for.

 You can offer categories in the form of links that visitors can click through or offer drop-down lists that visitors can drill down to find what they're looking for. Categories (called navigation) are usually listed on the left or right side of the page for quick access.

- ✔ **Breadcrumb links:** Breadcrumb links are useful navigation tools so visitors don't get lost in your website. These links show visitors the path they've taken to get to the page they're currently viewing. These are generally links at the top or bottom of the page that matches the navigation, and visitors can click to move back to where they've been in the path.

- ✔ **Suggested items:** If you already know a customer is interested in a product — based on a search term or past browsing (or buying) history — you can also offer a list of similar products. Something in that list might be exactly what your customer is looking for.

Figure 15-1 shows how one popular company, Amazon, uses these navigation features to enhance its findability.

The capability to find the right item or function can mean the difference between a potential customer completing a sale or moving on to another website. You have to make sure that your findability is as good as it can be in order to prevent losing those customers.

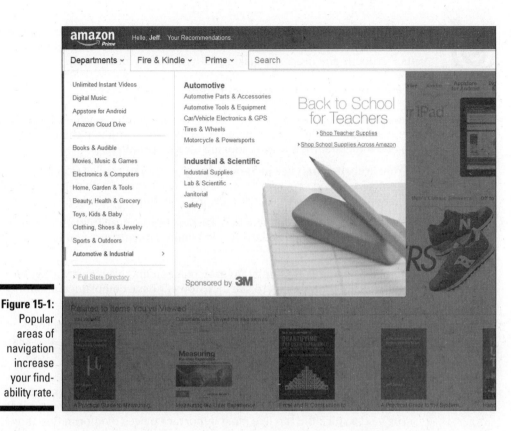

Figure 15-1:
Popular
areas of
navigation
increase
your find-
ability rate.

Identifying What Customers Want

The first step in understanding findability is to know what your customers are looking for. If you have a diverse customer base, you need to identify a target segment and persona to use for your findability study. Check out Chapters 4 and 5 to split your customer base into segments and then create a persona for each segment.

If you have a diverse customer base that buys different products, you'll need to conduct your findability study for each target segment.

Identify a good cross-section of products or pieces of information that your target segment would likely look for on the website. Although you might have thousands of products, pages, and content, you don't need to be comprehensive; just pick a representative sample.

Narrow the list to no more than 30 items. You should only ask participants in a study to spend no more than around 30 minutes. Anything more and participants lose focus and drop out, making data collection more costly.

Here are some ideas on how to identify those items:

- ✔ **Search logs:** See what users are searching for on the website's internal search function. If customers are searching for a product, then it's a good indication that they're looking for that product.

- ✔ **Your website analytics program:** Analytics programs like Google Analytics provide key words and traffic logs to see which pages are most visited and what external search words customers are using.

- ✔ **Purchase records:** Products that are purchased more frequently will have the most traffic, and even small improvements in findability can result in substantially higher revenue.

- ✔ **Comments and complaints:** An easy place to find problems with your categorization system is to see if customers have complained about not being able to locate items.

- ✔ **Your existing customers:** Ask customers to pick their top five products or things they look for when browsing or purchasing. You can also ask them which product, if any, they recall looking for and whether they were able to find it.

  You can ask website visitors to take a 5-minute survey using a website intercept. Questions to ask could be who they were, why they were visiting, and to pick the top five most important pieces of information they want to locate on the website.

- ✔ **New and known issues:** Sometimes you'll know that items can't be found. In other cases, you have a new product that you'll want to know if customers can find.

  For example, maybe you have a seasonal item that you only offer during certain times of the year. You know ahead of time that visitors might not be able to find the item or not know that you carry it (because it's seasonal), and you can figure out ways to make it more findable.

People usually search for products by category (for example, barbeque grills) and by brand (for example, Weber Grill). Look at existing customer data to see how customers search for items. If they use brands or generic categories when searching, you'll want to use the same terms because you're measuring findability.

Prepping for a Findability Test

Before you can launch your findability study, you have to do some things to prepare for it. You need to know what your existing findability is — after all, you need to know where you're at *now* to know what changes you need to make your findability and navigation better in the future. Setting up your existing navigation in a tree test can aid in your findability study. These tasks set you up for a successful findability study.

Finding your baseline

You need to find what your existing findability rate is — *baseline findability* — for items before you start making changes. You need to understand how well customers can find the items using your existing navigation structure. It's important to know how findable items are now so that when you make changes to labels, names, and navigation structures you have something to compare them to. Make sure you aren't making it harder for customers to find products!

For a baseline findability study, you need participants who represent your customer base to try to locate a typical set of items using your current website navigation. The resulting metrics will become your baseline findability.

You may think that customers always use the search box on your website. But research I've conducted shows that around half of customers start with a "browse-first" approach on most websites.

Although the fonts, layout, colors, and overall look and feel of a website play a major role in helping or hindering customers from finding items, isolate problems with the *taxonomy* — the order, labels, structure, and hierarchy of categories that contain the products or information — as a separate issue from navigation. After you have a good navigation structure, you can then test the design and know that the navigation is likely not the culprit causing problems.

Designing the study

For electronic product searches (websites, software, mobile apps), the best way to test findability is to replicate your existing navigation structure into a tree test. It's called a tree test because it looks like a tree trunk and branches, much like old versions of Windows Explorer.

While you can conduct a tree test using pencil and paper, the most efficient way to test a navigation structure is using software. Software can streamline the process by automating a lot of the functions and doing the hard work for you. You can find software from companies like UserZoom (`www.userzoom.com`) and Optimal Workshop (`www.optimalworkshop.com`).

The following steps show you how to conduct a tree test using UserZoom:

1. **Replicate your website navigation structure.**

   This should be the top two to three levels of your navigation structure. Figure 15-2 shows the navigation structure for the National Multiple Sclerosis Society replicated in UserZoom.

   About MS
   Living with MS
   Treating MS
      Symptoms
      New Treatments
      Diet and Exercise
      Medications
      Adherence
      Exacerbations
      Rehabilitation
      Complementary & Alternative Medicine
      Clinical Trials
      Research News
   Community & Support
   Get Involved
   News & Research
   Events
   Donate
   Find a Local Chapter

Figure 15-2: A navigation structure in UserZoom mirroring the actual navigation from the website.

2. **Add the items you want to test, and the search terms visitors typically use to find those items.**

   To understand what items visitors were looking for, review the page views and search logs for what pages and terms were the most popular, ask the web and content teams for what kind of content people typically want, and conduct a survey on the website. If you aren't sure what your customers are looking for, see the earlier section "Identifying What Customers Want."

3. **Identify the correct paths users should take to find each item.**

   As part of the study setup, identify which locations (the leaves in the tree) are correct paths users can take to find the information. The software tracks the paths users take and compares them to the paths you've identified as correct. Figure 15-3 shows the navigation tree with the correct paths identified.

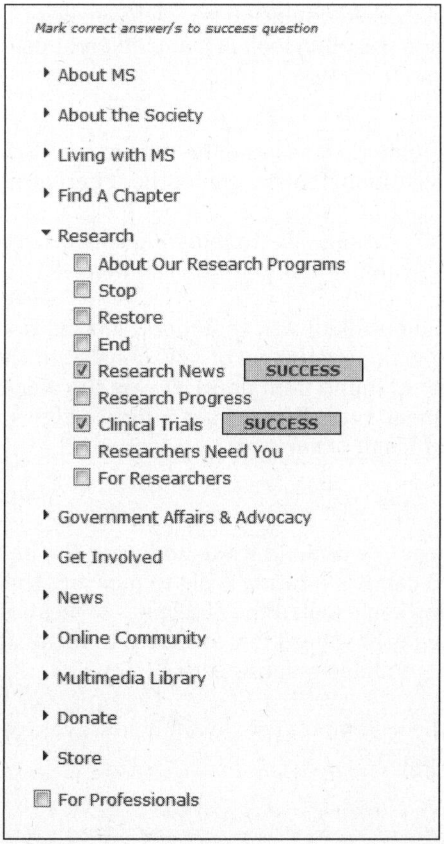

Mark correct answer/s to success question

▸ About MS

▸ About the Society

▸ Living with MS

▸ Find A Chapter

▾ Research
    ☐ About Our Research Programs
    ☐ Stop
    ☐ Restore
    ☐ End
    ☑ Research News   **SUCCESS**
    ☐ Research Progress
    ☑ Clinical Trials   **SUCCESS**
    ☐ Researchers Need You
    ☐ For Researchers

▸ Government Affairs & Advocacy

▸ Get Involved

▸ News

▸ Online Community

▸ Multimedia Library

▸ Donate

▸ Store

☐ For Professionals

Figure 15-3: Paths that users should take to find items are mapped.

Looking at your findability metrics

Before you launch your findability study, you need to know which data UserZoom collects for your baseline metrics. I discuss the most common metrics in the following sections.

Findability

Your key metric is findability or findability rate: whether the customer successfully finds the product or piece of information successfully. This is just like the completion rate in a usability study (see Chapter 14). Did the customer find the intended item (yes/no)? This answer gets coded as 1 for Found and 0 for Not Found. For example, if 70 out of 100 participants found the item, then the findability rate is 70%.

An item can live in multiple places, so double-check "right answers." Remember: Participants and real customers will often look in many different places.

Time to find

If you ask users to locate an item, they assume the item can be found. Otherwise, why would you ask them? This is one of the inherent biases in findability testing. If users eventually find the item but it takes them a long time, then you have a findability issue. The tree-testing software records how long it takes participants to locate (or fail to locate) an item.

The median time on task is an excellent way to understand the average time it takes participants. To also gain perspective of how consistent the experience is, look at the variability of found item times. Divide the standard deviation of the task time by the mean time. High values indicate high variability (this metric is called the *coefficient of variation*).

Task Difficulty

If you ask participants how easy or difficult it was to locate the item after they finish looking for it, you can use a rating scale to measure the perceived difficulty. A seven-point rating scale called the Single Ease Question (SEQ) (discussed in Chapter 9) gauges how hard it is for users to locate items. So if there are 12 items to locate, you have responses to 12 items.

Scores below about a 6 on the seven-point scale are below average in ease (and therefore are more difficult).

Open-Ended responses

If participants rate an item as relatively difficult to locate, you can ask them to describe in their own words the problem they encountered. These remarks become excellent ideas for improving the navigation and findability. They help provide the "why" behind the numbers.

Card sorting

If you want to test how clear your category labels are, ask participants to sort your items into their own categories and then label them (a technique called *card sorting*). Check responses against the way you have your categories labeled, which can help you understand the thought process your customers use in finding products.

National Multiple Sclerosis Society

The National Multiple Sclerosis Society (NMSS) wanted to redesign its website. Members and visitors loved the wealth of information that the NMSS maintained online, but had trouble finding information when they needed it. Instead of just starting with a brand new website with a new navigation structure, the NMSS conducted a findability study in UserZoom. First, it measured the baseline findability.

To understand what items visitors were looking for, page views and search logs for what pages and terms were the most popular were reviewed. The web and content teams were asked to create a list of information that people typically want. In total, people were looking for 64 pieces of information, including information about newly approved medications, information about specific symptoms, and ways of sharing information via social media.

To reduce the items for website visitors to find, the NMSS needed input from qualified participants. It's difficult to find participants in the MS community from a panel agency, so the society used a website intercept launched from its website (www.nmss.org). For two weeks, website visitors were asked to answer a five-minute survey about who they were and why they were visiting, and to pick the top five most important pieces of information they wanted to locate on the website. In total, data was collected from 1,300 website visitors using their desktop computers or mobile devices (tablets or smartphones).

Ranked in order, the top ten items were selected for the findability study. The terms the visitors used in the tasks were added into the UserZoom software for testing.

The discovery: 77% of participants found the location for information around new treatments, a reasonably high findability rate, as shown in the first figure. In comparison, only 44% found the information about vitamin D as a treatment, and an even smaller number of participants, only 9%, located information around financial assistance programs. Both these tasks have high difficulty ratings as well, which isn't surprising: the NMSS already knew the items were difficult for participants to find. But it did find out that although the New Treatments task had relatively high findability at 77%, participants thought it was about average in difficulty, as shown in the second figure. To find out how these problems were fixed, see the "Improving Findability" section.

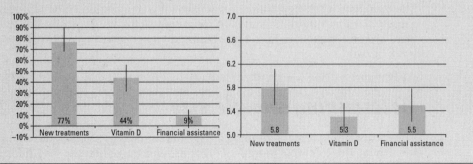

Conducting Your Findability Study

When you have your tree test set up the way you want it, you can add profile and demographic questions to the beginning or end of your study. You can also ask participants which items they found the most difficult to locate. Figure 15-4 shows a schematic for a typical tree test.

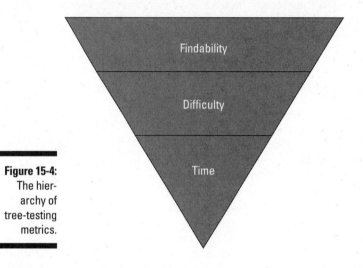

Figure 15-4:
The hier-
archy of
tree-testing
metrics.

Findability

Difficulty

Time

WARNING!

Be careful about what you ask your participants so they don't feel like you're invading their privacy. If you ask for income, age, or other personal questions, consider making these questions optional if it makes a difference between someone continuing your study and opting out.

The total time it takes to collect responses for a tree test depends on your sample size and how difficult it is to recruit participants. Typically, you need 50 to 300 participants to take a tree test and you collect the data within a week or two.

Determining sample size

The ideal sample size for running a baseline findability study is based on identifying the tolerable margin of error around the estimate (see Chapter 2 for a reminder on the margin of error). The following minitable, which is derived using the margin of error from a 50% binary (yes/no) response question, shows the approximate sample size needed to achieve a specific margin of error.

Margin of Error	90% Confidence (+/-)
24%	10
20%	15
15%	28
14%	32
13%	38
12%	45
11%	54
10%	65
9%	81
8%	103
7%	136
6%	186
5%	268
4%	421
3%	749

For example, if 103 customers completed a tree-test study and 50% found an item, you can be 90% confident the percentage of all customers locating the item in the tree test would be between 42% and 58%.

Recruiting users

Like a usability study or survey, you need to find qualified participants who represent your customer base, and then have them attempt to locate items. Generally, you can find customers to participate in a findability study in three places:

> ✔ **Customer lists:** If you keep lists of current customer contact information and have permission to contact them, then you can simply ask, and usually, you compensate these customers to participate in a study.

✔ **Panel agencies:** Companies such as Op4G (http://op4g.com), Toluna (www.toluna-group.com), and Research Now (www.researchnow. com) have active panels of millions of people with a range of profiles that mimic the U.S. or international populations. You provide these companies with the type of customer you want and then pay per completed study.

Panel agencies recruit physicians, engineers, IT administrators, CFOs, attorneys, and small-business owners to participate in findability studies. You can also recruit based on habits, such as people who have a Costco membership or who have recently purchased a car.

✔ **Website intercepts:** For testing website navigation, one of the best places to find qualified participants is from customers actively visiting the website. Using a pop-up intercept from companies like UserZoom (www.userzoom. com) and Ethnio (http://ethn.io), a simple line of code will pop up and ask website visitors to participate in a study. It will even redirect them to an online study, allowing for virtual real-time data collection.

Analyzing the results

With the data collected, summarize the findability metrics by task: findability, task difficulty, and task time.

1. **Calculate the findability rate as your first (or *gateway*) metric.**

   If users can't even locate the item, then it's a findability issue. While it's unrealistic to expect 100% of participants to find each item, you should aim for findability rates in the high 80%–90% range. Figure 15-5 shows findability rates for products on Target's website. Around half the products had reasonable findability rates, with a few, including the Wildkin Kaleidoscope Backpack, had very low findability rates.

   A high findability rate doesn't mean participants think an item is necessarily easy to locate. Participants may still take a long time or found the number of steps or choices too difficult. Finding an item is necessary but not sufficient to achieve high findability.

2. **Examine how difficult it was to find the item by looking at the average score to the difficulty question.**

   For 7-point rating scales, the average score should be above a 6 — that's the average level of difficulty. Figure 15-6 shows the perceived difficulty of finding the same items. Even though nine items had findability rates above 50%, only four items had difficulty ratings that were above average. These lower-rated items are good candidates for you to improve their findability.

3. **Calculate the median time to find the item.**

For the participants who did find the item successfully, compute the median time to find the item. The median is the middle value of a set of times. It can be found using the Excel function =Median(). While the actual time it should take to find an item depends on the complexity of the tree, aim for times to be less than 30 seconds.

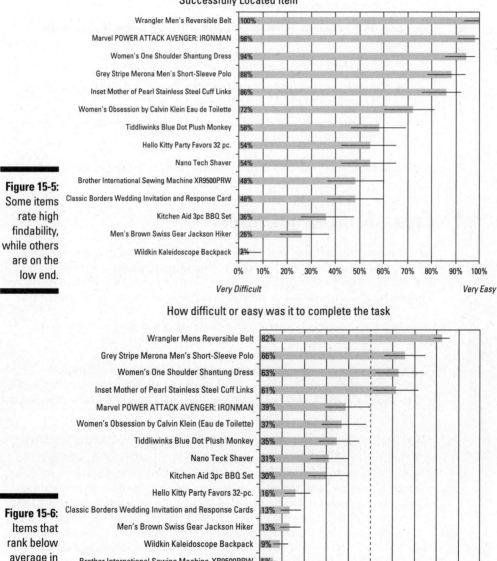

Successfully Located Item

Item	%
Wrangler Men's Reversible Belt	100%
Marvel POWER ATTACK AVENGER: IRONMAN	98%
Women's One Shoulder Shantung Dress	94%
Grey Stripe Merona Men's Short-Sleeve Polo	88%
Inset Mother of Pearl Stainless Steel Cuff Links	86%
Women's Obsession by Calvin Klein Eau de Toilette	72%
Tiddliwinks Blue Dot Plush Monkey	58%
Hello Kitty Party Favors 32 pc.	54%
Nano Tech Shaver	54%
Brother International Sewing Machine XR9500PRW	48%
Classic Borders Wedding Invitation and Response Card	48%
Kitchen Aid 3pc BBQ Set	36%
Men's Brown Swiss Gear Jackson Hiker	26%
Wildkin Kaleidoscope Backpack	2%

Very Difficult — *Very Easy* (0% to 100%)

Figure 15-5: Some items rate high findability, while others are on the low end.

How difficult or easy was it to complete the task

Item	%
Wrangler Mens Reversible Belt	82%
Grey Stripe Merona Men's Short-Sleeve Polo	66%
Women's One Shoulder Shantung Dress	63%
Inset Mother of Pearl Stainless Steel Cuff Links	61%
Marvel POWER ATTACK AVENGER: IRONMAN	39%
Women's Obsession by Calvin Klein (Eau de Toilette)	37%
Tiddliwinks Blue Dot Plush Monkey	35%
Nano Teck Shaver	31%
Kitchen Aid 3pc BBQ Set	30%
Hello Kitty Party Favors 32-pc.	16%
Classic Borders Wedding Invitation and Response Cards	13%
Men's Brown Swiss Gear Jackson Hiker	13%
Wildkin Kaleidoscope Backpack	9%
Brother International Sewing Machine-XR9500PRW	5%

Very Difficult — *Very Easy* (0% to 100%)

Figure 15-6: Items that rank below average in difficulty are areas to improve.

Percentages are normalized percentile ranks from across 200 tasks. 50% = Average.

Improving Findability

When you've collected all your baseline data, it's time to do something about improving the findability. Here's how to dissect the information gleaned from your tree-testing software:

1. **Look for items that were hardest to find.**

2. **Look for items that were rated more difficult (even if they were found).**

3. **Look for items where users took too long to locate.**

   Anything that takes over a minute to find is too long; ideally items should take less than 30 seconds to find.

4. **Examine the open-ended responses participants provided to see why items are difficult to find.**

In the following sections, I offer insights into how to fix the issues you find.

Cross-linking products

Tree-testing software tells you not only whether customers found the item, but also the paths they took, as well as the paths taken by customers who didn't successfully find the items. Look to see where customers are going and if possible, add a cross-link or recategorize your products or information.

Cross-linking is especially useful for websites and software where you don't need to physically place items.

For example, in a baseline findability study with the National Multiple Sclerosis Society's website, only 12% of participants found the correct location for financial assistance information — one of the top reasons people visit the website.

Figure 15-7 shows the output from part of the tree test. The correct location was "Society Programs and Services," as indicated with the checkmark and box. The first percentage shows that 12% of participants at some point considered this option, and the second percentage, 9%, shows the percentage of participants who ultimately selected this as the location. In looking at the options immediately above the Society and Program Services, a substantial percentage (44%) selected Insurance and Money Matters as the place they'd expect to find information on financial assistance programs. Adding a cross-link from Insurance and Money Matters or moving the content solves the problem.

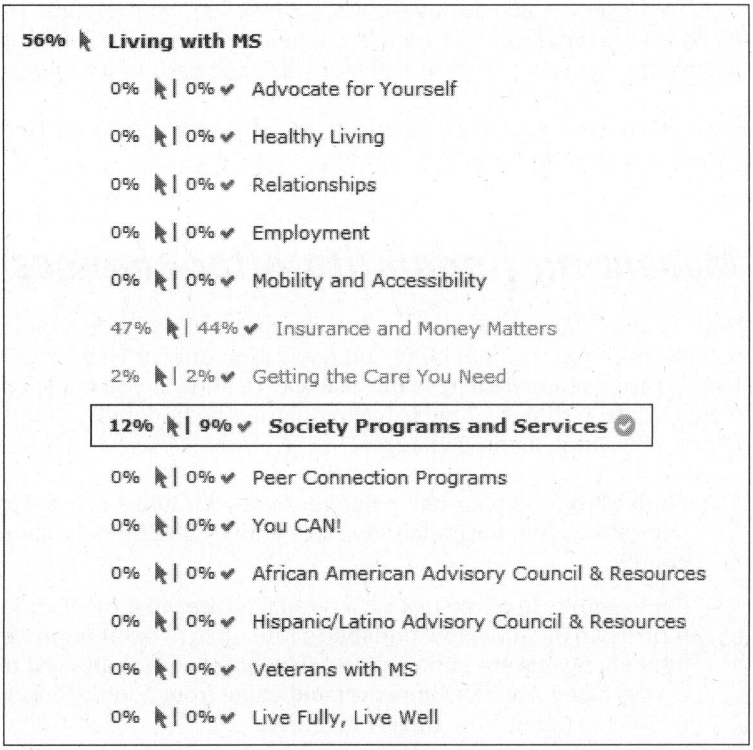

56% ↖ **Living with MS**

0% ↖ | 0% ✔ Advocate for Yourself

0% ↖ | 0% ✔ Healthy Living

0% ↖ | 0% ✔ Relationships

0% ↖ | 0% ✔ Employment

0% ↖ | 0% ✔ Mobility and Accessibility

47% ↖ | 44% ✔ Insurance and Money Matters

2% ↖ | 2% ✔ Getting the Care You Need

12% ↖ | 9% ✔ **Society Programs and Services** ◉

0% ↖ | 0% ✔ Peer Connection Programs

0% ↖ | 0% ✔ You CAN!

0% ↖ | 0% ✔ African American Advisory Council & Resources

0% ↖ | 0% ✔ Hispanic/Latino Advisory Council & Resources

0% ↖ | 0% ✔ Veterans with MS

0% ↖ | 0% ✔ Live Fully, Live Well

Figure 15-7:
In this example, 44% of participants looked in a category that didn't have the right information.

Regrouping categories

One of the biggest problems you might have with findability is the category names you use. You might use jargon or terms that are familiar with you, but less so with your customers. Your customers can have problems navigating your website if your categories aren't labeled properly — for them, not you.

Tree-testing software can show you what your customers expect category names to be. A complementary method, called *card sorting,* helps identify labeling problems. With card sorting, users take your products and sort them into categories and then give their categories names. Look at those customer-provided names and consider changing or adding to your categories to aid in better navigation.

Rephrasing the tasks

Sometimes, low findability rates can be caused by participants not fully understanding what they are looking for. For example, gift cards are popular purchases on retail websites. In a target.com tree test, the most difficult item to find was the "Iconic Puppy Gift Card $5–$1,000." Participants were confused when looking for the item. In reading the comments, participants didn't know if the item they were looking for was a gift card or a $5 puppy!

If you get a lot of similar comments, try rephrasing your tasks to be sure participants understand what to look for.

Measuring findability after changes

Now it's time to find out whether the changes you've made to your navigation actually improve the findability and navigation of your website. Here's where having the baseline data pays off. The way to know if you made improvements or made things worse is by comparing the findability of the same items after you've implemented changes.

- ✔ **Findability:** Did your users find more of your items using your new navigation? Aim for findability rates above 70% (but any improvement is good!).

  For example, in a tree test on a retail website, an item of children's furniture had an initial low findability rate of 29%, but it improved to 74% after changes were implemented. The baseline test showed users split across categories; the improvement came from adding links to the correct department from those categories.

  Figure 15-8 shows the 90% confidence intervals for the percent of users who found the item before and after the change. The difference was both statistically significant (p <.01) and practically significant (the findability rate more than doubled!). See the appendix for what p-values are and how to interpret them when comparing two percentages.

- ✔ **Difficulty:** Did users find it less difficult to find the items? You should find overall that the difficulty rate went from harder than average to easier than average.

  Figure 15-9 shows the perceived difficulty of finding the children's furniture using the rating scale of difficulty. Higher scores indicate an easier experience finding the item, compared to hundreds of other tasks. Before the findability fixes, the item scored easier than 37% of all tasks. After the change, the perceived ease score was easier than 59% of all tasks in the database.

  As with measuring the user experience in general, measuring findability in particular involves multiple metrics and multiple methods to show a quantifiable better navigation.

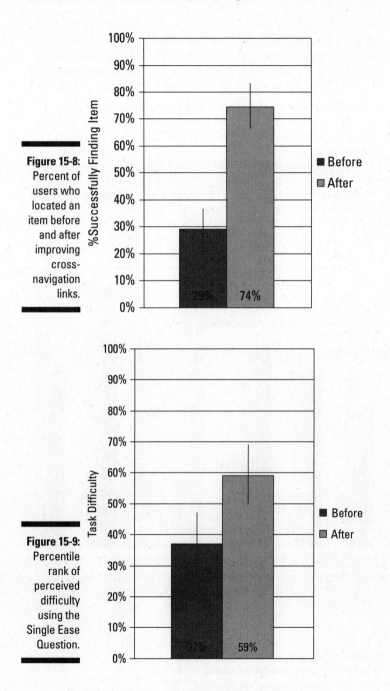

Figure 15-8:
Percent of
users who
located an
item before
and after
improving
cross-
navigation
links.

Figure 15-9:
Percentile
rank of
perceived
difficulty
using the
Single Ease
Question.

Figure 15-10 shows that only 1% of participants were able to locate a prom dress on a department store website using the old category "Guys and Juniors." After changing the category to "Teens," based on the input from participants in a card-sorting study, the findability rate improved to 74%!

✔ **Task time:** When users located the item both before and after the change, were they able to find it in the same amount of time or quicker after changes were made based on the first set of results? Figure 15-11 shows the median task time for three items found on a ski resort website. Customers were able to find vacation package deals faster on the improved navigation structure compared to the old. In the other two tasks, the times were not statistically different, suggesting changes that benefited one task didn't harm the others.

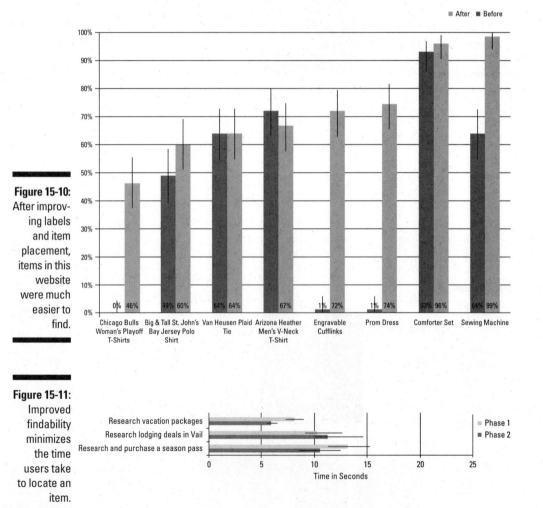

Figure 15-10:
After improving labels and item placement, items in this website were much easier to find.

Figure 15-11:
Improved findability minimizes the time users take to locate an item.

Chapter 16

Considering the Ethics of Customer Analytics

*I*n 1963, Yale Psychologist Stanley Milgram paid volunteers $4 to "teach" another volunteer new vocabulary words. If the learner got the words wrong, he or she received an electric shock! Or so the participants believed . . . no shocks were actually given. Regardless, a majority of participants believed that they were shocked, which led to a concern over the ethical treatment of study participants.

Even though no one is getting shock treatments for wrong answers anymore, the debate over ethical treatment continues. There will always be problems with the way some companies handle data, especially companies that exploit new technology that people aren't familiar with. But you can avoid being one of those companies.

If you don't treat your customers or study participants in a fair manner (or in a manner they expect), not only will you risk losing your current customers, but it also may turn loyal customers who are currently promoters into former customers who discourage others from purchasing or using a product or service.

Getting Informed Consent

In the years since the Milgram studies, it's become common to provide participants with an *informed consent* form. It lets participants know the general topic of the study, and informs them that they can stop (opt out) any time, regardless of what the experiment demands. Here's how you go about getting informed consent from your participants:

✔ **Get signatures.** Even when you're not conducting a lab-based study, you're collecting data from volunteers and subjecting them to questioning, analysis, and observation. If the data deals with sensitive information (financial data or other personal data), consider having them sign an informed consent document stating that they understand the purpose of the test, what their participation means, and what their remuneration (if any) is.

✔ **Offer a verbal explanation.** Whether or not you provide a formal document for participants to sign, always explain what participants will be asked to do (at least in high-level terms) and ask if participants understand or have questions.

✔ **Be as clear as possible.** A lot of user research happens well beyond the confines of a laboratory. No matter what environment you conduct your experiments in, always make it clear what users are volunteering for. New technology and methods can lead to a blurring of ethical lines.

✔ **Include how you are using their data.** Everyone always wants to know how his or her data is being used. Reassure participants that their data will remain private.

In the following sections, I discuss some interesting experiments conducted by well-known brands that ultimately went wrong because their users didn't understand what they were consenting to. I also explain how you can avoid the same mistakes.

Facebook

Early in 2014, Facebook made headlines for conducting a large-scale experiment on a small fraction of its billion users — small still being 700,000 users.

Users unknowingly had their newsfeeds manipulated for one week to show them either positive or negative postings. The results of the study showed that exposure to positive posts resulted in users producing positive posts, too. The same was true of the negative posts. In other words, emotional sentiments were contagious. Good news didn't lead to people feeling glum; it actually led them to feel better.

The results were quickly overshadowed by outrage over Facebook using information to manipulate users.

Facebook discloses the latitudes it can take in its privacy policy and terms of use, but few people read, much less understand, the implications of terms and conditions and privacy policies. For example, on average, customers spend just six seconds looking at the terms and conditions of their software products. These are documents that, if read in full, can take several minutes to read, so those six seconds probably represent the time it takes customers to click "Accept" without considering what they are consenting to.

The big takeaway for you is to always make sure your participants know they're agreeing to participate in a study, even if they sign a consent form. After all, those Facebook users all agreed to Facebook's terms of uses, but not many knew that meant Facebook could filter what they saw on their timelines.

OKCupid

The dating website OKCupid admitted that, among other things, it paired up people who were poor matches according to their dating algorithm. The results of the experiment suggested that the act of *telling* someone that she was a good match was as important as *actually being* a good match. Users were notified that they were involved in a study and were shown the correct compatibility percentages after it was concluded.

This sort of manipulation was likely covered under the terms and conditions the users agreed to when using the website. But just like with Facebook, most users probably didn't read or understand those terms and conditions.

Also, OKCupid told users about the study after it was over. To avoid the same mistake, be up front with customers about how information may be changed and give them a way to opt out. If you explain how the data manipulations and analysis will ultimately benefit them, you may have a high opt-in rate, and likely fewer irate customers.

Amazon and Orbitz

Amazon has been a pioneer of many things on the web. In 2000, it was revealed that Amazon was adjusting the pricing of some of its products based on past browsing behavior. So one customer would pay more or less than the next person who bought the same item.

Orbitz also came under fire for revealing that it prioritizes hotels based on data that showed Mac users were 40 percent more likely to book a 4- or 5-star hotel than PC users. Mac users would be shown more expensive alternatives when searching.

The line between using customer segments to personalize products and experiences is a fuzzy one. Be sure customers understand how recommendations will change based on their preferences or profile.

Mint.com

The financial planning website Mint.com invited some participants to use a new beta feature that separated business and personal accounts. After a year of collecting data from users who meticulously entered financial information, Mint.com turned off the feature without notice. Previously entered data and reports were no longer accessible. These actions were permissible under the terms of use.

Your takeaway is to always tell participants what you're doing with their data, and what access they'll have to their own data. Most people are reassured when their data ultimately remains under their control.

Deciding to Experiment

Most people understand that their actions and data are being monitored and used for commercial purposes. But you can minimize their concerns by following these tips:

- ✔ **Privacy/anonymity:** Where possible, ensure both privacy and anonymity. When you collect survey data or conduct a usability or findability study, avoid collecting personally identifiable information unless it's absolutely necessary. When it is, be sure the participant is informed and take effective measure to keep that information secure. The National Security Agency (NSA) has made headlines for how it has data on millions of Americans and that data is associated with names, Social Security Numbers, and addresses. In the commercial world, real names and identities are generally less important.

- ✔ **Disclosure:** At the very least, you need to disclose what you're doing — or might do — with user information. Write the language in the terms of use clearly. Avoid legalese that few understand.

- ✔ **Retention and access to customer data:** If you collect data from customers, especially data that requires labor (like providing content), make it available for those customers to download or use in other forms. The more sensitive the data (family photos, financial information, taxes), the more important it is. If that's not possible, make it clear up front.

Privacy, disclosure, and anonymity are necessary but not sufficient when your goal is to treat your participants in an ethical manner. You can take the additional step to make sure users comprehend what they're participating in. This gives users an opportunity to opt out of your study if they want to.

Test how well users actually understand the terms they're agreeing to. You can set up a study to assess how well participants comprehend the terms and conditions. For example, I worked with a large credit card issuer and presented several variations on wording and images so customers understood things like interest rates and fees. A series of open- and closed-ended questions was asked to assess their comprehension after being exposed to the terms. Terms were picked that led to the highest level of comprehension and helped iterate the language to write more understandable terms.

The popular practice of A/B testing is one of the most effective ways for website owners to understand which design elements lead to higher purchases, donations, or registration rates (see Chapter 10). But at what point does A/B testing — and other techniques that manipulate customers and their data — become unethical?

Professional organizations like the User Experience Professionals Association (UxPA) available at `http://www.usabilityprofessionals.org/about_upa/leadership/code_of_conduct.html` and Direct Marketing Association (DMA) have codes of conduct that offer a good guide for researchers (`https://thedma.org/wp-content/uploads/DMA-Ethics-Guidelines.pdf`). Among other things, the codes cover similar topics I discuss here, including consent and disclosure. The organizations' guides also delve into marketing to children and using sweepstakes.

Part V
The Part of Tens

In this part . . .

- ✔ Avoid common analytic mistakes.
- ✔ Find customers' unmet needs.
- ✔ Improve the customer experience.
- ✔ Visit www.dummies.com for great Dummies content online.

Chapter 17

Ten Customer Metrics You Should Collect

● ●

In This Chapter

▶ Identifying the most useful metrics

▶ Improving revenues by improving your knowledge about your customers

● ●

*Y*ou can quantify the value of your customers throughout the customer journey in myriad ways. While the "best" metrics depend on your goals and specific context, most organizations should collect these ten.

These metrics are a mix of the four types of customer analytics to collect: *descriptive, behavioral, interaction,* and *attitudinal* (as described in Chapter 2).

Customer Revenue

Understanding where, when, and how much top-line revenue is being generated is probably already being done. However, it's often not being effectively tracked on a customer-by-customer basis. Tracking how much revenue is generated by each customer allows you to understand both which customers and which customer segments are responsible for the majority of your revenue.

The Pareto Principle says that usually a *minority* of customers is responsible for the *majority* of your revenue.

See Chapter 4 for more details on using the Pareto Principle.

Customer Satisfaction

Revenue doesn't last if customers aren't happy. Fortunately, you can measure customer satisfaction in many ways. Ask customers how satisfied they are with your product or service on a numbered scale. The American Customer Satisfaction Index (ACSI) database, maintained by the University of Michigan, is a popular tool that consists of multiple questions and provides a reference database.

Don't worry too much about the phrasing of customer satisfaction questions or the total number of response options. It's more important to collect satisfaction data early and often.

Use multiple sources of data (existing customers, former customers, and third-party reports) and different points in time to understand how your product or service is perceived. Chapter 9 provides more information on measuring customer attitudes and Chapter 11 digs into customer satisfaction.

Customer Profitability

Companies don't stay in business (at least not for long) by selling for $5 products that cost $10 to make. Knowing revenue by customer is the first step. The next step is to understand the cost associated with that revenue.

Certain customer segments will be more profitable, due to factors such as low price sensitivity or less use of customer support. Identify these particularly valuable customers and, in most cases, treat them differently by offering customized incentives, perks (first-class upgrade, anyone?), product features, or other means of gaining and retaining their loyalty.

See Chapter 4 for guidance on segmenting your customers.

Customer Lifetime Value

Have you ever wondered why cable companies offer really low prices for the first few months then increase the rates? The total revenue over the lifetime as a customer (usually years) offsets the losses the providers absorb in the initial period to gain a customer. A long-term projection into the future profitability of a customer is called the customer lifetime value.

A customer lifetime isn't usually the life span of a person, but rather the days, months, or years a customer spends using your products or services. Acquiring a customer often comes with large initial costs, but these are (hopefully) offset by higher revenue over time.

The steps you need to compute the lifetime value of your customers (and segments) can be found in Chapter 6.

Brand Awareness

How many customers even know a product or company exists? You can measure brand awareness using unaided or aided recall. With unaided recall, you ask participants to name the brands or products that come to mind when considering a certain category — for example, toothpaste or luxury watches. You can also have customers or prospects rate how familiar they are with certain brands using simple scales from not at all familiar to familiar.

Methods for measuring brand awareness can be found in Chapter 8.

Top Tasks

Every product, website, or software application has multiple functions, but customers are usually interested in only a handful of them. Identify these tasks and be sure users can effectively complete them and are satisfied with the experience. A top-task analysis helps to separate the many trivial tasks from the critical few that matter to your customers.

Think about all the tasks Microsoft Word can do: mail-merging, macros, desktop publishing. Yet, most users only want to accomplish a few core tasks, such as writing and formatting documents.

The same observation applies to health-insurance websites: They are full of places to click, information to read, and features to use. Yet, when my company conducted a top-task analysis with customers, it found that only two actions — finding a doctor and seeing if insurance would pay for a specific procedure — were top tasks. Unfortunately, many insurance provider websites don't make accomplishing these tasks easy. This affects both customer satisfaction and loyalty.

Read Chapter 13 for information about identifying customers' top tasks.

Customer Loyalty

Customers who come back, repurchase, or recommend a product to friends or colleagues, are key drivers of a product's long-term viability.

The popular Net Promoter Score (NPS) is one way to measure customers' likelihood to say positive or negative things about their experiences with products or services. The likelihood to recommend is often a good indicator of future company growth. To measure loyalty, you should track both

- ✔ Intentions (are you likely to repurchase or recommend?)
- ✔ Actions (did customers actually repurchase or recommend?)

See Chapter 12 for a detailed discussion on measuring customer loyalty.

Conversion Rate

For online campaigns, direct marketing, donations, or just sales copy, it is useful to determine the percentage of customers who are exposed and who ultimately purchase a product (or sign up for a service). It enables you to understand how small changes in design, pricing, features, or content can increase or decrease the percentage of prospective customers who are gained or kept.

When I helped the Wikipedia team understand the differences in donation rates they saw on their website, we looked at the different images, copy, and the time of day that led to higher rates of browsers becoming donating customers.

See Chapter 10 for tracking conversion rates and customer purchases.

Completion Rate

Customers want to get things done. If they can't complete tasks, especially their top tasks, with a product or website, not much else matters.

I often call completion rates the gateway customer experience metric.

Completion rates are applicable to activities like finding products, searching for information on websites, solving tasks in architecture software, entering a journal entry in accounting software, or getting a problem solved by a customer service representative. Poor task completion rates lead to lower satisfaction levels and a drop in the likelihood to recommend.

Chapter 15 provides more information on measuring completion rates as part of usability evaluations.

Churn Rate

It isn't just about getting customers; it's also about keeping them. If customers never repurchase a product or service, or abandon as soon as they can, that has a long-term negative effect on profitability.

This so-called churn rate is especially true because the cost of acquiring customers is generally higher than the cost of keeping them. Valuable pieces of information include the percentage of customers who abandon at time intervals (for example, after one or two years) or stages (for example, renewal time or product upgrades) and the reason for abandonment. For example, while offering products like a cable subscription at a low price for a few months to lure customers may generate more total customers, if too many abandon when the prices increase, it may outweigh the new customer incentives and drive potential customers away.

Chapter 12 shows the effects of churn and customer retention rates.

Chapter 18

Ten Methods to Improve the Customer Experience

In This Chapter

▶ Understanding your customers

▶ Improving your customers' experience

▶ Prioritizing improvements

Measuring, managing, and improving the customer experience involves collecting good metrics and keeping track of them. Following are ten methods to use to improve the customer experience with websites, mobile apps, software, and hardware and services.

True Intent/Voice of Customer Study

You can be a successful company for quite a while without really knowing who your customers are. At some point, though, it makes financial sense to understand the basic demographics of the people who purchase, repeat purchase, and recommend your company and products to friends.

For companies with a strong web presence, a True Intent Study with a web intercept or conspicuous link and survey allows willing customers to let you know who they are (age, gender, occupation, salary) and what they are trying to do (goals, tasks, and interests). This becomes vital information for subsequent customer metrics and methods.

In addition to website intercepts, you should also target past customers to understand the same core aspects of who they are and what they do or want to do with your product and company. This way, you aren't relying exclusively on website visitors who may not be representative of your customer base.

Customer Segmentation

All customers are not created equal. With data from a True Intent Study, Voice of Customer Survey, and other data sources, you can begin to understand what differentiates your customers based on demographics, behaviors, and profitability. Not only does segmenting customers tell you how to better serve current customer demographics, but it also allows you to discover any unmet needs and deliver better products and services in the future.

Read Chapter 4 to learn how to segment your customer base.

Persona Development

It's hard to develop for a conceptual group of hypothetical customers. A persona helps focus product development and marketing efforts on real customer needs and goals rather than just abstract demographics. It embodies the key characteristics of a customer segment by highlighting salient demographics, goals, and top tasks for development teams.

Personas represent fictional customers but should be based on real data obtained from customer segmentation analyses, ethnographic research, surveys, and interviews. Chapter 5 provides more information on personas and their development process.

Journey Mapping

Rarely do customers follow a simple linear path from prospect to customer. A customer journey map helps identify problem areas customers encounter while engaging a product or service and can locate opportunities for improvement. It can also help unify often disparate and competing efforts within the same organization by providing different departments with a single document that maps the customer's entire experience with a product, service, or company.

In Chapter 7, I explain how to map the customer journey more precisely.

Top-Task Analysis

A product or website can't do everything for everyone. Despite there being dozens to hundreds of features and functions supported by products and websites, customers usually want to perform only a small number of tasks.

A top-task analysis helps separate the critical few tasks from the trivial many by having customers pick their most essential tasks. Targeting your efforts on significant tasks and delivering a solid experience where it has the biggest impact means more satisfied customers and customers who are more willing to repeat purchase, return, and recommend to friends.

See Chapter 13 for more details on conducting top-task analyses.

Usability Study

Just because a product has all the right features and is priced right doesn't mean it will be a big seller. If customers find it difficult to use your product or website, they'll look for easier alternatives and are less likely to reuse, repurchase, and recommend.

Observing just a few customers who use the product can uncover most of the common problems with an interface. Use data from a top-tasks analysis to understand what users want to accomplish and find users who match your customer segments. The most important concept to understand in a usability study is that it is not what customers think or want that matters, but to observe them using the product.

Read Chapter 14 for conducting usability studies.

Findability Study

One of the biggest pain points on the web and with software is just trying to find where features are buried. A findability study is a specialized usability study that focuses on the *taxonomy (labels and hierarchy)* and ignores distractions such as the design, layout, and search capabilities. It's used for testing everything from cable TV interfaces and the Settings screen on an iPhone to product categories on a large e-commerce website.

Findability studies use the methods of tree testing and card sorting to uncover problems and identify fixes. If this sounds complicated, Chapter 15 can help you understand better.

Conjoint Analysis

Customers usually want a lot of features for a low price, or for free. Just asking customers what they want is usually insufficient for understanding what really matters. A statistical technique called *Choice Based Conjoint*

Analysis produces a more accurate view of customer ratings by isolating which features have the biggest impact on preference. A conjoint analysis is typically used in the product development stages to understand which features to build or how changing price or options affects customers' future behavior. The conjoint analysis is one of a number of prioritization techniques used to help get the biggest bang for the development buck.

See Chapter 13 for more details on prioritizing customer requirements.

Key Driver Analysis

A key driver analysis identifies which features contribute the most to customer satisfaction, customer loyalty, or any other key variable of interest. Have customers rate their satisfaction with the most important features or functional areas of an experience. Include items on quality, features, value, service, and usability where appropriate. A key driver analysis provides the relative weight of each of these ratings using multiple regression analysis. A key driver analysis is typically performed after a product, website, or service has been in use for a while to evaluate what to improve, add, or remove.

Read the appendix and Chapter 12 to learn how to conduct a key driver analysis.

Gap Analysis

Conjoint analyses and key driver analyses usually require advanced software and some statistical sophistication to conduct and interpret. Another prioritization technique, called a gap analysis, can be performed more easily by asking customers to first rate or rank the most important features and aspects of a product or service. Then, have the same customers rate or rank how satisfied they are with each of the features. For each feature, find the "gap" by subtracting the average satisfaction rating from the average importance rating. The largest gap identifies the features that are the most important but with which customers are least satisfied and therefore presents the best opportunities for improvement.

In Chapter 13, I cover how to conduct a gap analysis.

Chapter 19

Ten Common Analytic Mistakes

Collecting, analyzing, and making decisions from data is the heart of customer analytics. But whether you're new to data analysis or have been doing it a while, ten common mistakes can affect the quality of your results. You should be on the lookout for them. They follow, and I include some ideas on how to avoid them as well.

Optimizing around the Wrong Metric

Metrics exist for just about anything in an organization and most probably are collected for a good reason. Be sure the metric you want to optimize will achieve not just your goals, but also your customers' goals.

If airlines optimize around on-time departure instead of on-time arrival, an airplane that pulls away from the gate and sits on the tarmac is a metric success even though the customers feel the experience is disappointing as they arrive at their destination an hour late. If you optimize around the number of calls answered in one hour at a call center, you are placing quantity over quality. While customers generally want to get resolution quickly, are their issues being properly addressed?

Be sure your metrics are meaningful to your customer and that optimizing those metrics makes for a better experience.

Relying Too Much on Behavioral or Attitudinal Data

Mining customer transactions can reveal a lot of patterns in things like what products customers purchase together or the average time between purchases. But this behavioral data doesn't necessarily help you understand the attitudes and motivations behind why customers purchase things together. This attitudinal data can more easily be collected using surveys or other methods of asking customers.

Not Having a Large Enough Sample Size

If you're looking to detect small differences in metrics, like conversion rates or customer attitudes, and you're measuring a sample of customers or data, be sure your sample size is large enough to detect that difference. Use the sample size tables in this book or consult a statistician to know what sample size you'll need ahead of time.

A lot of cost and effort are wasted on looking for very small differences in customer attitudes, such as satisfaction, perception of usability, or likelihood to recommend after making very small changes to products or websites with too small of a sample size.

Eyeballing Data and Patterns

I call it "eyeballing statistics." It's the tendency to think you can detect patterns from data by examining it without any statistics. For very large patterns, you can see these easily without any computations, but these sorts of obvious patterns rarely show up. To minimize the chance that you're being fooled by randomness in data, use statistics and mathematical computations to differentiate the news from the noise.

Confusing Statistical Significance with Practical Significance

With a large sample size, you'll be able to detect very small differences and patterns that are statistically significant. Statistical significance just means that the pattern or difference is not due to random noise in your data. But that doesn't mean that what's detected will have much practical importance. Analytics programs will flag different patterns and differences, but you need to determine if a 1% difference in conversion rates results will have a major or negligible impact. This depends on the context but means you'll need to exercise judgment and not blindly follow the software. Don't immediately think every statistically significant result is meaningful. Think through the business implications of the result carefully. See the appendix for more of a discussion on statistical versus practical significance.

Not Having an Interdisciplinary Team

If you have a stats PhD crunching numbers in your company basement, it may generate the right insights; but if sales, marketing, service, or product teams aren't involved, it's going to be difficult to get buy-in and implement the insights. Get the right people and teams involved in your initiative early and look to have complementary skills, including mathematical, software, business, marketing, and product experience.

Not Cleaning Your Data First

Garbage In, Garbage Out (GIGO) is a common phrase data junkies like to use to explain that data that has problems *before* analysis will have problems *after* analysis. This can be anything from mismatched data pulled from databases (customer names don't match transactions) or missing values. If the data is bad going in, you'll have bad insights coming out. Before running any analysis, do a quality check on your data by selecting a sample of data and auditing it for quality. Corroborate it with other sources to verify its accuracy.

Improperly Formatted Data

When you analyze your data, at least half of the effort is spent formatting the data so your software can properly analyze it. This often involves disaggregating and getting customer transactions or survey data in rows and columns.

Skimping on proper formatting usually means a lot of rework later, so be sure your data is formatted properly — and early.

Not Having Clear Research Questions to Answer

Sometimes it's fine to have a fishing expedition and examine patterns in data. But don't stop with the fishing expedition; use what you find to form hypotheses about customer behavior and look to confirm, refine, or reject these hypotheses with additional data.

Waiting for Perfect Data

Every dataset tends to have some problem of some sort. Some are minor, like a few missing fields; others are major, with lots of missing fields and mismatched data. For survey data, there always seems to be a concern about how a question was asked and to whom it was asked. That said, expect some imperfection in all your datasets and surveys. But don't let it stop you from working with what you have. Just be cautious about your interpretation.

Chapter 20

Ten Methods for Identifying Customer Needs

An innovative product doesn't come from a law passed by the government. It also doesn't come from venture capitalists looking for a higher return on an investment. Innovation comes from identifying customers' needs and providing solutions that meet those needs.

Companies like Uber, Airbnb, and Intuit understand this. Uber's success, for example, has come not from building new, better taxis, but from seeing — and then solving — people's transportation problems.

Want to know where to put your innovation efforts? Uncover your customers' unmet needs using the methods I discuss in this chapter.

Although you might not be working on the next Airbnb, Uber, or even a product you think is exciting, like business software, or temperature controls, understanding and identifying customer needs may lead to a revolutionary innovation. After all, Nest revolutionized the rather mundane industry of thermostats and changed how everyone heats and cools houses.

Starting with Existing Data

You most likely have existing data at your fingertips. Review past surveys, customer interviews, and customer-support call logs. There's no point in funding an extensive and expensive research campaign if the data you need is already collected.

Save the budget for data you don't have and more advanced questions you need answered.

Interviewing Stakeholders

Why not begin with the data you don't have to pay for: the collective knowledge stakeholders have. Start with sales and support teams. They know the product and the customer. They often have a list of feature requests, bug reports, and enhancements — straight from the customer's mouth.

Combine these to generate a preliminary list of requirements. Look for patterns, but don't automatically dismiss one-offs — look to corroborate them with findings from other methods.

Mapping the Customer Process

If you know your customer's process, map it out.

For example, before Uber, to get a ride you called a taxi company, waited to reach a dispatcher, waited for a car to be dispatched, hoped the driver would find you, and hoped you had enough cash when you reached your destination. With Uber, you open your smartphone and summon the nearest car with one tap; you already know how far away the car is because you can see it in real time on a map. The driver also sees your location so he or she can come right to you. Figure 20-1 shows a simple process map comparing these experiences.

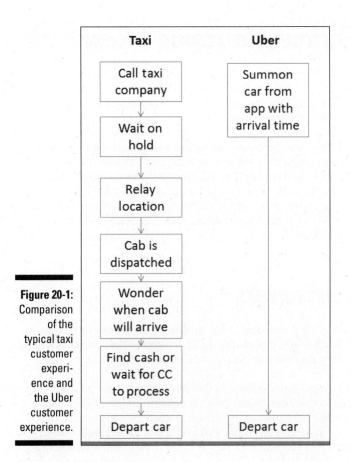

Taxi	Uber
Call taxi company	Summon car from app with arrival time
Wait on hold	
Relay location	
Cab is dispatched	
Wonder when cab will arrive	
Find cash or wait for CC to process	
Depart car	Depart car

Figure 20-1: Comparison of the typical taxi customer experience and the Uber customer experience.

Mapping the Customer Journey

A customer journey map is a visualization of the process a customer goes through when engaging with a product or service. It takes process mapping to a new level by including multiple phases and touchpoints a person goes through — from prospect to loyal customer. It's a document meant to unify fragmented efforts and identify points of friction and opportunities for improvement.

Finding and fixing the pain points in a customer's journey isn't just about damage control: It's also about the innovation that comes from fixing the pain. See Chapter 7 for examples and how to map the customer journey.

Conducting "Follow Me Home" Research

"Follow me home" research relies on observation by literally following a customer home or to work. You follow a customer to her workplace, spending the day watching her do her job. You observe process pain points and then look for opportunities for improvement.

For example, during a "follow me home" exercise, a team of researchers at Intuit noticed that retail customers were exporting their transactions from their point-of-sale cash registers into QuickBooks to manage their books. This step took time and sometimes led to failure and frustration. The innovative solution? Developers integrated QuickBooks into a cash register and eliminated the export step for customers and created a new version called QuickBooks Point of Sale (POS).

Interviewing Customers

Go right to the source: Ask customers what problems they have and what features they want. Even when customers can't articulate their needs clearly, you can often gain insights that lead to successful innovations.

Use the "Five Whys" technique to help you discover what needs people don't even know they have, needs that no one has recognized before: Keep asking why until you get at the root cause of the problem and not a symptom. (It's called "Five Whys" because you often have to go through five levels before you get to the point where you can make a change that addresses the problem.)

Conducting Voice of Customer Surveys

Voice of Customer surveys collect data, from email or from a pop-up on a website, about the attitudes and expectations of existing or prospective customers. Use a mix of open- and closed-ended questions to see what produces the most useful data.

Although customers aren't necessarily good at identifying their needs, this type of survey often yields data from which you can discern customer goals, challenges, problems, and attitudes, and then recommend opportunities for improvement.

Analyzing Your Competition

Consider using research firms that might present a more objective face to customers who engage with your organization and its competition. Consider using the SWOT rule: Identify your competitors' *strengths, weaknesses, opportunities,* and *threats.* You can use a SWOT for a brand, product, or even an experience.

Define the competition both narrowly and broadly. Don't just look at your competition in the same industry, but other industries as well. For example, when I tested the online-checkout experiences for a U.S.-based mobile carrier, I considered the competitors in the same industry (Sprint, Verizon, and AT&T) as well as companies in other industries (DirecTV and Comcast) whose websites have a checkout process that integrates products and service contracts.

Analyzing Cause-and-Effect Relationships

No one will disagree that it's usually good to think positively, but sometimes, negative thinking can solve problems more effectively. Through observations, surveys, and other data sources, you may find problems that are actually just symptoms of other root cause problems.

Task failures, errors, and long task times are usually the symptoms of multiple underlying problems. These can be problems in the interface or a disconnection with the user's goals. Through the process of asking "Why?" multiple times and segmenting different causes, you can help identify and address root problems in the user experience.

Recording Experiences through Diary Studies

Sometimes opportunities reveal themselves over time. One cost-effective longitudinal method is a diary study. Ask participants to record problems, frustrations, positive experiences, or thoughts at intervals throughout a day, week, or even a year. This can be low tech, with customers writing their experiences and thoughts down on paper and mailing it in, or high tech, in which you send text messages or emailed surveys to customers at particular intervals.

Because you're asking your customer to do the data collection for you, be sure you have targeted questions and clear hypotheses you want to test with all the data that gets collected.

Expect a good percentage of customers to drop out or not be 100% diligent about filling out their diaries. Still, any information you can garner is better than no information at all. After all, you can't fix what you don't know about.

Appendix

Predicting with Customer Analytics

. . . .

In This Appendix

▶ Recognizing relationships

▶ Predicting performance

. . . .

*P*redictive analytics comprises several methods to analyze what happened in the past to predict what will most likely happen in the future. You use your historical and transactional customer data to identify risks and opportunities.

You've almost surely encountered the results of predictive analytics as a customer yourself. Some examples you likely encounter include

✔ **Amazon's recommendation:** Probably one of the most famous examples of predictive analytics that touch the customer is Amazon's recommendation engine. This includes the "customers who purchased this book, also purchased this book."

✔ **Facebook and LinkedIn:** Social media websites like Facebook and LinkedIn use algorithms to determine both whom you might want to connect to and which stories and updates you want in your timeline based on patterns in your viewing behavior and people with similar behavior to you.

✔ **Netflix:** Netflix recommends which movie or TV show you'll like based on your past views and matching that to customers with similar behavior.

✔ **Return rates:** I worked with a mobile carrier to predict which phones customers would return most often based on the opinion of customers evaluating the phone's usability.

✔ **Credit cards:** Your credit score and credit report are the results of the banking and credit industry wanting to predict who is more likely to pay on time and those who will more likely default.

✔ **Insurance:** Life insurance, car insurance, and health insurance providers notoriously collect a number of data points about customers to predict which customers will more likely get sick and need care, have a higher chance of dying prematurely, or are more likely to get into a car accident.

In all these examples, some past customer data is being used to predict future events. The same principle applies to customer analytics: using past customer behavior to predict future behavior. Throughout this book, I've covered both what customer analytics to collect and methods to collect them. With these analytics collected to describe the customers' current and past experience with products and services, you can also predict the future. This appendix is a primer to help you get started with the skills needed to predict with customer analytics.

Three essential techniques to make predictions with customer analytics include

✔ **Finding similarities:** Identify how customers are similar, either based on behavior like purchase history or attitudes like customer satisfaction

✔ **Identifying trends and patterns:** Predict when customers will purchase, future revenue, website page views, subscription rates, or same-store sales.

✔ **Detecting differences:** Understand how customers differ or respond differently to product features and designs, which allows for customizing products, experiences, and pricing.

Finding Similarities and Associations

Finding similarities and associations with customer analytics data is the most common analysis technique to predict future customer behavior. Some examples of the types of questions based on making associations with customer data include:

✔ For customers who purchase product A, what other products do they purchase?

✔ Will coupons increase same-store sales?

✔ Does a longer time on a website result in more purchases?

✔ Will a reduced price mean higher sales?

✔ Is customer loyalty tied to future company growth?

✔ Does the change in home page design cause higher conversions?

Understanding the relationship between variables, how strong that association is, and ultimately the cause of outcome variables, is a fundamental and useful skill for predicting with customer analytics.

Visualizing associations

You can visualize the relationship between two variables by graphing them in a scatterplot. Scatterplots are a useful tool to identify associations and examine the strength of the relationship.

Figure A-1 shows the relationship between the time it takes customers to make a purchase on a website using their mobile phone and how many finger taps the purchase took. This data came from a usability study (see Chapter 14) from 181 participants on an e-commerce mobile site.

Figure A-1: A scatterplot between mobile phone "taps" and the amount of time it took to make a purchase.

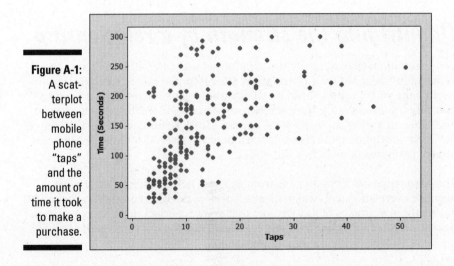

In Figure A-1, each dot represents 1 of the 181 customers' time and how many taps it took them to make the purchase:

- ✔ The horizontal axis (called the *x*-axis) shows the number of taps.
- ✔ The vertical axis (called the *y*-axis) shows the number of seconds it took for each participant to check out.

Figure A-2 shows the same scatterplot with an arrow pointing to one customer who took 50 seconds to make the purchase with 16 taps.

As the number of taps increase, so too does the time it takes the customer to check out. You can infer a positive association between the two pieces of data.

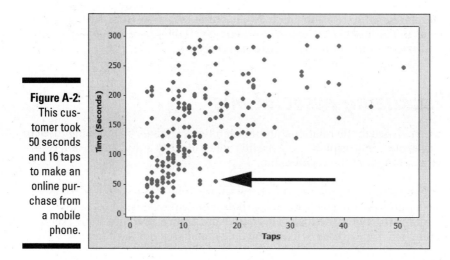

Figure A-2:
This customer took 50 seconds and 16 taps to make an online purchase from a mobile phone.

Quantifying the strength of a relationship

You can numerically quantify the strength of an association by using the Pearson Product Moment Correlation. It's often just called the correlation coefficient and is represented by the symbol r. The correlation is used to quantify the association between two continuous variables, (such as revenue, time, or rating scales). (See Chapter 2 for a reminder on the difference between continuous and discrete variables.) I cover associations between binary variables later in this appendix.

The correlation coefficient varies from an r of -1, which indicates a perfect negative correlation to 1, which means a perfect positive correlation. Figure A-3 shows three examples of scatterplots that show a perfect negative correlation ($r = -1$), no relationships ($r = 0$), and a perfect positive relationship ($r = 1$).

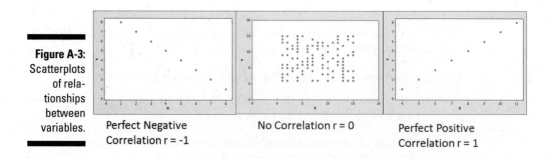

Figure A-3:
Scatterplots of relationships between variables.

Perfect Negative
Correlation r = -1

No Correlation r = 0

Perfect Positive
Correlation r = 1

Using two perfectly correlated variables isn't helpful. They're redundant; if you have the value for one variable, you can perfectly predict the other.

In practice, correlations are weak to strong. Some examples of correlations of different strengths include:

- ✔ **Height and Weight:** $r = .8$
- ✔ **Scholastic Aptitude Test (SAT) and First-Year College Grades:** $r = .5$
- ✔ **Usability and Customer Loyalty:** $r = .7$

The correlation between variables means that one variable can predict the value of the other variable:

- ✔ If you know a customer's height, you can estimate his weight.
- ✔ If you know a customer's weight, you can estimate his height.

But because these aren't perfect correlations, the further a correlation is from 1 or -1, the more error you have in predicting one variable based on the other.

Computing a correlation

You can compute the correlation coefficient by hand, or use software like Excel to compute it for you.

To compute a correlation on a set of data using the Pearson Correlation formula, follow these steps. (Refer to Figure A-1 for the data I'm using.)

1. **Set up the data in rows and columns in Excel.**

   Have one column for each variable and the customers' IDs. Each row should represent the same customer's data on two variables. Figure A-4 shows 17 customers' time to make the purchase and the number of taps needed for the purchase.

2. **In any cell, type**

   ```
   =PEARSON(
   ```

3. **Select all the values for the first variable.**

   My data for time appears in column B and the data goes from cell B2 to cell B182.

4. **Type a comma (,) and select all the values for the second variable.**

   My data appears in column C and the data goes from cell C2 to cell C182.

   Be sure to select the same number of values for both variables.

5. **Close the parenthesis and then press Enter to get the correlation.**

   `=PEARSON(B2:B182,C2:C182)`

   The correlation for this data, between taps and time, is .560666. As the scatterplot in Figure A-1 shows, there's a positive correlation between time and taps.

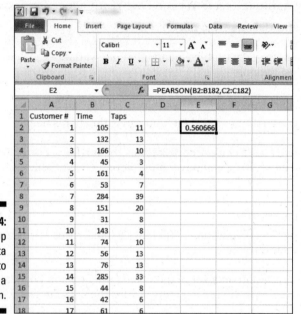

Figure A-4:
Setting up
the data
in Excel to
compute a
correlation.

Interpreting the strength of a correlation

Once you compute a correlation, you need to interpret the strength of the relationship. The correlation between taps and time is $r = .56$. Is that a strong correlation? It depends.

The strength of a correlation is context dependent. A "strong" correlation in one context may be a weak correlation in another. It depends on how much error you can tolerate and the consequences for being wrong in your predictions. Predicting time from taps probably won't involve a loss of life or money, so it's strong enough to be useful. In fact, it's about the same strength of an association as between the SAT and first-year college grades — where there's a lot at stake!

While correlations are context dependent, it can help to have some guidance on what you'll likely see with customer analytics data. A famous researcher by the name of Jacob Cohen examined correlations in the behavioral sciences, something similar to measuring customer behavior, and provided the following rules based on how common the correlations were reported in the peer-review literature:

   ✔ Small r = .10

   ✔ Medium: r = .30

   ✔ Large r = .50

Therefore, one simple interpretation of correlation of r = .56 between taps and time is that it's large. But there is another way of interpreting the correlation coefficient, which I cover next.

Coefficient of determination r^2

Multiplying the correlation coefficient by itself (squaring it) produces a metric known as the *coefficient of determination.* It's represented as r^2 (pronounced *r-squared)* and provides a better way of interpreting the strength of a relationship.

For example, a correlation of r = .5 squared becomes .25. Note that r^2 is often expressed as a percentage, 25%. For the correlation between taps and time, the r^2 is 31%. That means taps can explain 31% of the variation in time. And conversely, time explains 31% of the variation in taps. As you can see, even a strong correlation of above r = .5 still explains a minority of the differences between variables.

Height, for example, explains around 64% of the variation in weight. That means that knowing people's heights will explain most — but not all — of why they are a certain weight. Other factors explain 36% of the variation. That would include things like exercise, eating habits, or genetic factors that make some people weigh more at a certain height than others of the same height.

Use this same approach when correlating customer analytics. Find the correlation, square it, and then interpret the *r*-squared value. When stakes are high, you want to have high correlations and explain most of the variation between variables. With customer analytics, there are usually multiple variables that predict another variable. I get to multiple regression later in this appendix.

Correlation is not causation

One of the most important concepts about correlation that you will hear repeated, because it's worth repeating, is that correlation is not causation. That means just because one variable is correlated with another, doesn't mean one variable is caused by another variable. Time doesn't cause taps. SAT scores don't cause higher grades. Net Promoter Scores don't cause higher revenue (see Chapter 12).

You can say there is an association, but that association doesn't imply causation. See the later section on ways to determine causation.

It could be that a new design causes higher website conversion rates or it could be that a coupon increases same-store sales. However, there could be other variables that are actually affecting the outcome variable. For example, it could be that same-store sales were already increasing because of an increase in customers. Or it could be that more customers are converting on a website (making a purchase) because the competitor website sold out of the same product — not because of your website design change. Always consider what other variables might be affecting the relationship when making statements about causation.

Associations between binary variables

Very often in customer analytics, you encounter binary data that takes the form of yes/no, purchase/didn't purchase, agree/disagree, and so forth (see Chapter 2). You need to understand the association between binary variables just as you need to understand the association between continuous variables that I describe in the preceding section. While the principle of correlation is the same with binary data, however, the computations are different.

One of the most famous and visible examples of predictive analytics with binary data is the Amazon recommendation engine, as shown in Figure A-5.

Figure A-5:
Amazon's recommendation engine.

While the exact algorithm Amazon uses is proprietary, it's known that much of it is based on an association that indicates that a person who purchases one book also purchases another book. The recommendations are based on binary variables. To generate a recommendation, Amazon computes the proportion of customers who purchase one book and the proportion of the same customers who purchase any number of other books. (See Chapter 2 for a reminder on binary data and proportions.) Books with the highest association are recommended first, the next-highest associations next, and so forth. Figure A-6 shows transactions from 15 customers across four books. These could just as likely be software, groceries, songs in a playlist, TV shows, or any products or services customers can select from.

If the customer purchased the book, there's a 1 in the row; if she didn't, there's a 0. For example, Customer 1 purchased Book A and Book B, but not C or D. Customer 2 purchased only Book B.

Customer	Book A	Book B	Book C	Book D
1	1	1	0	0
2	0	1	0	0
3	1	1	0	0
4	1	0	0	1
5	0	0	0	0
6	1	1	0	0
7	1	0	1	0
8	0	0	1	0
9	1	1	0	0
10	1	1	0	0
11	0	1	0	0
12	0	1	0	0
13	1	1	0	0
14	0	0	0	0
15	0	0	0	0

Figure A-6: Purchases per customer represented as a yes/no choice.

To compute the association between any two book purchases, follow these steps:

1. **Count the number of customers who purchased each of these combinations of books:**
   - Neither book
   - Both books
   - Only Book A
   - Only Book B

2. **Put the totals in a table, like this:**

	Book B	
Book A	Y	N
Y	6	2
N	3	4

For example, six customers bought both Books A and B.

3. Label the table cells A to D, like this:

	Book B	
Book A	**Y**	**N**
Y	a	b
N	c	d

4. Use the formula for the correlation between binary variables:

$$\varphi = \frac{ad - bc}{\sqrt{(a+b)(c+d)(a+c)(b+d)}}$$

5. Fill in the values for the books to find the correlation between binary variables, like this:

$$\varphi = \frac{6(4) - 2(3)}{\sqrt{(6+2)(3+4)(6+3)(2+4)}}$$

$$\varphi = \frac{18}{\sqrt{3024}} = .327$$

In this case, the correlation between customers who purchase Book A and Book B is .327.

A correlation between binary variables is called *phi,* and is represented with the Greek symbol φ.

You can interpret the association between binary numbers the same way as the Pearson Correlation *r.* In fact, phi is a shortcut method for computing *r.* You get the same results by using the Excel Pearson formula and computing the correlation for all sets of data.

Figure A-7 shows the data setup in Excel. I computed the correlation between all pairs of books using the =PEARSON() Excel function.

I then created a matrix of correlations for each pair of books, as shown in Figure A-8.

Confirming the earlier result, the correlation between Book A and B is .33. The second-highest correlation is between Book A and Book D at .25.

The correlation between Book B and Book C is -.48. This negative correlation means that customers who purchase Book B are less likely to purchase Book C.

So if a customer is viewing and considering purchasing Book A, it would make sense to recommend (and possibly offer that customer an incentive) to also purchase Book B and D, but not Book C.

You may hear the terms *Basket Analysis* or *Affinity Analysis.* Both of these are just other names for finding associations and correlations between variables. It's like examining customers' shopping baskets in a grocery store to see what items are purchased together.

Figure A-7: The correlation between books using the Pearson Excel function.

| SUM | =PEARSON(E3:E17,F3:F17) |

	A	B	C	D	E	F	G	H
1								
2		Customer	Book A	Book B	Book C	Book D		
3		1	1	1	0	0		
4		2	0	1	0	0		
5		3	1	1	0	0		
6		4	1	0	0	1		
7		5	0	0	0	0		
8		6	1	1	0	0		
9		7	1	0	1	0		
10		8	0	0	1	0		
11		9	1	1	0	0		
12		10	1	1	0	0		
13		11	0	1	0	0		
14		12	0	1	0	0		
15		13	1	1	0	0		
16		14	0	0	0	0		
17		15	0	0	0	0		
18								
19		Correlations						
20			A	B	C	D		
21		A						
22		B	0.33					
23		C	-0.03	-0.48				
24		D	0.25	-0.33	F3:F17)			
25								
26								
27								

Figure A-8: Correlations between book purchases.

Correlations	A	B	C	D
A				
B	0.33			
C	-0.03	-0.48		
D	0.25	-0.33	-0.10	

Determining Causation

While correlation alone is not causation, there are ways to determine and show causation between customer variables. The amount of faith you can have in claims of causation depends on the method used to collect the data. While you may think that a new web page design resulted in more page views, it could be that page views were already increasing.

You can use any of five methods to make claims about causation, starting from the strongest and proceeding through the weakest.

Randomized experimental study

Randomly assigning participants to different design treatments and/or a control in a research study is an experimental design. For example, if you wanted to know which design customers would understand the most on a check-out page, you can create three different designs:

- ✔ The dependent variable could be something like

    - Accuracy in answering questions

    - Difficulty in checking out

    - Confidence in checking out

    - Time to check out

- ✔ The independent variable is the design — with three variations.

The hallmark of experimental research is randomly assigning participants to different treatments. You identify the design that users correctly selected and were most confident in using to make their selection.

There are all sorts of variables you can't control for — or are unaware of — that could impact results. But by randomly assigning participants to different designs or treatment conditions, you spread those nuisance variables evenly across designs. This increases the internal validity and generalizability of the findings.

As another example, researchers in Europe conducted an experiment in which they manipulated both the usability and visual appeal of an online e-commerce website. They essentially took one website, made the navigation intuitive or not intuitive, and then changed the colors and contrast to be appealing or unattractive. They found that customers find more usable websites more attractive. The researchers concluded that better usability increases opinions about attractiveness. Their conclusion is well-substantiated because they used a randomized experimental design.

Experiments (with random assignment) provide the strongest controls against extraneous variables and provide the highest levels of internal validity. These generate the strongest types of research results. But what happens if you cannot randomly assign participants?

Quasi-experimental design

If you want to test different conditions, but you cannot randomly assign participants to the different conditions, then the study is quasi-experimental. For example, you might want to know if customers find the beta version of a software product more usable than an existing version. Customers of beta software usually volunteer to use the software during the beta-test period. This self-selection (non-random) assignment introduces a potential source of bias into the results. It has higher external validity because these groups are naturally segmented, but has lower internal reliability.

When you compare attitudes of usability (say from the SUS or SUPR-Q, as discussed in Chapter 9) from the beta software customers to the existing version customers and find a difference, the difference could be due to differences in the type of people using the software and not actual differences in the attitude. This type of problem is confounding and makes the quasi-experimental design type less internally valid than the experimental condition.

As another example, I worked with a national retailer a few years ago that wanted to know the effects of direct mail coupons for in-store purchases. I used two markets: One received one new coupon (treatment) and the other acquired the standard coupon (control) from newspaper inserts mailed to homes. I compared the sales of stores prior to the coupon and after the coupon in both markets.

I couldn't randomly assign people to live in different cities, so I used two similarly sized midwestern advertising markets and looked to see what the new coupon did to sales. While I was able to show more sales with the new coupon, there was still some uncertainty about whether that difference was just due to other differences in the markets.

WARNING!

The weakness with quasi-experimental studies is that you can never be as sure as you can with random assignment that any increase in sales is attributable to the variable (in this case, sales) or to other nuisance variables (in this case, just differences between the markets).

Correlational study

A *correlational study,* as the name suggests, is when you look at the relation-ship between two variables and report the correlation. For example, the rela-tionship between product usability and likelihood to recommend is a strong positive correlation (meaning ease is strongly associated with, and likely pre-dicts, much of why users do and don't recommend products).

While correlational studies provide valuable results, they don't have random assignment and the independent variables aren't manipulated, which lessens the internal validity of the findings and weakens the case for causation.

The next time you hear that one customer metric causes another metric, look to identify how that was determined. Chances are it was done with either a correlational study or a quasi-experimental design. That doesn't mean one variable doesn't cause another; it just means you can't be as confident.

Single-subjects study

It's often the case that getting access to customers is extremely difficult. For example, you might be interested in whether a new interface to a PET scan-ner reduces the time it takes attending radiologists to adjust a setting on the scanner.

If you had access to one of these customers, you could ask her to perform a task on the existing software version three times, record how long it took to complete, have her attempt the same task three times on the new soft-ware, and finally, have her attempt it again three times on the old version. Figure A-9 shows how this data looks on a scatterplot.

This type of single-subject study uses what's called an ABA condition (where A is the existing software and B is the new software). The repeated trials help establish stability in the measures and increase the internal validity of the finding (as much as you can from a single subject).

The obvious limitation with the single-subject design is generalizability. All you know is that when you manipulate an independent variable (the software), task time goes down for one user. There could be a number of variables you're not accounting for. For this reason, single-subject designs aren't used very often in customer research.

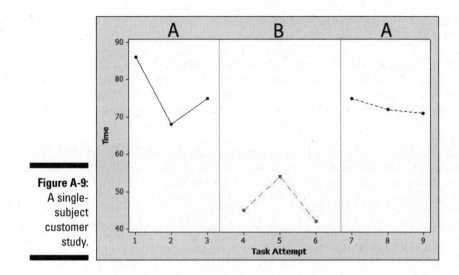

Figure A-9:
A single-subject customer study.

You can actually use more than one participant in a single-subject design (for example, two or three radiologists) and use the same technique to establish the pattern. To be more sophisticated in your analysis, you can also use time series analysis to examine trends over time and by condition for each user or the data in aggregate (I discuss time series analysis later in this chapter).

Anecdotes

Unfortunately, many business decisions are made based on opinion or hearing from a vocal customer or sales rep. While a good story of a successful product strategy can be convincing emotionally, it carries little weight when establishing causation.

Predicting with Regression

While a correlation speaks to the strength of a relationship between two variables, and the r^2 helps explain that strength of the relationship, what you need to do to predict one variable from another is to use an extension of correlation called regression analysis. *Regression analysis* is known as a "workhorse" in predictive analytics. The math isn't too complicated, and most software packages support regression analysis.

Regression analysis extends the idea of the scatterplot used in correlation and adds a line that best "fits" the data.

One of the requirements of using correlations and regression analysis is that the data is linear. *Linear* means a line can reasonably describe the relationship between variables and then be used to predict values that don't appear in your data (future customer data points). If the scatterplot of your data forms a curve, or any shape that a line doesn't fit well, you may get misleading results.

While there are many ways to draw lines through the data, the least squares analysis is a mathematical way that reduces the distance between the line and each dot in the scatterplot. This analysis can be done by hand or by using software such as Minitab, SPSS, SAS, R, or Excel.

Figure A-10 shows the least squares regression line from the scatterplot of taps and time (refer to Figure A-1).

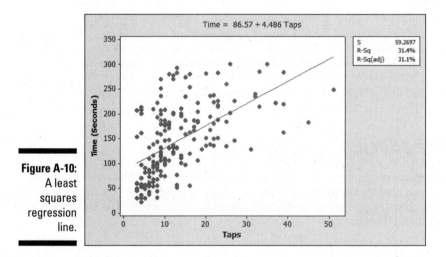

Figure A-10: A least squares regression line.

The software gives you the equation to the regression line above the graph:

```
Time = 86.57 + 4.486 Taps
```

The regression equation takes the general form of

$\widehat{Y} = b_0 + b_1 X + e$. Here's an explanation of each part of the equation:

- $\hat{Y}$ **(pronounced y-hat):** This is the predicted value of the dependent variable: predicted time.

- b_0: Called the *y*-intercept, this is where the line would cross (or intercept) with the *y*-axis.

- b_1: This is the slope of the predicted line (how steep it is).

- **X:** This represents a particular value of the independent variable: taps.

- *e:* represents the inevitable error the prediction will contain.

So in this example, the regression equation indicates that the predicted amount of time it takes a customer to make a purchase is equal to 86.57 (the *y*-intercept) plus 4.486 (the slope) multiplied by the number of taps (X).

Predicting with the regression line

It's the regression formula that allows you to predict customer values that don't exist in your data. It allows you to perform "what-if" analyses on future customer values. This is the "predictive" part of predictive customer analytics.

For example, using the regression equation from the preceding example, you can predict how long a customer takes to make a purchase with 38 taps. You just fill 38 in the regression equation.

```
Time = 86.57 + 4.486(38)
Time = 86.57 + 170.47 = 257.04
```

A customer needs 257 seconds, or a bit longer than four minutes, to make a purchase that requires 38 taps.

The dependent variable is denoted "Y" and is displayed on the y (vertical) axis. The independent variable is called X and is displayed on the horizontal (x) axis. (See Chapter 2 for discussion about independent and dependent variables.)

Instead of predicting a customer's task time from taps, this same approach can be used to predict other customer analytics, including:

- Customer revenue from advertising revenue

- Likelihood to recommend from usability data

- Number of conversions from website page views

Creating a regression equation in Excel

To create a regression equation using Excel, follow these steps:

1. **Insert a scatterplot graph into a blank space or sheet in an Excel file with your data.**

    You can find the scatterplot graph on the Insert ribbon in Excel 2007 and later.

2. **Select the *x*-axis (horizontal) and *y*-axis data and click OK.**

    Put what you want to predict in the *y*-axis (so my time data is in column B). The taps are in column C.

    You now have a scatterplot.

3. **Right-click on any of the dots and select "Add Trendline" from the menu.**

    The Format Trendline dialog box opens, as shown in Figure A-11.

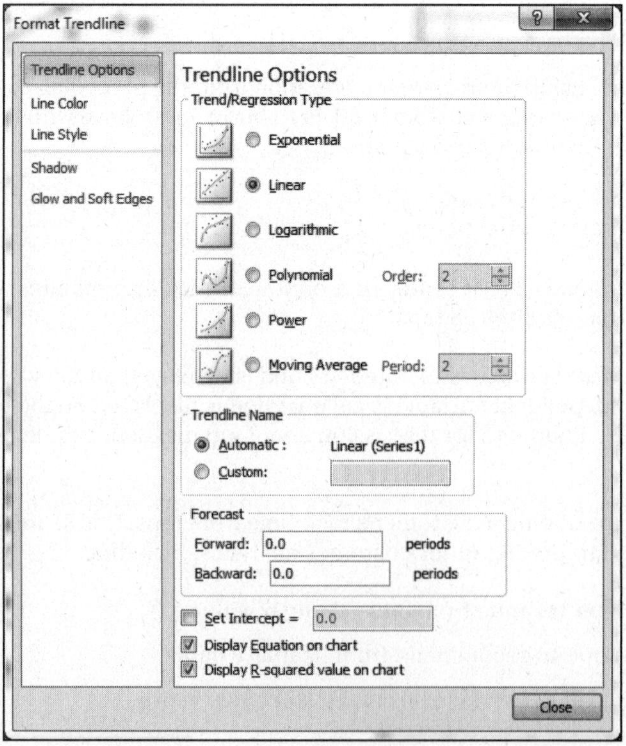

Figure A-11:
Add the
regression
equa-
tion and
r-squared
value to the
trendline.

4. **Select Trendline Options on the left, if necessary, then select the Display Equation on Chart and Display R-Squared Value on Chart boxes.**

You now have a scatterplot with trendline, equation, and r-squared value, as shown in Figure A-12. The regression equation is $Y = 4.486x + 86.57$. This is the same regression equation from the earlier "Predicting with the regression line" section, except that the y-intercept (86.57) is after the slope.

The r^2 value of .3143 tells you that taps can explain around 31% of the variation in time. It tells you how well the best-fitting line actually fits the data.

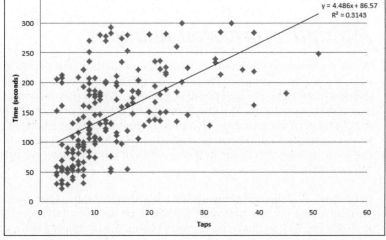

Figure A-12: Scatterplot, regression line, and equation computed in Excel.

Going beyond the ends of observed values is risky when using a regression equation. There's no guarantee that the regression line will continue to be linear because it extends before and after the data points.

Watch out for the following three things when correlating customer analytics data and using regression analysis:

✔ **Range restriction:** Two variables might have a low correlation because you're only measuring in a narrow range. For example, height and weight have a strong positive correlation, but if you measure only National Basketball Association (NBA) players, the correlation would mostly go away. This can happen, for example, if you are looking at a narrow range of customers — say, the ones with the highest incomes or most transactions.

- **Third variables:** It's often the case that another variable you aren't measuring is actually the cause of the relationship. For example, high school grades are correlated with college grades. It may seem like better studying in high school leads to better grades in college. However, it's often the case that a third variable, Socio Economic Status (SES) is a better explanation of both high school and college grades. Students in families with higher SES tend to have higher grades in high school and college than students from families with low SES. In customer analytics an improving economy or a growing company may be the reason for increases in sales, and not your marketing campaign or feature changes.

- **Nonlinearity:** The relationship between variables needs to be linear — that is, follow a line somewhat. If the relationship curves downward or upward, a correlation and regression equation will not properly describe the relationship.

Multiple regression analysis

When you have one independent variable predicting one dependent variable, it's called *bivariate regression.* You can extend the idea of regression to include more than one independent variable, which then becomes multiple regression. As with the Tap and Time data, taps only predict 31% of the variation in time. Other variables also predict customer time. Multiple regression analysis includes additional variables to see how much, if at all, they contribute to explaining variations in the dependent variable, beyond the variables already included.

In Chapter 12, I discuss the value of a key driver analysis for predicting which variables best predict customer loyalty. A key driver analysis typically uses multiple regression analysis (another technique is Shapley Value Analysis, which uses a different algorithm but provides similar output).

With multiple regression, you build the regression equation with two or more variables. You can then see how important each independent variable is, relative to the others included.

With another independent variable, the regression formula becomes $\hat{Y} = b_0 + b_1 X_1 + b_2 X_1 + e$:

- **$\hat{Y}$ (pronounced y-hat):** Represents the predicted value of the dependent variable: predicted time.

- **b_0:** This is the *y*-intercept.

- **b_1:** The regression coefficient "weight" for variable 1.

- **b_2:** The regression coefficient "weight" for variable 2.

- **X_1:** Represents a particular value of independent variable 1

✔ X_2: Represents a particular value of independent variable 2

✔ *e:* Represents the inevitable error a prediction will contain

For example, 2,584 customers rated their likelihood to recommend a learning management system (LMS) used at a university:

✔ They rated their likelihood to recommend on a 0 to 10 scale (0= not at all likely to recommend and 10 = extremely likely).

✔ These customers rated their satisfaction on several other variables using a five-point scale from not at all satisfied (1) to very satisfied (5). They rated attributes including

- Stability of the system (whether it crashed)

- Satisfaction with customer support

- Efficiency (how quickly customers get their tasks done)

  See Chapter 9 for ideas on measuring customer attitudes.

- Usability of the product across four 5-point questions for a total of 20 points.

Here's how I used a bivariate regression equation to see how much customers' satisfaction with the product's stability predicts their likelihood to recommend it.

1. I computed the correlation and found that satisfaction with stability has a reasonably strong correlation $r = .49$.

2. I performed a regression analysis using the statistical software SPSS.

   You can also use Minitab, SAS, and R, and online calculators, to perform a multiple regression analysis.

   In SPSS, I chose Analyze➪Regression➪Linear Regression. In the Linear Regression dialog box, I used the satisfaction with the product stability (labeled Stability) of the software to predict the likelihood to recommend (labeled NPS), as shown in Figure A-13.

   I got the following table of results shown in Figure A-14. While there are a lot of numbers, what you're interested in is the regression equation in the B column. This column contains the B's in the regression equation described earlier (the *y*-intercept and slope). The estimate of likelihood to recommend = 1.950 + 1.423 (Stability). The "Sig" column values show that the predictor of Stability Satisfaction is statistically significant (not just a chance association) because the values of .000 are less than .05. See the sidebar discussion on statistical significance. The r^2 value is .24, meaning stability explains around 24% of customers' likelihood to recommend (this is found from squaring the correlation of .49).

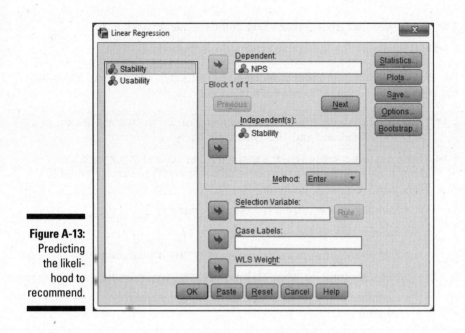

Figure A-13:
Predicting
the likeli-
hood to
recommend.

Figure A-14:
Regression
output from
SPSS.

Coefficients^a

Model		Unstandardized Coefficients		Standardized Coefficients	t	Sig.
		B	Std. Error	Beta		
1	(Constant)	1.950	.200		9.764	.000
	Stability	1.423	.049	.494	28.833	.000

a. Dependent Variable: NPS

Next I wanted to see if usability adds any predictive power to customers'
likelihood to recommend, beyond what is being explained by their satisfaction toward the stability.

3. I ran the correlation between usability and likelihood and got a strong
   correlation of $r = .733$.

   The correlation between usability and stability is also medium-strong,
   $r = .477$. It's often the case that independent variables will correlate with
   each other and the dependent variable. But you don't want to include
   variables that provide completely redundant information. It could be
   that when customers rate the usability of the software, they are already
   considering its stability. Multiple regression can tell you if the stability
   satisfaction is adding anything that usability isn't already adding (and
   vice versa).

4. I repeated the procedure with the updated table of results.

5. I added in usability to the regression equation. The results are shown in Figure A-15.

Figure A-15:
Multiple
regression
output from
SPSS.

Coefficients[a]

Model		Unstandardized Coefficients		Standardized Coefficients	t	Sig.
		B	Std. Error	Beta		
1	(Constant)	-.937	.168		-5.579	.000
	Stability	.541	.043	.188	12.570	.000
	Usability	.419	.010	.641	42.887	.000

a. Dependent Variable: NPS

Look at the B column to see the regression weights and to build the equation for likelihood to recommend:

```
Likelihood to Recommend = -.937 + .541 (Stability)+ .419 (Usability)
```

Again, both predictors are statistically significant because the values in the "Sig" column are under .05. The r^2 for this equation is .561, meaning these two variables together predict around 56% of likelihood to recommend.

If the correlation between independent variables is too high, an undesirable condition called *multicollinearity* occurs, which can provide a misleading regression equation. I get concerned when the correlations exceed $r > .9$ and I use additional tests to be sure multicollinearity isn't occurring.

This regression equation output reveals a few things.

✔ Adding usability as a variable substantially increased the explanatory power compared to just stability alone:

• With stability alone, you could predict 24% of likelihood to recommend.

• When you add in usability along with stability satisfaction, the explanatory power more than doubles to 56%, which is the majority of variation.

✔ You can predict a customer's likelihood of recommending the software product by inserting values for stability and usability ratings.

For example, a stability satisfaction rating of 4 (out of 5) and a usability score of 15 (out of 20) would result in a likelihood to recommend score of

```
Likelihood to Recommend = -.937 + .541 (4)+ .419 (15) = 7.5
```

That would place this customer in the Passive category, not terribly likely to recommend, but probably someone who also won't detract (see Chapter 12).

✔ The relative importance of each of these two variables in predicting likelihood to recommend.

The weights of each value are the coefficients in the regression equation (.541 for stability and .419 for usability). While this appears to show that stability has the higher weight, and therefore importance, this is misleading because the items used different scales (a 5-point versus a 20-point scale).

To better understand the importance, look at the standardized coefficients to find the relative importance. The standardization process converts each raw score into a standard score, making the values comparable. You see this value in the Standardized Coefficients column (refer to Figure A-15). The stability has a standardized weight of .188. This means that increasing customers' satisfaction with the stability increases the likelihood to recommend by .188 points. In comparison, the standardized weight of usability is .641. That means a 1-point increase in the standardized usability score increases the likelihood to recommend by .641. In other words, usability is more than three times as important as stability in predicting customer loyalty (.641 / .188 = 3.4).

Predicting with binary data

The regression examples used in the preceding section both use continuous dependent and continuous independent variables. You can use also use categorical predictor variables with two, three, or more specific categories — for example, task-completion, agree-disagree, or a customer segment (high income, medium income, or low income), as long as they are dummy coded with 1's and 0's, where the 1 represents the category presence and 0 the absence. See Chapter 2 for a reminder on dummy coding. For regression analysis, the dependent variable needs to be a continuous variable. A special form of regression analysis called *logistic regression* can handle categorical data as the dependent variable.

Statistical significance and p-values

When dealing with customer analytics in general, you'll encounter the phrase *statistically significant*. You'll also run into something called a *p-value*. There's a lot packed in that little p and there are books written on the subject. Here's what you need to know.

In principle, a statistically significant result (usually a difference) is a result that's not attributed to chance. More technically, it means that if the Null Hypothesis is true (which means there really is no difference), there's a low probability of getting a result that large or larger.

Consider these two important factors.

- ✔ Sampling Error. There's always a chance that the differences we observe when measuring a sample of customers is just the result of random noise; chance fluctuations; happenstance.

- ✔ Probability; never certainty. Statistics is about probability; you cannot buy 100% certainty. Statistics is about managing risk. Can we live with a 10-percent likelihood that our decision is wrong? A 5-percent likelihood? 33 percent? The answer depends on context: What does it cost to increase the probability of making the right choice, and what is the consequence (or potential consequence) of making the wrong choice? Most publications suggest a cutoff of 5% — it's okay to be fooled by randomness 1 time out of 20. That's a reasonably high standard,

and it may match your circumstances. It could just as easily be overkill, or it could expose you to far more risk than you can afford.

The p-value is one of the outcomes of a statistical test when making a comparison, say, between the conversion rate in a test of one marketing campaign compared to another. The p-value stands for *probability value*. The p-value is the probability of obtaining the difference you see in a comparison from a sample (or a larger one) if there really isn't a difference for all customers.

Some examples of p-values are .012, .21, or .0001; a p-value of .012 indicates that the difference observed would only be seen about 1.2% of the time, if there really is no difference in the entire customer population.

Given that this is a pretty low percentage, in most cases, researchers conclude that the difference observed is not due to chance and call it statistically significant. By convention, journals and statisticians say something is statistically significant if the p-value is less than .05. There's nothing sacred about .05, though; in applied research, the difference between .04 and .06 is usually negligible.

Statistical significance doesn't mean practical significance. Only by considering context can you determine whether a difference is practically significant (that is, whether it requires action).

Predicting Trends with Time Series Analysis

A natural extension of regression analysis is time series analysis, which uses past customer data collected over regular intervals to predict future customer data on the same intervals. Time series analysis can be used to predict things like

✔ Subscription rates

✔ Train ridership

✔ Product sales

✔ Web page views

For example, requiring customers to register for updates with a website is a way to nurture lead generation. With customers providing their email addresses, they are also giving permission for an organization to directly communicate, market, and (attempt to) convert them into paying customers.

Figure A-16 shows the total number of subscribers from January 2012 through February 2014 from a B2B services company website. With this data, you can use the past pattern of subscribers to predict what the future number of subscribers will be.

Month	Year	Sequence	Raw Number	Cumulative
Jan	2012	1	68	2075
Feb	2012	2	65	2140
Mar	2012	3	70	2210
April	2012	4	59	2269
May	2012	5	79	2348
Jun	2012	6	67	2415
Jul	2012	7	56	2471
Aug	2012	8	64	2535
Sep	2012	9	48	2583
Oct	2012	10	72	2655
Nov	2012	11	70	2725
Dec	2012	12	53	2778
Jan	2013	13	66	2844
Feb	2013	14	75	2919
Mar	2013	15	122	3041
April	2013	16	90	3131
May	2013	17	103	3234
Jun	2013	18	91	3325
Jul	2013	19	77	3402
Aug	2013	20	94	3496
Sep	2013	21	87	3583
Oct	2013	22	139	3722
Nov	2013	23	92	3814
Dec	2013	24	109	3923
Jan	2014	25	104	4027
Feb	2014	26	94	4121

Figure A-16: Number of website subscribers for the specified time frame.

To estimate the cumulative number of subscribers in the future, follow these steps to use time series analysis in Excel:

1. **Create a line graph from the data by month and year in Excel. Insert a line graph into an Excel sheet with the data.**

2. **Add the cumulative column as the series values in the graph in the Edit Series dialog box.**

3. **To create *x*-axis date labels, select both the month and year columns in the Axis Labels dialog box.**

   Figure A-17 shows the cumulative number of subscribers by month and year.

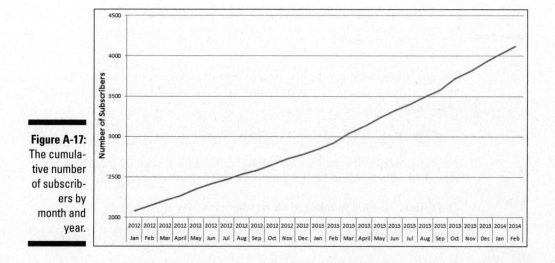

Figure A-17: The cumulative number of subscribers by month and year.

You can see that pattern of cumulative subscribers is generally linear (forming a line going up). By adding a regression equation, you can predict the future number of subscribers (assuming subscriber growth continues to exhibit this linear pattern).

4. **Add a regression equation:**

   • Click on the data line and right-click "Add Trendline."

   • In the Format Trendline dialog box, select the Display Equation on Chart" and Display R-Squared Value on Chart boxes.

Figure A-18 shows a linear regression equation. The best fitting line does a good job of describing the relationship. This r^2 value is .988, meaning this line explains 98.8% of the variation in subscriber rates, which is excellent.

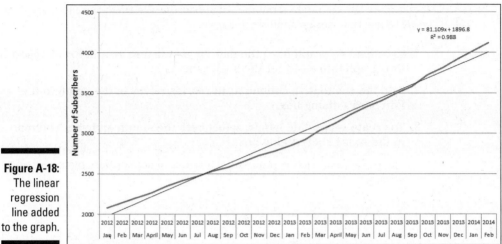

Figure A-18:
The linear
regression
line added
to the graph.

The only independent variable used here is the sequence of time over 26 months (from 1 to 26). The regression equation for subscribers for the 26 months is:

```
Subscribers = 81.109(x) +1896.8
```

You can now predict the number of subscribers for a specific month — say, May 2014, which would be the 29th data point (3 into the future).

The estimated total number of subscribers for May is:

```
May Subscribers = 81.109(29) +1896.8 = 4249
```

Any judgment about the future is susceptible to errors. It's important to understand the limitations of using past data to predict the future.

Exponential (non-linear) growth

One of the benefits of first graphing data is that you can examine the relationship to be sure a line does a good job of fitting it. Customer growth is a key metric for social media companies like Facebook, LinkedIn, and Twitter. Over short intervals (weeks and months), growth looks linear, but over longer periods of time, the growth is exponential. It will often be the case that an exponential (non-linear) equation fits your data better and will provide a better prediction.

You can see if an exponential trendline better describes the subscriber growth than a linear one:

1. **Right-click the data and choose Format Trendline.**
2. **Choose Exponential in the Format Trendline dialog box.**

An updated trendline with an exponential regression equation is shown in Figure A-19.

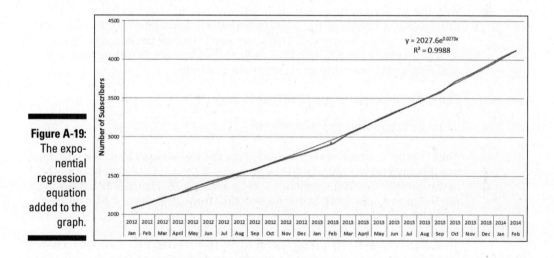

Figure A-19:
The exponential regression equation added to the graph.

Here is the new regression equation.

$$\text{Number of Subscribers} = 2027.6e^{0.0273\ (x)} = 4249$$

The "e" represents a constant, which is approximately 2.71828, and is raised to the power of .0273 and multiplied times the number of months. You can see why it's called an exponential equation, as the month is now part of an exponent. The r^2 value is 0.9988, which is actually higher than the linear equation (which had an r^2 value of 0.988), meaning this equation fits better.

The prediction for May, the 29th data point, is:

$$\text{May Subscribers} = 2027.6e^{0.0273\ (29)} = 4475$$

In Excel, use the function =EXP(0.0273*29) × 2027.6 to get 4475.

Training and validation periods

A more sophisticated and often essential approach to time series analysis involves partitioning your customer data into training and validation periods. In the training period, you build a regression equation on the earliest section of data (approximately two-thirds to three-fourths of your data). You then apply the regression equation to the later part of your data in the validation period to see how well the earlier data actually predicts the later data.

With the subscriber data, you could use the first 20 months (January 2012 through August 2013) as the training period and September 2013 to February 2014 as the validation period. This approach is testing the equation using data you already have, which is as close as you can get to testing how well a prediction might perform when new data comes in.

The regression equation for the first 20 months is:

```
Subscribers = 2033.9e^0.0269x
```

The $r^2 = 0.9979$, which shows a good fit for the exponential line. You can then use this regression equation to see how well it predicts the final six months of the dataset. The last six months are 21 through 26. Figure A-20 shows the predicted and actual values for August 2013 through February 2014, labeled the Validation (in the Period column).

To assess how well this prediction actually is, I created two additional columns. The first is the raw error from the actual number to the prediction. For example, in September 2013, the prediction was short by 5 subscribers. In February 2014, it was short by 28. This sort of raw error can itself be understandable, if you're familiar with the customer data you're working with. When communicating how much error your predicted values have, it's often easier to speak in terms of percentage error.

The Mean Absolute Percentage Error (MAPE) can be a bit more understandable to stakeholders. It's computed by finding the absolute value of the difference between the actual and predicted values, then dividing that difference by the actual value to compute the absolute percentage error. This is then averaged for each value.

$$\frac{1}{n} \sum_{t=1}^{n} \left| \frac{A_t - F_t}{A_t} \right|$$

The APE column shows the absolute percentage error. For example, for January 2013, the regression equation predicted 2,885 subscribers; the actual number of subscribers was 2,844, meaning the equation overpredicted by 41 subscribers.

Month	Year	Sequence	Cumulative Subscribers	Predicted Values	Difference	APE	Period
Jan	2012	1	2075	2089	14	0.7%	Training
Feb	2012	2	2140	2146	6	0.3%	Training
Mar	2012	3	2210	2205	-5	0.2%	Training
April	2012	4	2269	2265	-4	0.2%	Training
May	2012	5	2348	2327	-21	0.9%	Training
Jun	2012	6	2415	2390	-25	1.0%	Training
Jul	2012	7	2471	2455	-16	0.6%	Training
Aug	2012	8	2535	2522	-13	0.5%	Training
Sep	2012	9	2583	2591	8	0.3%	Training
Oct	2012	10	2655	2662	7	0.3%	Training
Nov	2012	11	2725	2734	9	0.3%	Training
Dec	2012	12	2778	2809	31	1.1%	Training
Jan	2013	13	2844	2885	41	1.5%	Training
Feb	2013	14	2919	2964	45	1.5%	Training
Mar	2013	15	3041	3045	4	0.1%	Training
April	2013	16	3131	3128	-3	0.1%	Training
May	2013	17	3234	3213	-21	0.6%	Training
Jun	2013	18	3325	3301	-24	0.7%	Training
Jul	2013	19	3402	3391	-11	0.3%	Training
Aug	2013	20	3496	3483	-13	0.4%	Training
Sep	2013	21	3583	3578	-5	0.1%	Validation
Oct	2013	22	3722	3676	-46	1.2%	Validation
Nov	2013	23	3814	3776	-38	1.0%	Validation
Dec	2013	24	3923	3879	-44	1.1%	Validation
Jan	2014	25	4027	3985	-42	1.1%	Validation
Feb	2014	26	4121	4093	-28	0.7%	Validation
Mar	2014	27		4205			Prediction
April	2014	28		4320			Prediction
May	2014	29		4437			Prediction

Figure A-20: The predicted and actual values for certain months.

Applying the Excel formula for the absolute percentage error (APE) generates an error of 1.4%:

```
=ABS(2885-2844)/2885 = .014 or 1.4%
```

The MAPE for the training period is .589%. The MAPE for the validation period is .870%, which is a bit higher, but both are still under 1%.

Finally, the predictions for March, April, and May 2014 are 4,205, 4,320, and 4,437.

```
=EXP(0.0269*27)*2033.9= 4205
=EXP(0.0269*28)*2033.9= 4320
=EXP(0.0269*29)*2033.9= 4437
```

There are a number of more sophisticated techniques that can make more accurate models by taking into account seasonality and autocorrelation, and then smoothing the data to better interpret patterns. Software such as JMP and Minitab have these features built in.

Predicting the future is always risky because you're assuming the future will have similar patterns as the past. In most cases it does and can be an excellent predictor of customer behavior. However, unusual events (outraged customers on social media, a terrorist attack, or recession) that are unpredictable can substantially affect the accuracy of your predictions. Treat predictions as a guide, not an absolute.

Detecting Differences

Determining if differences are statistically significant is another valuable tool for predicting with customer analytics. In fact, I cover three different applications in other parts of this book: A/B tests (see Chapter 10), usability tests (see Chapter 14), and findability tests (see Chapter 15). All three of these tests use sample customer data to make inferences about a larger customer population.

The particular statistical test you use depends on the type of data you have. Because binary data is so common in customer analytics, I cover comparing two proportions (recall that a percentage is just a proportion times 100) in this section.

Common questions include

- Do higher-income customers purchase at a higher rate than lower-income customers?
- Is there a difference in buying habits between men and women?
- Does one online advertisement result in more click-through than another?
- Will a green button lead to more purchases than a blue button?

To determine if there are statistical differences between proportions, you use a similar contingency table just as you do when computing correlations between binary variables.

A key difference here is that you're working with between-subjects data:

- Of the customers who considered Book A, which proportion ultimately purchased Book A?

✔ Of the customers who considered Book B, what proportion of customers ultimately purchased Book B?

✔ Is the difference in proportions from a sample of customers greater than what you'd expect from chance alone?

Even if you don't sample your customer data, but instead compute analytics on all transactions in a given period (for example, on a website for a month), you're interested in what will happen in the future. So you are using the current customer data as a sample of all future customer data. For that reason, you need to take into account chance variation, which is what computing statistical significance is all about.

Say you want to know if more customers are likely to click on an advertisement using one marketing message (Ad A) or are more likely to click through using an alternate message (Ad B). Imagine 435 customers were randomly served either Advertisement A or Advertisement B on a web page during a week. If 18 out of 220 clicked through on Ad A (8%) and 6 out of 215 clicked through on Ad B (3%), is there enough evidence that more future customers will click on Ad A over Ad B? There is a 5 percentage point difference in click-through rates, but is this difference just random variation or does it represent a real difference in the effectiveness of ads?

The type of statistical test used for detecting statistical differences between binary variables is a Chi-Square test. It is represented with the Greek symbol X^2 (Chi). Follow these steps to conduct a Chi-Square test.:

1. **Set up the data, like this:**

	Purchased	*Didn't Purchase*	*Totals*
Ad A	a	b	m
Ad B	c	d	n
Total	r	s	N

2. **Apply the X^2 formula (which works for small and large sample sizes):**

$$X^2 = \frac{(ad - bc)^2(N-1)}{mnrs}$$

Here are the values filled in.

	Purchased	*Didn't Purchase*	*Totals*
Ad A	18	202	220
Ad B	6	209	215
Total	24	411	435

3. **Fill in the values in the formula to get the Chi-Square statistic.**

$$X^2 = \frac{(18*209 - 202*6)^2(435-1)}{220*215*411*24} = 6.05$$

4. **Apply the Excel formula and obtain a p-value.**

In this case, you use the Chi-Square statistic of 6.05:

```
=CHIDIST(6.05, 1) = .014
```

A p-value this low indicates that a difference of 5 percentage points or greater would only happen about 1.4 times in 100, if there really was no difference. A difference this large is probably not just random noise (see the earlier sidebar on statistical significance and p-values). So Advertisement A would likely get more customers to click through and would be a more effective ad to implement going forward.

Index

About the Author

Jeff Sauro is a Six-Sigma trained statistical analyst and pioneer in quantifying the customer experience. He specializes in making statistical concepts understandable and actionable.

He is the founding principal of MeasuringU, a customer experience and quantitative research firm based in Denver, Colorado USA. Clients include Walmart, PayPal, eBay, Lenovo, Google, and Charter Communications.

Jeff has published over twenty peer-reviewed research articles on statistics and the user experience. He has written four books, including *Quantifying the User Experience: Practical Statistics for User Research* and *A Practical Guide to the System Usability Scale*.

Jeff is completing his Ph.D in Research Methods & Statistics from the University of Denver. Prior to DU, Jeff received his Masters in Learning, Design and Technology from Stanford University, and Bachelors in TV, Radio & Film and Information Technology from Syracuse University. Prior to starting his own company, he worked for Oracle, PeopleSoft, Intuit and General Electric.

He is married to his wife Shannon of 11 years; together, they have three children (5, 6, and 9).

He publishes weekly articles online at www.measuringu.com, and daily updates on Twitter (@MeasuringU).

Dedication

To Dr. Wayne Bausch, a great mentor, dentist, and father-in-law. He showed by example that patience and perseverance open many doors, but not to forget to enjoy the life that those doors open. You will be missed, but never forgotten.

Author's Acknowledgments

I'd like to thank those who helped in the creation of this book, including Parker Malenke, Rebecca Senninger, Ariana Wolf, Pascale Meysing, Alicia Cartwright, Elizabeth Baker, Dr. Jim Lewis, Amy Fandrei, and Pat O'Brien.

Most of all, I couldn't have written this book without the loving support, and patience, from my family.

Publisher's Acknowledgments

Acquisitions Editor: Amy Fandrei

Project Editor: Pat O'Brien

Copy Editor: Debbye Butler

Technical Editor: Dr. Smita Rajpal Kachroo, Post Doctorate Fellow, University of Waterloo

Editorial Assistant: Claire Brock

Sr. Editorial Assistant: Cherie Case

Project Coordinator: Melissa Cossell

Cover Image: ©iStock.com/denphumi